CARE, COMMUNITY AND CITIZENSHIP

Research and practice in a changing policy context

Edited by Susan Balloch and Michael

First published in Great Britain in 2007 by

The Policy Press
University of Bristol
Fourth Floor
Beacon House
Queen's Road
Bristol BS8 1QU
UK

Tel +44 (0)117 331 4054
Fax +44 (0)117 331 4093
e-mail tpp-info@bristol.ac.uk
www.policypress.org.uk

British Library Cataloguing in Publication Data
A catalogue record for this book is available from the British Library.

Library of Congress Cataloging-in-Publication Data
A catalog record for this book has been requested.

ISBN 978 1 86134 870 8 (paperback)
ISBN 978 1 86134 871 5 (hardback)

Cover design by Qube Design Associates, Bristol.
Front cover: photograph supplied by kind permission of Jason Antony.
Printed and bound in Great Britain by Hobbs the Printers, Southampton.

Contents

List of tables and figures   v

Acknowledgements   vii

Notes on contributors   viii

Introduction   I
Susan Balloch and Michael Hill

Part One: Care, community and citizenship in the delivery of welfare

one   The role of communities in care   5
Michael Hill

two   Care, citizenship and community in the UK   21
Susan Balloch

three   Care, citizenship and community in Scotland   41
Alison Petch

Part Two: Ethics, care and community

four   Participation, citizenship and a feminist ethic of care   59
Marian Barnes

five   Ethical dilemmas of front-line regeneration workers   75
Marjorie Mayo, Paul Hoggett and Chris Miller

six   Citizenship and care for people with dementia: 89
values and approaches
Tula Brannelly

Part Three: Bridging the gaps: a practice-based approach

seven   Rough justice, enforcement or support: young people   105
and their families in the community
Dawn E. Stephen and Peter Squires

eight   Survivors of domestic violence, community and care   121
Paula Wilcox

nine   Promoting choice and control: black and minority ethnic   141
communities' experience of social care in Britain
Jabeer Butt

ten   Community care development: developing the capacity   159
of local communities to respond to their own support
and care needs
Deborah Quilgars

eleven Neighbourhood Care Scheme: the 'Coronation Street' 177
model of community care
Marylynn Fyvie-Gauld and Sean de Podesta

twelve Challenging stigma and combating social exclusion 193
through befriending
Bill McGowan and Claire Jowitt

thirteen Paid care workers in the community: an Australian study 211
Jane Mears

Part Four: Comparative perspectives

fourteen The care of older people in Sweden 229
Christina Hjorth Aronsson

fifteen From old to new forms of civic engagement: communities 247
and care in Germany
Frank Bönker

sixteen The social care system for older people in Japan and 261
the role of informal care: Long-term Care Insurance
five years on
Michihiko Tokoro

Conclusion 281
Susan Balloch and Michael Hill

Index 287

List of tables and figures

Tables

2.1	Costs of long-term care	35
6.1	Number of people with dementia by age in England	89
6.2	Care outcomes for people with dementia	92
14.1	Total costs for care of elderly (thousands of million SEK)	237

Figures

11.1	Comparison of figures, April 1999–March 2005	179
11.2	Factors that influence volunteering	183
11.3	Most important support	185
11.4	Volunteer jobs	187
14.1	Medical/specialist treatment, primary healthcare and municipal social care (home help and special housing), cost (thousands of SEK) per person, by gender and age group, 2003	237
14.2	Percentage of persons aged 65 and over permanently living in special housing or with home-help service on 1 October 2005	238
14.3	Percentage of the population aged 65 and over with home-help service living in ordinary housing on 1 October 2005	239
14.4	Percentage of the population receiving home-help services plotted against allocated help hours/month on 1 October 2005	239
14.5	Percentage of the population aged 65 and over living permanently in special housing on 1 October 2005	241
16.1	Type of household and level of care needs	264
16.2	Choice of community-based service by level of care needs	265
16.3	Reason for not using services	266
16.4	Reason for not using services, older people and carers compared (Level 1)	267
16.5	Main carer's relation to the older person	268
16.6	Carer's age	269
16.7	Average time of care by carer's work status, 2001/04	269
16.8	Carer's health by the care need, 2001/04	270
16.9	Intention of using institutional care, answered by the main carer	270

16.10   Intention of using institutional care by care needs   271
16.11   Monthly spending on services by level of care need (yen)   272
16.12   Spending on care services by income level (the band   274
        of LTCI contribution, yen)

Acknowledgements

We would like to express our appreciation to all who contributed to the conference on Communities and Care in April 2005 from which the idea for this book was developed. In particular we would like to thank those who chaired the conference, including Sir David Watson, Angie Hart and Fred Gray, and our contributors including Marian Barnes, Marjorie Mayo, Bill Jordan, Charlie Jordan, Nick Cutforth and Daphne Statham. Two of our speakers have chapters in this book and our thanks go to both of them and to the other authors for their contributions. Thanks go too to our office staff Sallie White and Pippa Lewis. Most importantly, we should like to express our gratitude to the staff of The Policy Press who have supported us throughout the preparation of the book, including Alison Shaw, Philip de Bary, Emily Watt, Jo Morton, Dave Worth, and to Rowena Mayhew for copy editing the book. The final responsibility rests of course with us as editors.

Susan Balloch and Michael Hill
University of Brighton

Notes on contributors

Susan Balloch is Professor of Health and Social Care, and Director of the Health and Social Policy Research Centre at the University of Brighton, UK. Previously she was Policy Director for the National Institute of Social Work, Anti-poverty Officer for the Association of Metropolitan Authorities and a Lecturer in Social Policy at Goldsmiths College, University of London. Other co-edited publications have included *Partnership Working: Policy and Practice*, with Marilyn Taylor (2001), and *The Politics of Evaluation: Participation and Policy Implementation,* with David Taylor (2005), both published by The Policy Press.

Marian Barnes is Professor of Social Policy in the School of Applied Social Science, University of Brighton, UK. She has previously worked at the Universities of Birmingham, Leeds and Sheffield. She has researched and published widely on issues of care, citizenship and public participation. Her books include *Caring and Social Justice* (2005, Palgrave), *Taking over the Asylum: Empowerment and Mental Health*, co-authored with Ric Bowl (2000, Palgrave) and *Power, Participation and Political Renewal: Case Studies in Public Participation*, with Janet Newman and Helen Sullivan, (2007, The Policy Press).

Frank Bönker is a lecturer at the Department of Economics, European University Viadrina, Frankfurt (Oder), Germany. His main fields of interests are post-communist economic transformation and social service and welfare state reform in Germany. From 2001 to 2004, he participated in the EU-financed comparative research project 'Welfare Reform and the Management of Societal Change' (directed by Peter Taylor-Gooby).

Tula Brannelly is Senior Lecturer in Mental Health at Massey University, Wellington, New Zealand, having recently moved from the University of Birmingham. Her interests are in mental health and participation in care, particularly for older people. Her research and teaching interests have evolved from her practice background working as a psychiatric nurse with older people with mental health problems.

Jabeer Butt is the Deputy Director of the Race Equality Unit, a UK charity promoting race equality in social support and social care.

He was the Principal Investigator on an ESRC-funded investigation of the relationship between social and support networks of black and minority ethnic older people and quality of life. He is presently completing a study of voluntary organisations for the Joseph Rowntree Foundation.

Sean de Podesta has held a variety of posts in the fields of training, staff development and community education. In the mid 1990s, he served as a Voluntary Service Overseas volunteer in Romania for two years. He has over 20 years' experience working with volunteers. Sean has been running Brighton & Hove Neighbourhood Care Scheme for over eight years.

Marylynn Fyvie-Gauld is a research fellow with the Health and Social Policy Research Centre, University of Brighton, UK. Recent work has involved an evaluation of service user participation in residential domiciliary care for the Commission for Social Care Inspection and a comprehensive research project on Carers in East Sussex for East Sussex Social Services. Her work with the Neighbourhood Care Scheme, described in this volume, is nearing the end of a three-year evaluation.

Michael Hill is Visiting Professor in the Health and Social Policy Research Centre, University of Brighton, UK and at Queen Mary, University of London, and Emeritus Professor of Social Policy, University of Newcastle, UK. Publications include *Understanding Social Policy* (1980 [7th edition, 2003], Blackwell), *The Public Policy Process* (2004, Pearson Education Ltd), *Social Policy in the Modern World* (2006, Blackwell) and *Implementing Public Policy,* with Peter Hupe (2002, Sage Publications).

Christina Hjorth Aronsson is a Senior Lecturer in Social Work in the Department of Behavioural, Social and Legal Sciences at Örebro University, Sweden. Her research focus concerns the social care of older people and of disabled people. She is leader of the social work programme at the university, with an orientation towards ageing and disability.

Paul Hoggett is Professor of Politics and Director of the Centre for Psycho-social Studies at the University of the West of England (UWE), Bristol, UK. He has over 20 years' experience researching welfare change and the politics of community life for funders such as the ESRC, the Home Office and the European Foundation. He is also a psychotherapist with a strong interest in the role of emotions in politics. His books include *Partisans in an Uncertain World* (1992, Free Association Books), *Contested Communities* (1997, The Policy Press), *Emotional Life and the Politics of Welfare* (2000, Macmillan), *The Politics of Decentralisation*, with colleagues Robin Hambleton and Danny Burns (1994, Macmillan) and *Emotions, Politics and Society*, with colleagues Simon Clarke and Simon Thompson (eds) (2006, Palgrave).

Claire Jowitt has worked with individuals and groups in a number of different settings for over 20 years. Initially she worked in the youth service, and on moving to Hastings in 1988 became involved with the needs of adults through her work with homeless people and with those experiencing isolation as a result of mental health problems. She is currently studying for an MA in Psychoanalytic Psychotherapy at the Tavistock and Portman NHS Institute and continues to be involved in the training of new volunteer befrienders within a local voluntary sector befriending scheme.

Marjorie Mayo is Professor in Community Development at Goldsmiths, University of London. Her research interests focus on strategies for participation and empowerment. She has been working on an ESRC-funded project on 'Ethical Dilemmas in Contested Communities' with colleagues at the University of the West of England and on the evaluation of the Civil Renewal Unit's Active Learning for Active Citizenship programme. Publications include: *Communities and Caring: The Mixed Economy of Welfare* (1994, Macmillan), *Imagining Tomorrow: Adult Education for Transformation* (1997, NIACE), *Cultures, Communities, Identities: Cultural Strategies for Participation and Empowerment* (2000, Palgrave) and *Global Citizens* (2005, Zed Books).

Bill McGowan is a Senior Lecturer in Mental Health at the University of Brighton, UK and is involved in health and social care research and the education of mental health professionals. He has worked for 15 years with the Hastings APCMI (the Association for the Pastoral Care of the Mentally Ill) Befriending Scheme both as a training advisor and facilitator. He is currently involved with colleagues in the development of a social mentoring network within a local community.

Jane Mears is an Associate Professor in Social Policy at the University of Western Sydney, Australia. She has a history of researching issues of concern to women, such as care work, paid and unpaid. Relevant publications include *Women, Work and Care of the Elderly* (1999, Ashgate), with Liz Watson. She is particularly interested in utilising qualitative research methodologies that enable us to listen to and hear women's voices.

Chris Miller is a Reader in Health, Community and Policy studies, in the Faculty of Health and Social Care, University of the West of England (UWE), Bristol, UK. He is the Director of the Centre for Local Democracy at UWE, and the editor of the *International Community Development Journal*. His research interests include the organisation and delivery of social welfare, non-governmental action and community development. Recent publications include: *Producing Welfare: A modern agenda* (2004, Macmillan/Palgrave) and 'Public Health in the Local Authority Context', in J. Orme et al (eds) *Public Health for the 21st Century: New Perspectives on Policy, Participation and Practice* (2007, Open University Press).

Alison Petch has spent most of her career involved with research and policy, latterly in health and social care. From 1985 to 1993 she worked at the Social Work Research Centre at Stirling University. In 1993 she moved to Glasgow University as Director of the Nuffield Centre for Community Care Studies. In autumn 2005 she was tempted south to develop **research in practice** *for adults*, based at the Dartington Hall Trust and established to promote the use of evidence-informed policy and practice in the planning and delivery of adult support services.

Deborah Quilgars is a Senior Research Fellow in the Centre for Housing Policy at the University of York, UK. Her main research interests are in: homelessness, housing, care and support services, the risks of home ownership and comparative housing policy. Deborah has recently conducted research on housing and support for homeless families and people with alleged anti-social behaviour issues (for Shelter); on youth homelessness (Joseph Rowntree Foundation; Foyer Federation; Communities and Local Government); and on integrated housing provision for risk groups (European Commission).

Peter Squires is Professor of Criminology and Public Policy at the University of Brighton, UK, where he has worked since 1986. His more recent research interests have focused upon contemporary concerns with youth offending and the government's 'anti-social behaviour' agenda, while continuing to develop approaches to researching firearms, culture, crime and violence. While many people seem to see these as rather disparate interests, he remains convinced that they share important connections.

Dawn E. Stephen is a Senior Lecturer in Criminology at the University of Brighton, UK. Her research interests are driven by the desire to promote justice for marginalised young people and this imperative is most evident in her critical writings on anti-social behaviour measures, most recently 'Community safety and young people: 21st century homo sacer and the politics of injustice', in P. Squires (ed), *Community Safety: Critical Perspectives on Policy and Practice* (2006, The Policy Press).

Michihiko Tokoro is a lecturer in social policy and social security at the Graduate School of Human Life Science, Osaka City University Osaka, Japan. He has an MA in Social Policy and Administration from Nottingham University, UK and a doctorate from the University of York, UK. Recent publications in English include: 'Social Policy and Lone Parenthood in Japan: A Workfare Tradition?' in (2003) *The Japanese Journal of Social Security Policy*, vol 2, no 2, pp 45-58, and 'A Comparative Perspective on Family Policy Development: Britain and Japan' in (2001) *The Journal of Social Policy and Labor Studies*, no 5, pp 257-77.

Paula Wilcox is Course Leader, MA Criminology, at the University of Brighton, UK. Her research interests are in women's experiences of domestic violence and the development of effective support systems and in gender-based violence. Her recent publications include: *Surviving Domestic Violence: Gender, Poverty and Agency* (2006, Palgrave/Macmillan); 'Community safety, family and domestic violence' in P. Squires (ed) *Community Safety: Critical Perspectives on Policy and Practice* (2006, The Policy Press); and 'Beauty and the beast: Gendered and raced discourse in the news' in (2005) *Social and Legal Studies*, vol 14, no 4, pp 515-32.

Introduction

Susan Balloch and Michael Hill

The first aim of this book is to question current approaches to 'community care' in which the meaning of community is ill-defined and the concept of care is taken for granted. Although seen as a much preferred option to residential care, community care has often proved to be isolating and impersonal, offering few of the benefits of inclusion with which communities are strongly associated, hugely dependent on the unpaid services of relatives and friends and limited to meeting needs rather than supporting rights.

The book's second aim is to identify effective strategies and practices, and the thinking that lies behind these, through which individuals may be supported to live normally and safely within communities regardless of income and wealth, age, impairment, gender or ethnicity. This includes not only those who come under the conventional community care umbrella – older people and those with physical and sensory impairments and mental health problems – but also families with young people under anti-social behaviour orders and women experiencing domestic violence.

Part One of this book opens with a chapter reflecting on the key concepts of care, community and citizenship and their importance in the delivery of welfare (Chapter One, Michael Hill). Their translation into policy and practice in the UK is then considered, with questions raised about the lack of relationship between community development and social care (Chapter Two, Susan Balloch). In the third chapter the focus is on Scotland alone, where a tradition of community social work has been sustained and personal care costs are now paid by the state (Chapter Three, Alison Petch).

Part Two contributes to unpacking the concept of care by reflecting on the 'ethic of care', which characterises both personal relationships and professional behaviour. The first chapter reflects on this ethic in relation to community cohesion, social inclusion, community involvement and civil renewal (Chapter Four, Marian Barnes). Chapter Five then considers how front-line professionals are coping in a context of increasing ethical uncertainty, shifting professional boundaries and increasing pressures from New Public Management agendas. It examines how professionals hold on to their ethics, avoiding total moral relativisim and/or terminal burn-out (Chapter Five, Marjorie

Mayo, Paul Hogget and Chris Miller). The final chapter in Part Two focuses on people with dementia and asks what happens in their care when the ethical elements of an ethic of care are practised and when they are not (Chapter Six, Tula Brannelly).

Part Three reflects on the delivery of support and care in a wide range of settings and discusses the interface of care and communities in greater detail. Seven chapters cover the following issues: supporting young people and their families in the community (Chapter Seven, Dawn E. Stephen and Peter Squires); community responses to domestic violence and their impact on women's citizenship (Chapter Eight, Paula Wilcox); care and citizenship in black and minority ethnic communities (Chapter Nine, Jabeer Butt); a pilot project in Hull to discover if the community sector could provide low-level support and care needs (Chapter Ten, Deborah Quilgars); a neighbourhood care scheme run by volunteers (Chapter Eleven, Marylynn Fyvie-Gauld and Sean de Podesta); a befriending scheme for people with mental health problems (Chapter Twelve, Bill McGowan and Claire Jowitt); and home care in Australia (Chapter Thirteen, Jane Mears). This part of the book both shows the potential within communities to provide effective care and support as well as identifying the many barriers.

Part Four recognises the global significance of the many issues raised and that they are not unique to the UK. Three chapters, from Sweden, Germany and Japan, illustrate the different paths being taken to provide support and care in the 21st century. Sweden is the country that has gone most strongly down the state provision road but is now beginning to experiment with a mixed economy of welfare and the first chapter in Part Four traces the reasons and effects of recent change (Chapter Fourteen, Christina Hjorth Aronsson). The next chapter analyses the changing forms of civic engagement in German social care with a view to identifying major trends and policy issues (Chapter Fifteen, Frank Bönker). Finally a chapter on Japan reviews the first five years of its Long-term Care Insurance scheme and its impact on family care (Chapter Sixteen, Michihiko Tokoro).

In conclusion, the editors review the authors' contributions and draw together the shared issues, policy dilemmas and possible ways forward.

Part One
Care, community and citizenship in the delivery of welfare

ONE

The role of communities in care

Michael Hill

Introduction

What do people, including of course particularly governments, mean when they expect communities to be involved in care? The answers that are given to that question depend on what communities are understood to be. This chapter will therefore examine some of the problems about uses of the concept of community, particularly when it is related to issues about care. What kinds of assumptions are made about what communities are, and how various subgroups and families are (or are not) embedded in them?

Community

Community is a concept that is used very widely and very loosely. That is a topic the author explored many years ago in a book with Ruth Issacharoff (1971). We identified a range of problems with uses of the concept of community. We reported an American article that claimed to have identified 94 different definitions of community (Hillery, 1955) and we quoted Halsey as suggesting that usage of the concept of community tends to involve:

> The persistent residue of a romantic protest against the complexity of modern urban society – the idea of a decentralised world in which neighbours could and should completely satisfy each other's needs and legitimate demands for health, wealth and happiness. (Halsey, 1969)

Since those days the water has been further muddied by the rise – and to some extent fall – of an official usage directly pertinent for this book, the use of 'community' in tandem with 'care' to describe, in effect, *either* all care outside institutional settings *or*, more confusingly still, all care outside hospitals. These usages carry with them meanings that it suits government to imply. As Means et al (2003, chapter 1), among others, have pointed out, the wider implication is that the 'community' is intrinsically a better place for care, with the implications that it is cheaper for the government as far as possible obscured. Now of course that usage has largely been replaced by 'social care', but the questions remain about the caring capacity of the community (or perhaps more appropriately of the many different social contexts) and of the role of the government in supporting and sustaining this. Dawn Stephen and Peter Squires (in Chapter Seven) explore a related usage in the field of criminal justice, where the word 'community' is used similarly very loosely (in this case to describe control measures outside prison) but again carries implications of inclusion and care.

So has the concept of community reached the point at which at least we need to abandon it? Marjorie Mayo (1994) offers a good modern exploration of this issue, recognising drawbacks to its use like those outlined above. Having explored the use of the concept in sociological theory she argues that it remains important to recognise the notions of social solidarity embodied within it, as celebrated in Raymond Williams' (1976) emphasis on the quality of relationships where people 'have something in common'. She also invokes the distinction made by the sociologist Toennies (1936) between 'community' and the more impersonal form which many modern social relationships take of limited 'association'. Mayo (1994, p 58) also stresses the political dimension in which community struggles 'may be seen in the context of wider alliances ... to promote the empowerment of the disempowered to take more control over their own destinies'. Hence, for her:

> Despite all the ambiguities and contradictions inherent in
> the very concept of community, and in policies to promote
> community development, there remain strands that have
> continuing relevance in developing more democratic
> approaches to welfare.... (p 68)

This chapter takes it leads from Mayo's point of view, exploring some of its application in relation to issues about care (hopefully using the concept with as much precision as possible).

Community and geography

A crucial problem about the use of 'community' concerns the fact that it is often given a specific geographical referent. This is particularly the case in discussions of public policy, inasmuch as government too (the topic of a later section) generally implies activities within the confines of a specified area (often, but not always, a nation state). *The Chambers Dictionary* starts by defining community as 'a body of people in the same locality' but goes on to include 'a group of people who have common interests' among its later definitions (note also that Martin Bulmer, 1987, emphasises this as both a contrast and an overlapping usage). Clearly, for a great deal of discourse about community it is important to ask to what extent these alternatives are being conflated. Sometimes people in the same area have many interests in common, sometimes they have few. Several of the chapters in this book (particularly Six, Eight and Twelve) concern people who will often be very isolated from those who live around them. Conversely, interest 'communities' may have quite narrow geographical locations but sometimes very broad ones.

It is important to recognise that both 'locality' and 'interests' in those two dictionary quotes are open to multiple interpretations. Locality may be interpreted very narrowly or quite broadly, and in each case there will be very different ways of drawing boundaries. Interests – as the use of the plural implies – may be multiple, and overlapping in complex ways. Loose usages of either approach to defining communities often disregard these problems.

Clearly, however, what is involved in very many cases where community is discussed in geographical terms is an implication that it is possible to define a relatively specific area within which people with closely shared interests are located. There are then, however, difficulties in delineating such areas, something that is complicated by questions about how many people there can be in such an area. Work carried out in the 1960s in connection with English local government reform got into considerable difficulty in the search for ways of defining appropriate geographical units (HMSO, 1969).

A great deal of contemporary analysis of community as a geographical concept has suggested that the extent to which this is the case is diminishing in modern societies. These analyses often go on to explore the factors that influence variation in this respect. It does seem important here to be very sensitive to interest diversity, and the factors that may enlarge or reduce this. Relatives of the author used to live in a very anonymous suburban estate under threat from flooding. That clearly gave everyone in that locality a shared interest. Fortunately, that was not tested severely; had it been it would have been interesting and important to see to what extent solidaristic responses to emergencies occurred and to what extent they enhanced other collaborative actions. As far as the topic of this book is concerned the issue is about the extent to which the presence in such a location of some people with rather specific care needs would have been given special attention (but see Chapter Eleven by Marylynn Fyvie-Gauld and Sean de Podesta for an account of some very positive developments on a geographical basis).

On the other hand, leaving behind the geographical dimension, the alternative questions are about the extent to which interest links lead to solidaristic action despite the distances between people, which, in the case of care, may impose severe practical limitations on action. This is an issue pertinent to the retirement decisions of many better-off people where locations are chosen – in the remote countryside or even abroad – where relatives are far away and care networks, let alone services, are rudimentary (Hardill et al, 2005).

Studies of occupational groups (including professions) have drawn distinctions between 'cosmopolitans' with widespread reference groups and 'locals' for whom attachments are primarily to the colleagues – and indeed the organisations – with whom they are working (the distinction originates from Merton, 1957, chapter 10). This issue is clearly pertinent to the professional ethics discussed by Marjorie Mayo and her colleagues in Chapter Five. While occupations may differ in their orientations, and thus the relative importance of a cosmopolitan perspective, it seems also to be the case that individual preferences and personality characteristics influence the choice between these orientations. Inasmuch, then, as these alternative orientations influence other lifestyle choices – the characteristics of friendship networks and even residential locations – people may to some extent choose whether their 'community' is or is not geographically constrained. Such choices will then have an impact on the way potential care networks are constructed.

Community and diversity

However, it is inappropriate to see networks as simply matters of choice. They are influenced by cultural, ethnic and linguistic characteristics too. This brings us back to the assumptions discussed above about the extent to which there are communities, formed of people with strong shared characteristics. And, closely related to this are issues about the extent to which the processes that form these communities are imposed on them by the attitudes of others, engaging in various forms of discrimination. Relevant here is not only the obvious case of racial discrimination but also the extent to which people may be excluded from interaction with others because of their lifestyles (or assumptions about their lifestyles).

Hence, in the absence of actual pressures towards residential segregation (ghettoisation) the extent to which these kinds of community bonds will have a territorial dimension will vary greatly. Several important points follow from this.

The use of the concept of community is particularly problematic in contexts where it to all intents and purposes stereotypes a group to which the speaker does not belong. If we consider the various subgroups in society – whether identified by class, ethnicity, sexual orientation or other cultural identification – there will be differences in the extent to which those groups identify shared interests in the way implied by the concept of community. This is particularly evident in the way the concept of community is used with reference to ethnic groups. On the one hand, shared experience of discrimination and of difficulties in settlement in a new land may bring some very diverse groups together with common awareness and common action. On the other hand, other factors may divide. Consider, for example, the diverse island societies that first-generation immigrants from the Caribbean came from (the bigger islands of Jamaica, Trinidad and Barbados far apart – unwilling to participate in a federation and often even uneasy partners on the cricket field – and then alongside them the many from small islands often regarded contemptuously by people from the bigger islands but also with very different cultures themselves). Furthermore, they brought with them views about gradations of colour and class (Andrea Levy's novels illustrate this brilliantly) and wider ethnic divisions (illustrated in V. S. Naipaul's early novels). Even more seriously we regularly hear members of that vast, complex and diverse world religion – Islam – described in terms in which they are seen as belonging to a common 'community' and with, worse still, a limited number of identifiable 'community leaders'.

Much of the literature on communities within Britain has explored issues about class differences and homogeneities. In some of the literature there is a tendency to romanticise a working-class past characterised by high degrees of solidarity. There is little point in getting here into a discussion about the extent to which this involved an idealised vision. What is clearly evident is that such solidarity is now hard to find. However, an important aspect of that literature, as Mayo (1994) shows, is the extent to which such solidarity derives from a need to work together in the face of shared impoverishment and shared oppression.

Another feature of the debate about class and community is the extent to which there is (or has been) a strong connection between class solidarity and the geographical concentration of people with shared class characteristics. There are some pertinent issues here about the relationship between social mobility and geographical mobility. It

–

9

may be the case both that the most deprived are the least mobile – in either sense – and that such upward social mobility as occurs tends to increase homogeneity among those left behind. Once upon a time social engineers sought to create cross-class community identifications through deliberate mixing of people (witness the early ideal for the new towns and Aneurin Bevan speaking of creating in council estates 'the living tapestry of a mixed community', quoted in Foot, 1975, at p 76). Such ideals have long been abandoned, undermined if nothing else by the popularity of owner-occupation. However, while highly homogeneous communities can often be observed, accidents of history have also created some unexpectedly mixed neighbourhoods (particularly where the partial gentrification of old residential areas has occurred).

A more serious challenge for efforts to engender community feelings has occurred in areas where concentrated social housing has become what can only easily be described pejoratively as 'dumping grounds' for diverse groups of people – those who are desperate for housing, those evicted from preferred areas because of failures to pay rents or anti-social behaviour, those forced to turn to social housing because of disability, ex-prisoners and so on (Lee and Murie, 1998). Again, differential mobility out of such areas can add to this 'dumping' effect, note, for example, the way in which opportunities for owner-occupation, including of course the subsidised sale of social housing, play a part. Can community solidarity develop among a diverse group of people who have nothing to share but their deprivation? Brave social crusaders like Bob Holman have devoted much of their lives to trying to help it to develop, but in most cases surely the outlook is fairly bleak. Perhaps the most hopeful developments occur among subgroups within such neighbourhoods – here again is perhaps a reason for holding on to the notion of the feasibly of communitarian developments without there necessarily being a strong geographical connection.

Community and families

There are obviously connections between patterns of family life and community relationships. The issues about the relationship between family life and community life are relevant to the concerns of this book inasmuch as families are very important for social care.

Family connections are the building blocks of the more cohesive communities (although even here, as Shakespeare reminds us in *Romeo and Juliet*, families can divide as well as unite communities!). The family/community connection may be seen in a particularly strong form in the Confucian model of family life, in which kin ties are traced widely and far back and are, in Chinese rural societies, in many respects the lowest tier of government. Conversely, therefore, it may be quite difficult to separate out in situations in which traditional communities are seen to be being destroyed or in decline – as explored in the classic studies of East London by Willmot and Young (1957, 1960) – issues about disappearing neighbourhood ties and issues about the dispersal of extended families. As far as issues about care are concerned there must surely be similar reinforcing interactions.

As far as the policy issues are concerned, however, the fact that families go to considerable trouble to maintain links despite geographical separation is a matter deserving of attention, but it may be doubted whether similar considerations apply to attenuated non-kin ties. It is appropriate to note here that one of the characteristics of the issues about care is that they involve particularly sensitive interactions between people – both in terms of physical tasks and psychological difficulties. There is perhaps a paradox here that there are difficulties about relationships that lie in the middle ground between the impersonality of paid service by strangers and the intimate relations between family members. We return to this below.

Community and government

While it may seem to be taking us rather far from the issue of communities and care it is in fact not irrelevant to recognise that the modern concept of the nation state – as enshrined in the perspectives of many nationalist movements and given sustenance by the way in which national self-determination has (intermittently) been taken into account in determining territorial boundaries since 1919 – embodies a view of the desirability of equating a broad concept of community with the idea of democratic self-government. Indeed, that is implicit in the concept of citizenship. We are, of course, continually reminded of this in situations in which this ideal cannot be or has not been attained, as for example in the case of the Balkans or Northern Ireland. Of course, in most cases the community ideal in relation to nationhood involves population and geographical units much too large for notions of close caring networks, but it is appropriate to start from this point inasmuch as the legitimation of the assumption of a collective responsibility for care on the part of the government stems from this notion. This will therefore be explored a little more before proceeding to issues about smaller – local – units of government.

So the issue here is about the extent to which notions of solidarity through citizenship can be effectively seen to legitimise a consistent set of government policies for care holding across a specific area. Clearly, such a view is implicit in expectations that government has a key role in the provision of care, often reinforced (and not merely by politicians) by concerns about territorial justice – often given popular form in assertions that who gets what should not be a 'postcode lottery'.

Such a perspective seems, then, to come into conflict with an increasingly widespread view that a single government for a large territory (however defined) cannot realistically claim to represent us all. Leaving aside for a moment issues about more localised alternatives within a nation state, the general thrust of this argument requires a search for new approaches to self-government. That search tends to involve two alternative lines of argument.

One of these takes an individualistic character, stressing the need for consumer choice. This gives government the role of regulator of markets in which individual purchasing decisions may be made. It is not appropriate in this chapter, then, to go into the issues about the extent to which markets are non-existent, or rigged, or about the large number of situations in which consumers lack the resources to make choices of their own. Those deficiencies of markets can be addressed, notably through income maintenance measures. In some countries (see particularly the contributions on Germany and Japan in Chapters Fifteen and Sixteen respectively) care insurance offers another approach to this, although in the field of care – as these chapters show – it is impossible to escape forms of rationing through official need determination. In the UK the provision of 'direct payments' to people in need of care similarly extends individual choice to some extent.

It is, then, the other approach to the problem of the increasing irrelevance of the representative government approach to citizenship that particularly embodies a search for communitarian approaches to the government of caring services. Inasmuch as attention is paid to the geographical dimension of community this involves the exploration of ways to coordinate and consult on services at the local level, and at the same time therefore to strengthen locality-based networks. But perhaps their more concrete manifestations have been the growth of user groups – both as self-help groups and as participants in (or aspirants to participate in) policy processes at the local level. Such developments, important for the growth of the participatory ethic of care advocated by Marian Barnes in Chapter Four – although often locality specific – are likely (particularly as far as an issue like social care is concerned – by contrast with, for example, tenants' movements) to be less geographically concentrated and thus to involve highlighting some interests and concerns that will not be shared with others in the same locality. Inasmuch as this is the case, such movements may be more appropriately seen as 'consumerist' – perhaps connecting up with developments like direct payments in which market notions are present – rather than 'communitarian'. The consumerist emphasis may indeed be destructive of community approaches to serve organisation and control, interestingly a point made both by Alison Petch (Chapter Three) in her discussion of the importance of local government services in Scotland and by Frank Bönker (Chapter Fifteen) in exploring the replacement of non-profit organisations 'with deep roots in the local community' by commercial providers in Germany.

So far, this section has tended to pose two extremes for community involvement – one based on citizenship and oriented to the generally very large nation state, the other based on micro-level involvements. But, particularly given the extent to which interests may be expressed through movements that are localised in a broad rather than a narrow and very specific sense, is there a middle-level alternative? From the formal organisational point of view the obvious candidate for such a role is local government.

An interesting paper by Hellmut Wollmann (unpublished) explores the extent to which the roots of local government in European countries lay in notions of the representation of local communities, but later diverged from that ideal in many countries. The alternative competing notion was of local government as an administrative activity, with powers dictated by central government, with boundaries influenced more by concerns about the most efficient units for policy delivery rather than by communities of interest. This has taken its most striking form in the UK with the consequence that the ratio of population to local government unit is much higher than in most other countries. In particular, the UK has been reluctant to go down the French road of accepting that units may remain – at least in the rural areas – as representative bodies even when they have to accept that most services will have to be provided through combinations with other authorities or bought in from outside.

In this sense, local authorities in the UK are not seen as fora for the exploration of community concerns, a fact most dramatically demonstrated by low electoral turnouts to vote for candidates most of whom come from the national political parties and with results that are seen by the media as indicators of the popularity of the central government.

However, there is within local government scope for rectifying this deficiency – although probably not in electoral terms – through the provision of facilities within individual local authority areas, for consultation closer to local communities. In the field of social care the interest in notions of integrated 'patch' teams in the years after the Seebohm reforms involved a search for ways to do this (Hadley and Young, 1990). Within local authorities as a whole there was a corresponding interest in integrated local offices, with perhaps appropriate local consultative committees, and in some places the organisation of the business of the authority itself through area committees (Hoggett and Hambleton, 1988). That impetus was subsequently lost; this may be attributed to a combination of the abandonment of integrated approaches within social services in favour of divisions along client group-based lines, the impact of privatisation in fragmenting integrated approaches to services and the emergence of more centralised approaches to local decision making through 'cabinet', 'city mayor' and 'city manager' initiatives. Contemporary approaches to consultation with the public are much more individualised, seeing citizens as separate consumers who should hopefully be in a position to make consumer choices and whose opinions may be sought by way of questionnaires. In Chapter Two, Susan Balloch explores other dimensions of this change of emphasis, particularly the difficulties involved in integrated approaches at the community level.

There is one other alternative here – that the voluntary sector can operate in this social 'middle ground'. It is embodied in notions of subsidiarity, particularly in the traditional approach to much social care and education in the Netherlands and Germany (although note the comments on the decline of this in Chapter Fifteen) of leaving service provision to faith-based community organisations. This does to some extent separate the geographical dimension from the community of interest dimension. But it is pertinent to note that this has been observed to be of diminishing importance with the declining importance of religious affiliation within Christendom. It has re-emerged on the agenda because of the establishment of significant minority groups from outside Christianity, but is then the subject of much controversy inasmuch as separate services may imply forms of discrimination and may enhance divisions within a society. This implies a need to balance universalism and communitarianism, the topic of the next section.

Universalism versus communitarianism?

The heading for this section opposes the concepts of universalism and communitarianism but adds a question mark, to indicate that the concepts are not necessarily in opposition. Running through the discussion so far are two key points – one that those links between people that are seen as important for the maintenance of 'community' are very likely (indeed, probably increasingly likely) dispersed across large areas, the other that organising principles for government (and also correspondingly for key representative groups that link people's interests and convey them to governments) are likely to involve large units of a kind to which the application of community notions cannot be more than symbolic. But while the justification for these large units has often been in terms of efficiency, there is another justification that is important for public policy: the case for territorial justice, ensuring if not equality of treatment at least compatibility of treatment across large areas.

The question is, then, how large should these areas be? As suggested in the last section, the 19th- and 20th-century concept of the nation state suggested the importance of a communitarian notion spreading across a nation. The reality has been, and remains, that many so-called nations have sharp divisions running through them. But now in the 21st century, notions of interconnectedness between nations are very much on the agenda, reinforced not merely by global economic ties but by massive population movements between states. In political science one of the justifications for talking of 'governance' rather than 'government' is that complex political and institutional connections run across traditional state boundaries (Pierre, 2000).

The recognition of this complex interconnectedness seems to conflict with efforts to define and work within quite narrow communities of interest, particularly ones that are defined in narrow geographical terms. But there is nothing new about this. For the Christian world the recognition of a universal caring responsibility is embodied in the parable (perhaps more honoured in the breach than the observance) of the 'good Samaritan', while there are similar universalist propositions within Islamic thinking. In more modern times, issues about a common humanity have been an important ingredient in humanistic thinking, offering a challenge to the more atavistic nationalist notions.

In the field of care there are some very important transnational connections to which there is a need to be sensitive. Gough and Wood (2004), in a book on social policy in the poorer countries of the world, stress the importance of remittances from family members working abroad for welfare in their countries of origin. It is, then, important to recognise that many of these remittances come from people who are carrying out paid care tasks in the countries within which they work. Looking at this from the other end of the telescope, then, Clare Ungerson (2004) has raised concerns about the exploitation of these workers.

In relation to social policy, universalist notions have been propounded, as already noted, in the concept of territorial justice, but also in the advocacy of policies that extend social rights in a non-discriminatory way. This universalism is thus crucial for the defence of tax-funded healthcare for all (Titmuss, 1974). Reference to the particularist needs of specific communities is, then, seen as in conflict with this principle.

The difficulty with social care is both the cost of universalist solutions and the fact that, even if that cost could be afforded, entitlement depends on far from straightforward decisions about need and on the formulation and implementation of very varied packages of care. The author's own preference here is for an approach to this topic by way of (a) good overall income maintenance packages and (b) supplementary cash benefits depending on relatively simple tests of need, which then leave the recipient with a choice about how to spend the money. In other words, much better state pensions and invalidity benefits, supplemented by benefits like Attendance Allowance uprated so that they pay the real costs of attendance and so on. But that is a utopian dream. Without that, much tailoring of state support to individuals' resources and circumstances including the care they can call upon from others is necessary. In which case, attention to issues about community are important and connect up with concerns about citizenship – not to enable the public burden to be pushed off on to others, but to enable those who receive care and their carers to participate in decision making about how the resources should be provided.

Many people need care from family members (and in the absence of this from communities, in the broad sense) simply because public services are inadequate. It is not appropriate to espouse an argument that these links should be neglected simply because of a belief that there should be more adequate public services. Looking at this issue from a comparative perspective, distinctions need to be made between systems where there has been a stress on delegating tasks seen hitherto as potentially public to the community, those where community organisation is traditionally strong and those where the public contribution is so little that inevitably governmental effort has been about trying to shore up community resources.

There is a case for strengthening community caring networks, just as there is a case for strengthening family caring networks. On the whole that seems to be an issue for *us*, for civil society, since when the state does it there is an ulterior motive – to save it the cost and responsibility. We should distrust communitarian arguments emanating from the mouths of politicians (see also comments in Chapter Four by Marian Barnes and in Chapter Seven by Dawn Stephen and Peter Squires on this theme). Bo Rothstein (1998) develops an interesting argument about traditional Swedish communitarianism – as embodied in a doctrine coming from the Left about policies for the 'people's home' – inasmuch as while it led to the development of some universalistic benefits it also implied uniform services imposed from above (he uses, for example, the case of maternity services imposed on mothers without consultation). This is also related to an authoritarian view that people who are in need are in a dependency relationship, less than full citizens with entitlements but rather subservient to those who consider they know what is best for them (an issue explored by Marian Barnes in Chapter Four).

The argument here is thus about the importance of universalist principles, and a warning about the too eager espousal of communitarian alternatives, with an important reservation. That reservation is about the viability of integrating universality and choice in the absence of real alternatives. Choice in situations where there has been no participation to determine the conditions under which those choices are made – a current danger with the enthusiastic advancement of direct payments for care – carries similar dangers. In any case, treating care as a commodity carries with it potential problems, inasmuch as it involves complex relationships between people that cannot simply be commodified within contracts.

Rothstein (1998, p 214) argues that 'every democratic system must strike a balance between a collectivist/communitarian and an individualistic/autonomist ideal of democracy'. Fair enough, but in relation to care the issues go beyond this dichotomy. Both universal services and choice within them are needed. But there are limitations to the solutions these offer, not merely because of finite resources, but also because caring *relationships* are needed as well as caring *services*. Hence there is need, too, for the nurturing of networks of care. But this cannot be done 'top down' by politicians, telling us what our obligations are to each other, but through the recognition of real communities of interest that, in our complex world, will not have a simple spatial identity.

References

Bulmer, M. (1987) *The Social Basis of Community Care*, London: Allen and Unwin.

Foot, M. (1975) *Aneurin Bevan*, vol 2, 1945-60 (paper edition), London: Granada.

Gough, I. and Wood, G. (2004) *Insecurity and Welfare Regimes in Asia, Africa and Latin America: Social Policy in Development Contexts*, Cambridge: Cambridge University Press.

Hadley, R. and Young, K. (1990) *Creating a Responsive Public Service*, Hemel Hempstead: Harvester Wheatsheaf.

Halsey, A. H. (1969) 'Community against poverty', Unpublished paper.

Hardill, I., Spradbery, J., Arnold-Boakes, J. and Marrugat, M. L. (2005) 'Severe health and social care issues among British migrants who retire to Spain', *Ageing and Society*, vol 25, no 5, pp 769-83.

Hill, M. and Issacharoff, R. (1971) *Community Action and Race Relations*, London: Oxford University Press.

Hillery, G. (1955) 'Definitions of community', *Rural Sociology*, no 20, pp 111-23.

HMSO (1969) *Community Attitudes Survey*, Research study no 9 for the Royal Commission on Local Government, London: HMSO.

Hoggett, P. and Hambleton, R. (eds) (1988) *Decentralisation and Democracy*, Occasional Paper 28, Bristol: School for Advanced Urban Studies, University of Bristol.

Lee, P. and Murie, A. (1998) 'Social exclusion and housing', in S. Wilcox (ed) *Housing Finance Review*, York: Joseph Rowntree Foundation, pp 30-7.

Mayo, M. (1994) *Communities and Caring*, London: St Martins Press.

Means, R., Richards, S. and Smith, R. (2003) *Community Care: Policy and Practice*, Basingstoke: Macmillan.

Merton, R. K. (1957) *Social Theory and Social Structure*, Glencoe, Ill: Free Press.

Pierre, J. (ed) (2000) *Debating Governance*, Oxford: Oxford University Press.

Rothstein, B. (1998) *Just Institutions Matter: The Moral and Political Logic of the Universal Welfare State*, Cambridge: Cambridge University Press.

Titmuss, R. M. (1974) *Social Policy: An Introduction*, London: Allen and Unwin.

Toennies, F. (1936) *Community and Association*, London: Routledge.

Ungerson, C. (2004) 'Whose empowerment and independence? A cross-national perspective on "cash for care" schemes', *Ageing and Society*, vol 24, pp 189-212.

Williams, R. (1976) *Keywords*, London: Croom Helm.

Wilmot, P. and Young, M. (1960) *Family and Class in a London Suburb*, London: Routledge.

Wollmann, H. , 'The fall and rise of the local community: a comparative and historical perspective', Unpublished paper.

Young, M. and Wilmot, P. (1957) *Family and Kinship in East London*, London: Routledge.

TWO

Care, citizenship and community in the UK

Susan Balloch

In Chapter One Michael Hill addressed the broad concepts of care, citizenship and community and their interface nationally and globally. In this chapter the focus is on recent policy developments in the UK that have revived concepts of citizenship and community within the context of care. The next chapter from Alison Petch will then look at some of the distinctive developments in Scotland.

Background

In the UK, central government policy has regularly emphasised the importance of community in the provision of social care. Both the Seebohm (1968) and Barclay (1982) Reports saw communities as fundamental to the provision of local social care services, the latter advocating a system of 'patch-based social work' to utilise community resources and meet local needs effectively. The demise of community social work in the 1980s coincided, ironically, with the growth of community care policies, the closure of long-stay mental hospitals and the growing popularity of policies for enabling people with complex needs to remain independent in their own homes for as long as possible. Parallel policies for children and families saw a major reduction in the number of children's homes and an emphasis on foster care.

Community social work became a victim of centralisation and cost-cutting in local government just as Sir Roy Griffiths (1989) was preparing his report on community care. As a result, 'community care' never became a community-based system of care, but rather a policy for deinstitutionalisation. In spite of this the 1980s saw a rapid growth in residential and nursing homes, particularly after 1984 when legislation enabled individuals receiving social security benefits to receive state funding for residential care if assessed as in need, fuelling an unplanned growth in privately owned homes.

The 1990 NHS and Community Care Act, implemented in 1993, transferred the entire state funding for residential and nursing care for older people to local government social services departments and effectively closed the financial loophole that had encouraged many into residential care. The Act designated the local authorities as 'enablers', purchasing residential, day and home care services, mainly from the private and voluntary sectors rather than providing them themselves. Thus, local authorities became 'care managers' responsible for delivery of 'packages of care' purchased from private and voluntary providers, often through block contracts. Those deemed eligible for local authority support were, and still are, means tested and required to pay for their own care if their income and capital resources were above a certain limit (set at £20,500 in 2006). This led to many selling their homes to be able to afford residential care. It also raised issues about the anomaly between 'free' healthcare and means-tested 'social care'. In 1999 a Royal Commission on Long Term Care recommended that both health and personal care costs should be paid for by the state for all residents but this proved acceptable only in Scotland. The funding situation still remains very complex and often unfair (OFT, 2005).

The 1980s and 1990s were therefore characterised by two main developments in services for adults – a shift to independent rather than statutory provision and to people increasingly being cared for in their own homes. Between 1991 and 2001, over half the local authority-run homes in England closed, with an increase in independent residential homes of 12%. However, overall there was still a decline in the total numbers of homes and residents, by 11.5% and 13.3% respectively in England. In 2005, 88% of residents paid for by their local authority were in independent sector homes compared to 82% in 2000 and 20% in 1993 (DH, 2005).

As one would expect, given a strategy for maintaining more people in their own homes, the number of hours of home care delivered by local authorities rose by 21% between 2000 and 2004. However, this was matched by a fall in the number of households receiving services, down since 2000 by 11%. This resulted from the intensification of services needed to keep very frail and vulnerable people at home (Netten, 2005). The percentage of households receiving intensive home care has increased by 27% since 2001 (DH, 2006).

Whereas earlier home care services would have provided house cleaning, shopping and other similar services, today their work is very focused on personal care. Those requiring a limited amount of help around the house or garden cannot obtain it from their local authority and must purchase it privately. The lack of this 'bit of help' has been severely criticised; it means that preventative services are simply not available, only for those in crisis (Clark et al, 1998). Delivery of home care services has also shifted from the statutory to the independent sector, which provided 73% of all home care hours in 2005, an increase of 22% since 2001 (DH, 2006). Minimal provision of home care services is reflected in the growing number of carers who provide informal care for partners, relatives and neighbours as well as the growth of services purchased by individuals from private health and social care providers.

Reviewing developments since the 1970s, it is clear that the policy to deinstitutionalise care for adults has largely worked. We lack information, however, on those who purchase varying forms of care in the private market and only have detailed information on those poor enough or frail enough to receive local authority support. In fact, good research and data are lacking on many aspects of adults' and older people's care services (Knapp et al, 2004).

New Labour

Since New Labour came to power in 1997, policies focused around combating social exclusion, partnership working and user empowerment have revived interest in developing community-based services across the UK. Two policy agendas have been developed, more or less isolated from each other until 2004, one for renewal of impoverished neighbourhoods and the other for social care. Interestingly, in Northern Ireland, Heenan notes that, in spite of a new commitment to community development, this too remains on the margins of social work practice (Heenan, 2004).

The National Strategy Action Plan *A New Commitment to Neighbourhood Renewal* published by the Social Exclusion Unit in 2001 set out to 'narrow the gap between outcomes in deprived areas and the rest' (SEU, 2001, p 8) in 88 of the poorest areas, with Local Strategic Partnerships delivering and implementing local strategies. It pinpointed a broad spectrum of problems:

- the failure to address the problems of local economies and to promote safe and stable communities;
- poor core public services;
- the failure to involve communities;
- lack of leadership and joint working;
- and insufficient and poor use of information.

Five areas for change were identified:

- employment
- crime
- education and skills
- health, and
- housing and physical environment.

This heralded a new era for community development (Gilchrist, 2003). In all of this there was barely a word about social services. Where client groups such as children and young people (traditionally the preserve of social services) were considered, special initiatives were set up outside social services departments – for example, Sure Start, Connexions, the Children's Fund and a strategy for teenage pregnancy. It was therefore unsurprising to find an observation in an Audit Commission survey in 2002 that social services departments seemed to be sticking to their 'core business' rather than getting involved in neighbourhood renewal (Audit Commission, 2002, p 12).

While the neighbourhood renewal strategy might suggest a disregard for social services, the White Paper *Modernising Social Services* (DH, 1998) suggested that government itself was taking the social care agenda seriously: it introduced comprehensive National Service Frameworks for a range of groups and emphasised partnership working with health through Care Trusts, and user empowerment and independent living through direct payments. Other initiatives included workforce development through a General Social Care Council and the Training Organisation for the Personal Social Services (TOPSS), now Skills for Care, and the establishment of a Social Care Institute for Excellence (SCIE) supporting a firm belief in evidence-based practice. The establishment of the Commission for Social Care Inspection (CSCI) pulled previous functions of the Social Services Inspectorate, the Care Standards Commission and the Audit Commission together into a major initiative for improving services. Yet the social care agenda still seemed narrowly focused, with a greater focus on the workings of statutory social services and their contractual partners, and the interface with health and education, than on the potential role of services in communities.

As Quilgars (2004, p 2) has noted in her evaluation of the Hull Community Care Development Project (see also Chapter Ten):

> Community care and community have received little joint attention. Community care policy continues largely to be delivered in, rather than by, the community, with professionals primarily adopting an individualised approach

to delivering support and care. Whilst regeneration and social inclusion policy agendas have brought a renewed focus on communities and a heightened role for community development, care and support issues have been largely neglected in area-based work.

Similarly, commenting on the government's *Framework for the Assessment of Children in Need and their Families* (DH/DfEE, 2000), Jack (2004, p 1) pointed out that the core assessment forms included 14 pages in which child development and parenting capacity were considered together, but 'what is missing is a simultaneous consideration of the interactions between these issues and the wider family and environmental factors that are also involved'. *Working Together to Safeguard Children* (DH, 1999) only had six lines in a 100-page document on community influences. Jack (2004) also cited evidence from the national survey of children's health that the risk of developing a classifiable mental disorder is two to three times higher for children living in the poorest families, in privately rented or social housing, in deprived areas with limited friendship networks.

As often in the past, developing policy was challenged by a further shocking instance of child abuse and neglect. The Laming Report (2003) on the Victoria Climbié case produced a damning indictment of social services management; this added strength to a slow-burning fire, which for a number of years had fuelled the argument that children's services should be organised separately from those for adults. Thus, following publication of the Green Paper *Every Child Matters* (DfES, 2003) responsibility for children's social services was moved from the Department of Health to the Department for Education and Skills.

A prime example of tensions between neighbourhood renewal and social care may be found in the Anti-Social Behaviour Orders (ASBOs) currently being implemented around the country. Stephen and Squires (2004, Chapter Seven) have illustrated how the implementation of these by community safety officers in Brighton and Hove has left some families distraught, unsupported and fearful of eviction. 'Amongst most of the parents and young people the greatest contempt for and sense of "having been failed" was directed at two main agencies: education (mostly) and social services' (Stephen and Squires, 2004, p 66). Although social services had been involved with several of the families interviewed there was a perceived absence of support and an inability to provide the sorts of resources the families felt they needed.

Community development and social care

Tensions between community development/neighbourhood renewal and social care policy have several sources. Chief among these are historical factors, political divisions of responsibility, changing patterns in the delivery of welfare, education, training and workforce issues, and ideology.

Historical factors

The development of community work through the Charity Organisation Society (COS) and the Settlement Movement in the 19th century, and as a specialist branch of social work in the mid-20th century, can best be described as haphazard. It was transformed from 'an activity largely on the margins of the voluntary sector into an instrument of policy within the statutory sector' (Shaw, 2004, p 19), through the 1968 Calouste Gulbenkian Foundation report *Community Work and Social Change*, with both the Calouste Gulbenkian Foundation and Seebohm (1968) emphasising its role in creating active citizens from within deviant and depressed subcultures. The launch of the Community Development Project in 1968 confirmed community work's state role although this was challenged by an alternative, more radical approach, based on the perception of poverty as structurally created through capitalism.

Social work had similar origins, both through the COS and the Guilds of Help. While the influence of the COS is well established (Lewis, 1995) less is known about the Guilds, the first of which was launched in Bradford in September 1904 and which within a year had 500 helpers and 2,000 cases. By 1911 there were 60 Guilds in England and Wales with over 8,000 members and these provided the most important membership of the 1919 Council of Social Services. What was interesting about the Guilds was that their philosophy was one of citizenship, with a duty to provide help to those less fortunate than oneself, but:

> this civic consciousness did not, however, include a commitment to the city council directly providing services, for this would have been an acknowledgement by them that voluntary organisations could not cope with distress. (Cahill and Jowitt, 1980, p 398)

Nevertheless, like community work, social work moved steadily into the statutory sector from the mid-20th century, gradually leaving its voluntary origins behind. Unlike community work, political commitment, through the 1970 Local Authorities Social Services Act, and the creation of social services departments in 1971, confirmed social work institutionally, standardised training and initiated a long period of mounting statutory responsibilities. Although a 'radical social work' agenda in the 1960s and 1970s encouraged the development of a belief in individual empowerment in social work (Langan, 2002) this did not extend to empowering communities. Subsequently, not just crises in child protection but the development of community care's contract culture moved social work further away from the spirit of community work in the 1980s and 1990s with 'care in the community' rarely translating into 'care by the community' (Bulmer, 1987).

Political divisions of responsibility

In the Thatcher years no fewer than seven ministries held some responsibility for urban renewal. Today there may have been some streamlining of responsibility with the placing of the Neighbourhood Renewal Unit within a Department for Communities and Local Government, but this will still operate separately from the Social Exclusion Unit now based in the Cabinet Office and from those in the Home Office with responsibility for the voluntary sector. At local level, Local Strategic Partnerships have responsibility for community development but social services' main interests are concentrated in Care Trusts for adult services, and Partnership Boards and Children's Trusts for children's services. Partnership working between health and education therefore provides a more important focus than between neighbourhood renewal and social care. On the ground, interactions between front-line staff often remain difficult and there is a reliance on other agencies to bridge the gulf between community interests and social services' responsibilities.

Changing patterns in the delivery of welfare

Two features have distinguished the delivery of social care in recent years. The first has been the development of the market economy, with the once near monopoly of service provision by local authorities challenged and replaced, as explained earlier, by services contracted out to voluntary and private providers. Commitment to a mixed economy of care, promoted by the Conservatives and endorsed by the 1990 Community Care Act has intensified under New Labour. Second has been the separation of adults' and children's services, reflecting a pattern, albeit on a much smaller scale, that existed before the Second World War, and the growing relationship with health and education. The 2001 Health and Social Care Act has, for example, directed local authorities and health agencies to pool their budgets where services are failing. One assessment of the effect of these changes is that 'health and social care have now lost virtually all their ties into such processes as urban regeneration, widening participation and social inclusion' (Jordan, 2004, p 91).

Education, training and workforce issues

Although social workers and community workers are increasingly likely to work together in such settings as Children's Centres, they share little commonality in training.

Ideology

The fact that the education and training of community workers and social workers have travelled along different paths is both a cause and a result of the different discourses that characterise their activities. Concepts common to community development, such as governance, citizenship, community engagement, civic involvement, social capital, democracy and human rights, contrast with a social work training programme normally focused on anti-discriminatory practice, user empowerment, inter-professional working and meeting individual needs. This is not to suggest that such concepts are incompatible, but that they appear opposed because of the ways in which they are presented and interpreted. Jordan (1990), Beresford and Turner (1997), Lister (1998) and others have made the point that social workers are well placed to promote the citizenship of those in poverty and other marginalised groups. To quote Lister (1998, p 16):

> The concept of citizenship offers social work a framework which embraces anti-poverty work, principles of partnership and an anti-discriminatory or oppressive practice and an inclusionary stance.

Yet it is hard in the current situation to see this happening, in spite of the recent and apparently encouraging policy developments discussed below.

More recent policy developments

In the aftermath of the removal of responsibility for children's services to the Department for Education and Skills there was concern at the potential loss of a coherent and distinctive care agenda. The Green Paper on adult social care *Independence, Well-being and Choice* (DH, 2005), based on more or less identical principles to those of *Every Child Matters* (DfES, 2003), was seen as redressing this. Few challenged its 'new vision' based on the belief that 'everyone has a contribution to make and has the right to control their own lives' (DH, 2005, p 16). In the same year the Green Paper was joined by two other documents *Improving the Life Chances of Disabled People* (Cabinet Office, 2005) and *Opportunity Age* (HM Government, 2005), both of which, as Glendinning and Means (2006, p 18) point out, reflect 'an underlying shift from a paternalistic to a citizenship discourse', which emphasises rights rather than needs. It should be noted, however, that their discourse surrounding choice and empowerment was articulated in very similar fashion in the Seebohm (1968), Barclay (1982) and Griffiths (1989) Reports as well as in the 1989 White Paper on community care (DH, 1989). In many ways, therefore, there was little new in this Green Paper. The calls for preventative services, greater reliance on the community and voluntary sectors, support for carers and closer working with health had been made regularly down the years (Glasby, 2005).

In the Green Paper, ensuring that control and choice becomes a reality is reliant on four strategies:

* giving people more control through self-assessment and planning and managing their own services;
* developing new and innovative methods of support;
* building and harnessing the capacity of communities; and
* improving the social care workforce.

These and related issues are discussed below.

Direct payments and individual budgets

Individual budgets, an extension of direct payments, were defined as one of the main tools for implementing the new agenda. Direct payments had been based on a scheme pioneered in Hampshire with the Independent Living Association whereby individuals with physical disabilities were given a payment with which they could purchase the services they wanted. In many cases this involved employing a personal assistant, necessitating training and support in employment law and practice. Under the 1996 Direct Payments Act only people under the age of 65 were eligible, but the scheme was extended to older people in 2000 and also to people with learning disabilities, people with mental health problems and carers. Generally, take-up has been limited: out of 1.68 million adults using community care services in 2002/03 only 12,585 individuals were receiving direct payments, of whom only 2,000 were older people.

The introduction of individual budgets has been described as capable of radically altering the face of social care by promoting independence and recognising an individual's right to make their own choices. The budget will be held by the local authority on behalf of the person using services, who may choose to receive their support in a cash payment or through provision of services. The Green Paper (DH, 2005) argued that giving people individual budgets would drive up the quality of services, stimulating the social care market to provide the services people really want and shifting resources away from services that do not meet needs and expectations (para 4.35). It would also promote the development of different social work roles including:

- a person-centred planning facilitator to support the individual;
- a care manager to undertake the needs assessment and case manage the care package;
- a care navigator with knowledge of mainstream and specialist services;
- a care broker who might help the individual formulate the care plan.

There is no doubt that individual budgeting can open up an exciting range of possibilities, for example by allowing groups of individuals to purchase collectively, set up cooperatives and make real choices about what they would like. Budgets will also be available to carers, although the implications of this are far from clear. The system will only work, however, if the services they want to purchase are readily available and of good quality (Scourfield, 2005) and that is often far from the case.

Role of the community and voluntary sector

In the Green Paper a further component of planning for adult social care was greater reliance on the voluntary and community sector. At the moment the voluntary sector plays a relatively minor, although significant, role in social care. Kendall (2000) has suggested three reasons for this situation, which is unique to the UK:

- First, major statutory payments to the private sector for supported residents and those in receipt of home care have led to the growth of commercial care enterprises rather than the growth of the not-for-profit sector.
- Second, lack of support for the principle of welfare subsidiarity has meant that the voluntary sector has not been acknowledged as superior to the state in delivering services that people want and need.
- Third, the very low wages of those working in service delivery for older people have made the commercial care sector more profitable than in other parts of Europe.

To these we can add a fourth dimension. In their commissioning of services from the voluntary sector, local authorities have been accused of holding down prices, making it difficult for small voluntary bodies to cover their costs and requiring them to subsidise their services from funds raised from the public. This has been no recipe for expansion.

Added to all this is the fragmented nature of voluntary and community activity. In poorer areas, neighbourhood renewal funding has, as discussed, supported the development of community safety, better education, employment, housing and health, but has not embraced social care. The ideological and organisational gap between community work and social care services continues to restrict attempts to address the needs of the poorest and most vulnerable people.

This may all sound very negative when in fact there are many examples in the field of local projects designed to support people in their own homes through voluntary activity. The Neighbourhood Care Scheme in Brighton, described in Chapter Eleven, is one example of this. Yet, as was the case with the befriending scheme described in Chapter Twelve, voluntary projects are not self-sustaining and will close if mainstream funding is not made available.

The social care workforce

A third major component in implementing the new vision for adult social care is the social care workforce supported by a children's workforce strategy and the Skills for Care agency. Across the statutory, voluntary and private sectors well over a million people work in social care, a majority with adults and older people. Recruitment and retention are problematic in both inner-city and rural areas. The almost totally female workforce has a wide range of choices at a time of almost full employment and is not easily attracted to work and remain in organisations characterised by low pay, poor conditions of work and few career opportunities (Balloch, 2005). Mears makes the same points in her chapter on home care in Australia (Chapter Thirteen). Although in some areas these working conditions have improved, the security that workers had when employed by a local authority is lacking. Attempts to raise levels of qualification have been only partially successful, due to a lack of enthusiasm among older women, the high cost of training that has to be borne by the women or their employers, and the lack of assessors. Arguably, the greatest effect has been seen in social work itself with the BA Social Work and the Green Paper's view of social workers as brokers of services raising the profession's status. Although for other care staff the government has set targets for improved levels of qualification, these are proving difficult to meet due to a lack of funding and training facilities (Balloch et al, 2004). The employment of agency staff and overseas workers has addressed some of the recruitment difficulties but brought its own problems – not least the lack of the continuity of care that people value highly. Interestingly, in Japan, until the time of writing the employment of overseas staff in social care was banned, although now staff shortages have encouraged reconsideration of this.

Health and social care

The integration of health and social care services at the local level took centre stage in the White Paper *Our Health, Our Care, Our Say* (DH, 2006) on out-of-hospital and adult social care. This was designed to build on and take forward the Green Paper. It set out four main goals:

- better preventative services;
- more choice for patients and users;
- addressing inequalities and developing community resources; and
- providing more and better support for people with long-term needs.

Critics felt that it overemphasised health and underplayed the significance of social care. Others saw it as a good way forward for integrated health and social care in the community, to be achieved through aligning local authorities and Primary Care Trusts, strengthening Local Area

Agreements and Local Strategic Partnerships and, hopefully, linking up with the neighbourhood renewal agenda.

From 2007 councils' performance will be assessed against the White Paper's seven outcomes – health, quality of life, choice, freedom from discrimination, making a positive contribution, economic well-being and dignity, as well as judgements on leadership and commissioning. By 2009 joint outcomes for health and social care are proposed with performance indicators changed to reflect these and separate judgements for each client group (CSCI, 2006).

The White Paper recognised the important role of carers, acknowledging that those with responsibilities of over 50 hours a week are much more likely to be in poor health. Better support for carers came third in the 'people's options' at the national Citizens' Summit (para 5.50). It therefore proposed to update and extend the 1999 Strategy for Carers, encourage councils and Primary Care Trusts to nominate leads for carers' services, establish an information service/ helpline for carers, ensure that short-term, home-based respite support is established for emergency situations and allocate specific funding for an Expert Carers Programme. The words are fine, but the reality on the ground has been one of local authorities being forced into cutting support to carers' organisations as a direct result of enforced economies.

Partnership working

Partnership working is clearly seen as crucial to achieving the goals above. A consistent and central theme of New Labour's modernisation agenda, it has been given greater emphasis by the proposed shift to community-based services with the key to its success dependent on joint service and workforce planning. Developing team working through the NHS Large-scale Workforce Change programme and the Skills for Care New Types of Worker pilots is to be complemented through the Partnership for Older People Projects (POPs), other well-being pilots and multi-skilled teams (DH, 2006, paras 8.35–8.40). This is matched by the further aim of professionals working to support and empower people to make their own decisions wherever possible (para 8.41).

While widely accepted as positive, the effectiveness of partnership working in terms of improved outcomes for users has still to be demonstrated. Also, as Rummery (2006, p 300) has emphasised, there is a danger that an emphasis on partnership 'works against improvements in involving citizens in meaningful ways...' and '... strengthens the role of agencies in a way that can disempower citizens and lead to their social exclusion'. The tensions between partnership working and service user empowerment have several sources. First, there is, for example, an inherent difficulty where professionals must weigh a citizen's right to privacy against achieving effective, joined-up service delivery. This is particularly the case in settings such as mental health teams where one citizen may be perceived as posing risks to others (6 et al, 2006). Second, there is also a danger that a focus on integrated systems, such as hospital discharge procedures set up to avoid bed-blocking, may actually lose sight of a user's particular needs. Third, with user involvement much more extensively developed and incorporated into professional training in social care rather than in health, problems can arise between different models and ideologies of care. Ultimately, however, the core problem is one of power imbalances between the various partners involved. As we noted several years ago, 'inclusive partnerships can be developed, but only if fundamental inequalities between "partners", based on differences in income, culture, ethnicity, disability, age, education and training and other factors, are recognised, challenged and changed' (Balloch and Taylor, 2001, p 288). Joining up the care agenda with policies for local communities means, precisely, taking this into account.

Funding

One of the major difficulties with both the Green Paper (DH, 2005) and the White Paper (DH, 2006) was that they promised no extra resources for care, rather a 'shifting of resources'. Yet the care system already operates on a minimalist basis, with strict eligibility and means-tested rationing criteria operated by local authority adult social care departments. At the time of writing some local authorities had begun to restrict adult social services to people with 'critical' needs, due to the pressures on resources from increased demand, NHS cuts and tight government grants (Community Care, 2006). Many view this situation as grossly unfair, with a postcode lottery determining local authority charges and individuals often being required to sell their homes to afford residential care. It penalises, in particular, those just above the income threshold for assistance.

With an ageing population there is inevitably mounting concern over care costs. In 1999 the Royal Commission on Long Term Care had concluded that current arrangements for continuing long-term care were inadequate and recommended statutory funding not just for health costs (difficult to obtain in any case) but also personal care costs.

As noted earlier, only in Scotland was this recommendation accepted – one of the reasons for including a separate chapter on Scotland in this book (Chapter Three).

The way our social care system is funded, through a mix of social security benefits and local authority expenditure, has changed little since the end of the Second World War, with the exception of the substantial increase in local authority charging systems. In 2005 Hirsch quoted the main public resources spent on long-term care as shown in Table 2.1.

This does not take account of the substantial sums spent on home and residential/nursing care by private individuals for which there are no satisfactory statistics.

Hirsch (2005) estimated that a current expenditure of £14.2 billion could quadruple by the middle of the 21st century. Similarly, the Wanless (2006) review of social care estimated an increase to around £30 billion by 2026. To cover this, Wanless recommends a partnership model, rather than free personal care. In this Rawlsian model there would be a free-of-charge minimum guaranteed amount of care, supporting those on low incomes but guaranteeing everyone the basic minimum. All would contribute amounts matched by the state up to an agreed level, with people able to top up afterwards. This would do away with means testing, leaving this to the benefits system, with social care provision determined by need. While the system would cost more than the present one, its advantage would lie in its universal and inclusive character, mirroring that of health and education and recognising the right to care as well as the importance of meeting needs.

Table 2.1: Costs of long-term care

	£ billion
Attendance/Disability Allowance	6.7
Carers' Allowance	1.1
Local authority spending (England)	5.7
NHS spending on continuing healthcare	Not known
NHS spending on nursing care	0.7
Total	14.2

Source: Hirsch (2005, p 30)

Conclusion

In reviewing the complex issues surrounding care, community and citizenship, this chapter has identified positive developments such as the move away from institutional care to home care, the development of more integrated working between health and social care, the increasing emphasis on independence, choice, rights and citizenship and the drive to relate local services to local needs. It has also identified the welcome, renewed emphasis in the Green and White Papers on strengthening links between communities and social care.

But the picture is very mixed and the market in social care means that there are not only winners but losers. The high costs of care require rationing, with strict criteria to determine eligibility for statutory services and limits on the extent of statutory support. In spite of the move away from residential care towards more intensive home care, there are many in need who cannot benefit from either. For older people in particular, between residential and home care there are few alternatives in terms of very sheltered housing. Informal carers carry much of the burden of care and compensate for the lack of services, as do voluntary and community groups.

The biggest problems will, of course, continue to arise in the poorest communities where health inequalities and income differentials are greatest. That is why, if care in and by the community is finally to become a reality, we need to see the above policies underwritten by substantial funding. While the government's vision of improved independence and choice for all is widely acclaimed, the reality is that this vision will be difficult to implement if the above issues are not first addressed.

References

6, P., Bellamy, C., Raab, C. and Warren, A. (2006) 'Partnerships and privacy – tension or settlement? The case of adult mental health services', *Social Policy and Society*, vol 5, no 2, pp 237-48.

Audit Commission (2002) *Policy Focus: Neighbourhood Renewal*, London: Audit Commission.

Balloch, S. (2005) 'The social care workforce', A community care pre-election supplement, *Community Care*, 23 March, available at: www.communitycare.co.uk

Balloch, S. and Taylor, M. (eds) (2001) *Partnership Working: Policy and Practice*, Bristol: The Policy Press.

Balloch, S., Hill, M. and Banks, L. (2004) 'Securing quality in the mixed economy of care: issues about training standards', *Social Policy and Society*, vol 3, no 4, pp 365-73.

Barclay Report (1982) *Social Workers, their Role and Tasks*, London: National Institute for Social Work.

Beresford, P. and Turner, M. (1997) *It's Our Welfare*, London: National Institute for Social Work.

Bulmer, M. (1987) *The Social Basis of Community Care*, London: Allen and Unwin.

Cabinet Office (2005) *Improving the Life Chances of Disabled People*, London: Cabinet Office, Strategy Unit.

Cahill, M. and Jowitt, T. (1980) 'The new philanthropy: the emergence of the Bradford City Guild of Help', *Journal of Social Policy*, vol 9, no 3, pp 359-82.

Calouste Gulbenkian Foundation (1968) *Community Work and Social Change*, London: Longman.

Clark, H., Dyer, S. and Horwood, J. (1998) *'That Bit Of Help': The High Value of Low-level Preventative Services For Older People*, Bristol: The Policy Press.

CSCI (Commission for Social Care Inspection) (2006) Consultant paper, *A New Outcomes Framework for Performance Assessment of Adult Social Care*, Consultation document, London: CSCI.

Community Care (2006) 'Treasury spending review unlikely to resolve social care funding woes', *Community Care*, 10-16 August, p 8.

DfES (Department for Education and Skills) (2003) *Every Child Matters*, Cm 5860, London: The Stationery Office.

DH (Department of Health) (1989) *Caring for People: Community Care in the Next Decade and Beyond*, London: HMSO.

DH (1998) *Modernising Social Services: Promoting Independence, Improving Protection, Raising Standards*, Cm 4169, London: The Stationery Office.

DH (2005) *Independence, Well-being and Choice: Our Vision for the Future of Social Care for Adults in England*, Green Paper, London: DH.

DH (2006) *Our Health, Our Care, Our Say: A New Direction for Community Services*, London: The Stationery Office.

DH/DfEE (Department for Education and Employment)/Home Office (2000) *Framework for the Assessment of Children in Need and their Families*, London: The Stationery Office.

DH, Home Office and Department for Education and Employment (1999) *Working Together to Safeguard Children*, London: The Stationery Office.

Gilchrist, A. (2003) 'Community development in the UK: possibilities and paradoxes', *Community Development Journal*, vol 38, no 1, pp 16-25.

Glasby, J. (2005) 'The future of adult social care', *Research Policy and Planning*, vol 23, no 2, pp 61-70.

Glendinning, C. and Means, R. (2006) 'Personal social services: developments in adult social care', in *Social Policy Review 18: Analysis and Debate in Social Policy, 2006*, Bristol: The Policy Press with the Social Policy Association.

Griffiths, R. (1989) *Community Care: Agenda for Action: A Report to the Secretary of State for Social Services*, London: HMSO.

Heenan, D. (2004) 'Learning lessons from the past or re-visiting old mistakes: social work and community development in Northern Ireland', *British Journal of Social Work*, vol 34, no 6, pp 793-809.

Hirsch, D. (2005) *Facing the Cost of Long-term Care: Towards a Sustainable Funding System*, York: Joseph Rowntree Foundation.

HM Government (2005) *Opportunity Age: Meeting the Challenges of Ageing in the 21st Century*, London: Department for Work and Pensions.

Jack, G. (2004) 'The missing side of the triangle: analysing the influence of wider family and environmental factors on parenting and child development', Paper presented to the Royal Holloway's Making Research Count Policy Forum, London, 5 March.

Jordan, B. (1990) *Social Work in an Unjust Society*, London: Harvester Wheatsheaf.

Jordan, B. (2004) 'The personal social services', in N. Ellison, L. Bauld and M. Powell (eds) *Social Policy Review 16*, Bristol: The Policy Press for the Social Policy Association, pp 81-98.

Kendall, I. (2000) 'The voluntary sector and social care for older people', in B. Hudson (ed) *The Changing Role of Social Care*, London: Jessica Kingsley.

Knapp, M., Fernandes, J. L., Kendall, J., Beecham, J., Northy, S. and Richardson, A. (2005) *Developing Social Care: The Current Position*, London: PSSRU, London School of Economics and Political Science.

Laming, H. (2003) *The Victoria Climbié Inquiry*, Cm 5730, London: The Stationery Office.

Langan, M. (2002) 'The legacy of radical social work', in R. Adams, L. Dominelli and M. Payne (eds) *Social Work: Themes, Issues and Critical Debates* (2nd edition), Basingstoke: Palgrave in association with the Open University, pp 207-16.

Lewis, J. (1995) *Voluntary Sector, the State and Social Work in Britain: The Charity Organisation Society/Family Welfare Association since 1869,* Aldershot: Edward Elgar.

Lister, R. (1998) 'Citizenship, social work and social action', *European Journal of Social Work,* vol 1, no 1, pp 5-18.

Netten, A. (2005) 'Personal social services', in M. Powell, L. Bauld and K. Clarke (eds) *Social Policy Review 17: Analysis and Debate in Social Policy, 2005,* Bristol: The Policy Press on behalf of the Social Policy Association, pp 85-103.

OFT (Office of Fair Trading) (2005) *Care Homes for Older People in the UK: A Market Study,* London: Office of Fair Trading.

Quilgars, D. (2004) *Communities Caring and Developing: Lessons from Hull,* JRF Findings, Ref 534, York: Joseph Rowntree Foundation.

Royal Commission on Long Term Care (1999) *With Respect to Old Age: Long Term Care – Rights and Responsibilities,* London: The Stationery Office.

Rummery, K. (2006) 'Partnerships and collaborative governance in welfare: the citizenship challenge', *Social Policy and Society,* vol 5, no 2, pp 293-303.

Scourfield, P. (2005) 'Implementing the Community Care (Direct Payments) Act: will the supply of personal assistants meet the demand and at what price?', *Journal of Social Policy,* vol 34, no 3, pp 1-20.

Seebohm Report (1968) *Report of the Committee on Local Authority and Allied Personal Social Services,* Cmnd 3703, London: HMSO.

SEU (Social Exclusion Unit) (2001) *A New Commitment to Neighbourhood Renewal: National Strategy Action Plan,* London: Cabinet Office.

Shaw, M. (2004) *Community Work: Policy, Politics and Practice,* Working Papers in Social Sciences and Policy, Hull: University of Hull.

Stephen, D. and Squires, P. (2003) *Community Safety, Enforcement and Acceptable Behaviour Contracts: An Evaluation of the Work of the Community Safety Team in the East Brighton 'New Deal for Communities' Area,* Brighton: University of Brighton, Health and Social Policy Research Centre.

Wanless, D. (2006) *Securing Good Care for Older People: Taking a Long-term View,* London: King's Fund.

THREE

Care, citizenship and community in Scotland

Alison Petch

> Community in its fullest sense is thus what is achieved through social inclusion and social justice, including the reduction of inequalities. (Stewart, 2004, p 145)

This chapter explores the extent to which policy and practice in Scotland in the key areas of care, citizenship and community contrasts with that presented for the rest of the UK. The extent to which there is evidence for difference, both before and after devolution, is examined. It is suggested that a succession of shifts can be identified: from a privileging of community interests evident across social welfare, housing and community regeneration to a greater emphasis currently on partnership working, and from a concept of communal benefit to individual personalisation.

Traditionally, social welfare practice in Scotland has been portrayed as distinctive from that elsewhere in the UK. Section 12 of the 1968 Social Work (Scotland) Act is cited as placing a unique duty on every local authority:

> to promote social welfare by making advice, guidance and assistance on such a scale as may be appropriate for their area, and in that behalf make arrangements so to provide or secure the provision of such facilities as they may consider suitable and adequate.

There is a common perception that the community social work model promoted within the Barclay Report (1982) and subsequent initiatives (for example Hearn and Thomson, 1987; Darvill and Smale, 1990) gained a stronger following in Scotland. It is difficult to assemble definitive evidence on this argument but there have been well-regarded and well-documented examples through the former National Institute for Social Work of teams operating on this model (Crosbie et al, 1987, 1989; Smale and Bennett, 1989). Certainly a period spent with the Badenoch and Strathspey team in 1987 highlighted a way of working very much rooted in the local community. A more systematic evaluation, of the Age Concern Aberdeen Informal Support and Care Project, was reported by Gordon and Donald (1993) who considered the effectiveness of weaving together informal and formal networks in providing support for older people.

The features attributed to the community social work model can be linked to other initiatives within social welfare and the social economy in Scotland, which are characterised by a focus on community capital and on participation by local stakeholders. The development of the housing association movement in the west of Scotland during the 1970s and 1980s (Burns et al, 2001) with its focus on tenant participation and local regeneration strategies, for example the renewal of the Glasgow East End through the GEAR Project, was very much of this ilk. Scottish Office initiatives for housing renewal have also been predicated on principles of resident involvement, for example transfer of stock to community ownership schemes and the establishment of four Urban Partnerships in the late 1980s, multi-agency projects to transform run-down housing. The extent to which such developments engage effectively with community interests has, of course, varied and has been the focus for a raft of detailed studies. Kintrea (1996), for example, has explored the extent to which the principle of resident involvement was achieved in the oft-cited Ferguslie Park Urban Partnership (Paisley) and in particular the role of FLAG, the Ferguslie League of Action Groups, highlighting the potential for community participation to be managed and incorporated.

Also focused in the west of Scotland, and particularly within the former Strathclyde Region, has been the emphasis on social enterprise, with a tradition of locally grown businesses fostered by groups such as the WISE group and Community Enterprise. Most recently a number of social firms have been established in Scotland, including Rolls on Wheels and Six Mary's Place guesthouse, part of Forth Sector, which have had particular success. A number of Clubhouses, dedicated to the integration of individuals with mental ill-health into the workplace and the work-ordered day, have also flourished.

While each of these initiatives may on its own be modest, they attain greater significance in the context of different trajectories in the establishment of community-based provision (Hunter and Wistow, 1988) and when the relative balance across different providers north and south of the Border is explored. For example, whereas 73% of home care is delivered by the independent sector in England (September 2005), the comparative figure in Scotland is 30% (November 2005).

These variations have been explored further elsewhere (Petch, 1999; Curtice and Fraser, 2000).

Perhaps more telling, however, is the commentary presented by Cheetham (2001). She describes her return to Scotland in 1986:

> My strong impression, then and now, was of a greater public ownership of welfare in Scotland than in England. In middle class and professional circles you do not think twice about owning up to being a social worker for fear of a diatribe about delinquents, inadequate parents, neglectful social workers and dependent scroungers. (Cheetham, 2001, pp 625-6)

And she cites the first Scottish Minister for Health and Social Work who declared that 'welfare is part of the way Scotland does its business'. It may be considered significant that the first piece of legislation to be pursued by the Scottish Parliament was the 2000 Adults with Incapacity Act, a challenge only now being addressed in England. It should also not be forgotten that following the Kilbrandon Report (1964), the responsibility for making decisions in respect of children and young people within the juvenile justice system was placed on the lay children's hearings. This included the directive that selection for panel membership should seek to identify individuals familiar with, indeed representative of, the communities of origin of the children appearing before the panel. There is a sense, therefore, of something that hints at a Scottish difference, perhaps a legacy of a long tradition that can be traced back to the Scottish Enlightenment. Stewart (2004) presents an interesting exploration of this argument, focusing in particular on health and on education.

The place of community

The Joseph Rowntree Foundation and the Scottish Executive funded an important action research project designed to explore the contribution of the community development approach to community care (Barr et al, 2001), which is of relevance to this debate on the role of communities in care in Scotland. This built on an earlier research and training project (Barr et al, 1997), which from a number of case studies had evidenced the benefits:

- empowered user organisations;
- better services;
- increased user satisfaction;

- supportive communities; and
- community regeneration.

It also acknowledged earlier work by Barr (1995) on the complexity of empowering communities. The key theme emerging from the detailed activity in the four diverse communities in the second study was the broadening of focus from community care to more generic community involvement in response to the government's agenda of social inclusion and the call for local authorities to work with communities in the provision of 'joined-up solutions' and community-based regeneration.

> From a community and service user perspective, issues relating to community care services could not be conveniently isolated from many others that determined the quality of personal or community life. Exclusion was a powerful common denominator between care users and others in the community. Needs were consistently placed in a context that connected them to wider community concerns related, for example, to transport, safety, planning, leisure opportunities, accessible services or responsive governance. (Barr et al, 2001, p 5)

It should be noted that one of these projects focused on the involvement of users and carers from black and ethnic minority communities in Glasgow. Bowes and Sim (1997) argue that minority ethnic groups have been badly served by support services in Scotland; however, the comparative status of such assertions across different countries can be difficult to evidence.

A force in Scotland since the mid-1990s has been the development of local community care forums and their overarching body, the Scottish Community Care Forum. The particular focus of these forums has been the involvement of service users and carers in the process of community care planning and delivery. The forums in Borders and Highland have been particularly vigorous, the latter, for example, spawning the Highland Users Group, a highly effective voice for mental health service users. It is perhaps not entirely fanciful to consider such user-led initiatives, and indeed the increasing voice of the disability movement more generally, as a natural successor to the tenants' groups and community action groups of the earlier decades. The emergent rhetoric, however, is very much one of partnership, with this the mantra of the modernising adult social care agenda – partnership between social care and health, between professional and user, between formal and informal carer.

Aspirations for community involvement in planning structures have been evident in particular since the requirement for community care plans was introduced in the 1990 NHS and Community Care (Scotland) Act and, more recently, the establishment of a structure for community planning. A Green Paper in 2000, *A Power of Community Initiative* (Scottish Executive, 2000), recommended a general power of 'community initiative' and this was translated through the 2003 Local Government in Scotland Act. This introduced a statutory requirement on local authorities to engage in community planning with a range of bodies (police authorities, health boards, Scottish Enterprise, Highlands and Islands Enterprise, the Strathclyde Passenger Transport Authority and the fire boards), with the driver a holistic approach to the social, economic and environmental needs of an area and its communities. In particular, community planning was promoted as a means of ensuring a long-term commitment to effective partnership working with communities, and between local authorities and other key agencies, in order to promote the well-being of the community. Interestingly, 'communities of interest' as well as communities of place were specified as of relevance. A number of commentators have explored the extent to which community planning appears to be delivering on its goals (Stevenson, 2002; Audit Scotland, 2006), while Dewar et al (2004) have sought to translate more general wisdom on the involvement of older people into the specifics of community planning. Most recently this transformation of community engagement into formalised structures has been further centralised with the development of National Standards for Community Engagement through Communities Scotland (2005).

Policy divergence

The creation of the devolved Scottish Parliament has, of course, presented the opportunity for more overt differentiation of policy. The extent to which policy divergence is evident has been a natural focus for commentary (Paterson et al, 2001; Curtice et al, 2002; Parry, 2002; Bromley et al, 2003), whether Scotland is indeed 'a land of milk and honey' (Mooney and Poole, 2004). Mooney and Poole suggest that there have always been claims to Scottish distinctiveness based on four interrelated elements: institutional differences in how social welfare is organised and delivered; distinctive policy and implementation on a number of issues; a more discursive approach to social welfare; and a greater commitment to social democracy. These authors, however, question whether such variation has necessarily led to different outcomes, highlight the variation in interests and priorities *within* the country, and conclude that there may not (yet) be the distinctiveness post devolution that some perceive. Inevitably, there is a degree of relativity and selective emphasis in such debates. For the current context, however, two specific initiatives can be highlighted, the contribution of unpaid carers and the implementation of free personal care for older people.

The role of the unpaid carer

Carers Scotland and others concerned with the role and status of informal care have seized the opportunity of Scottish legislation to promote a distinctive identity for the unpaid carer. In 1999 a Strategy for Carers in Scotland was published (Scottish Executive, 1999), similar to the parallel strategies in England and in Wales, and in 2000 a Carers Legislation Working Group was established. The recommendations from the Group (Scottish Executive, 2001) included a number of key elements:

- The NHS, local authorities and others should regard carers as key *partners* in providing care.
- Support provided to carers in their caring role should not be regarded as services to clients but as resources to assist them in this role as partners in the provision of care.
- Carers should not be required to contribute to the cost of support or other resources that help them to continue caring.
- Local authorities should be required to provide information to carers about their rights and available support.

Similar to the 2000 Carers and Disabled Children Act in England, the 2002 Community Care and Health (Scotland) Act provided the legal right to a direct assessment as a carer, independent of whether the cared-for person is being assessed. The distinctive perspective in Scotland was the status of co-provider and co-producer of outcomes, one of the agencies providing support rather than themselves a care recipient. The minister at the time endorsed the underlying philosophy: 'I have made clear the Executive's full support for the principle of carers as partners in providing care. That means carers of all ages' (Malcolm Chisholm, Minister for Health and Community Care, 28 November 2001, Official Report, col 4268).

Most recently, Care 21 (2006) has published a major report on the future of unpaid care in Scotland. It concludes that 'recognition, partnership and joint working with carers currently remains more integrated in Scottish social policy' (p 43). Based on a framework of human rights and incorporating a number of research strands reported in a series of appendices, the report identifies two core principles and makes 22 recommendations. The core principles are greater recognition and respect for unpaid carers as key partners and providers of care, and the development of a rights-based approach to services for unpaid carers. In its response to the report, the Scottish Executive (2006b) identifies four priority areas for the immediate future: young carers, respite, health of carers and carer training. These will be revisited in 2008. With regard to respite, the Executive refused to adopt the report's recommendation of a statutory minimum entitlement, although was prepared to reconsider in the future. NHS boards are to develop local carers' information strategies to identify carers, inform them of their rights to support, and ensure they receive information and support. Carers Scotland is to be funded to provide a new training programme designed to develop the 'expert carer'.

Free personal care for older people

For many, the decision of the Scottish Parliament to implement free personal care for older people on the basis of assessed need was a sudden alert to the potentially divergent futures for social welfare (Marnoch, 2003). *Fair Care for Older People*, the report of the Care Development Group (2001) charged with detailing the implementation of free personal care, sought to take a holistic approach to the directive, building the community capacity to support older people in their own homes and seeking to shift further the balance of care towards non-institutional support. Despite media carping and some uncertainties around definition, the implementation of free personal care to date has generally been deemed a success (Bell and Bowes, 2006; Bell et al, 2006). In particular, a concern (in respect of financial estimates) that it might lead to a reduction in unpaid care, with substitution between formal and informal care, has not materialised, while older people with dementia have gained particular benefit.

The Scottish Executive (2006c) has published statistics on the first three years of free personal care. The numbers receiving free personal care rose from 24,200 in July 2002 to 40,900 at September 2005. In July 2002, 45% of home care clients received personal care; by 2005 it had risen to 68%. The proportion of self-funding residents in care homes rose from 23% in 2002-03 to 27% in 2004-05. In terms of expenditure in care homes on free personal care, for the first nine months, July 2002 to March 2003, this was £42 million, rising to £63 million for the 12 months of 2003-04 and £65 million for the 12 months of 2004-05. The equivalent figures for free nursing care were £12 million, £18 million and £19 million. For free personal care at home, expenditure figures rose from £69 million (over the first nine months) to £136 million (for the 12 months of 2004-05), but not all of this is new expenditure.

Haynes et al (2006) in a recent analysis of Census data have shown that Scotland was the only area of the UK in which the number of care homes increased between 1991 and 2001. Care home numbers were up by 11%, compared to a decline of 11% in England, while resident numbers rose by 21% (−13% in England). Much of the explanation for these figures lies in a time lag in the transfer from the former NHS 'geriatric beds' to nursing home provision. Subsequent statistics (Scottish Executive, 2006d) show that between 2000 and 2005 the number of care homes has again declined by 11% (1,684 to 1,504) and the number of residents (of all ages) from 40,332 to 38,433.

The Health Committee of the Scottish Parliament selected free personal care as the focus for its Care Inquiry. Its report (Scottish Parliament, 2006) was published as concerns emerged that half of the local authorities were placing individuals assessed as eligible for free personal care on a waiting list, and there was confusion stemming from the original guidance over eligibility around meal preparation. Nonetheless, the Inquiry concluded that 'the policy of free personal care for the elderly introduced by the Community Care and Health Act has been a success, and has been widely welcomed' (Scottish Parliament, 2006, p 1). In particular it has, in the main, been introduced swiftly and comprehensively, provided greater security and dignity, allowed people to be cared for more readily at home, reduced delayed discharges and largely ended disputes between local authorities and health boards over the care of older people. Areas that need to be addressed include increases for inflation, loopholes that can be used to 'ration' free personal care and delays in assessment. It is recommended that the Executive undertake a review of resources, including whether extension of free personal care to those under the age of 65 can be financially sustained.

Useful evidence relevant to both the above initiatives can be found in the annual Scottish Social Attitudes surveys, which have sought since 1999 to capture attitudes within Scotland on a range of diverse issues with, for a number of key areas, the opportunity for comparison with similar questions asked in England through the British Social Attitudes series. Curtice and Petch (2002) report on the use of four vignettes to explore the question 'does the community care?'. Responses from a sample of 1,605 suggested variations in who people thought should live in community settings (defined as own home, with family or in supported housing) and who people would feel comfortable having as neighbours. For example, three quarters felt that the frail older person should live in the community and would be comfortable with them living next door. Almost three quarters also considered that the person with mental illness should live in the community but less than half said they would be happy with them being next door, and while the vast majority chose a community setting for the person with a learning disability, only three in five would want them next door. For the person with dementia, fewer than three in five thought they should live in the community and only just over two in five would be comfortable with them as a neighbour. Interestingly, there were no gender differences (the vignettes were presented alternatively as male and female) save for women being more wary of a man with mental ill-health living next door.

The same survey also explored 'who should provide care' and 'who should pay for care'. In terms of formal versus informal care, formal provision was the preferred model for the person with mental ill-health (74% of respondents) whereas the pattern was reversed for the person with a learning disability. Believing that an individual should live in the community did not necessarily equate, however, with informal care: half of those who felt that the frail older person should live at home considered their care was best provided by a formal carer. There was a clear belief in a government responsibility for meeting care costs, irrespective of individual means (62% for the individual with a learning disability to 72% for the person with mental ill-health). What is interesting, however, is that the attitudes on this issue may be very similar north and south of the border. In response to a simple choice in meeting care home costs for older people between 'mainly the government' and 'mainly a person themselves and their family' the 88% in Scotland opting for the government was almost matched by the 86% in England. The conclusion is that although the adoption of free personal care in Scotland accords with the wishes of the Scottish population, the belief in a state responsibility is by no means unique to Scotland. Further analysis suggests that there is not a simple equation between those who believe individuals should live in the community and those who support government funding; rather (based on a liberal–authoritarian scale adopted for the study) government funding is associated with a more left-wing outlook while supporting more people in the community equates with a more liberal position.

Current developments

There have been two recent developments of particular interest to the discussion of this chapter. The first is the development of Community Health Partnerships. The second is the year-long exploration of the role of social work triggered by events in the Borders whereby a woman with learning disabilities had experienced long-term abuse.

Community Health Partnerships

Community Health Partnerships (CHPs) were first proposed in the 2003 White Paper *Partnership for Care* (Scottish Executive, 2003) and, following extensive consultation, given their statutory basis in the 2004 NHS Reform (Scotland) Act and the associated guidance. They built on the earlier Local Health Care Cooperatives but are charged in particular with providing the bridge between primary and secondary care and between health and social care, working in partnership to support the improvement of the health of local communities. They follow the service redesign of 2004 whereby NHS boards and trusts were unified into single bodies. The White Paper detailed that CHPs should:

- ensure that patients, carers and the full range of healthcare professionals are involved;
- establish a substantive partnership with local authority services (for example, social work, housing, education and regeneration);
- have greater responsibility and influence in the development of health board resources;
- play a central role in service redesign locally;
- focus on integrating primary and specialist health services at a local level;
- play a pivotal role in delivering health improvement.

The aspiration is to deliver on the key aims:

- delivering services more innovatively and effectively by bringing together those who deliver health and social care;
- improving the health of local communities, tackling inequalities and promoting policies that address poverty and deprivation by working within the community planning framework;

- securing effective public, patient and carer involvement by building on existing, or developing new, mechanisms.

Delivery should be manifest in better outcomes for individuals, with the CHPs expected to contribute, for example, to a reduction in waiting times for assessment, diagnosis, treatment and care, a reduction in the number of emergency admissions through better chronic disease management, a reduction in delayed discharges, and improved access to services through co-location and joint service provision.

Echoing earlier themes, each CHP is charged with developing a Public Partnership Forum as the mechanism for maintaining 'an effective and formal dialogue with their local communities'. The Forum should make people aware of what it is responsible for, engage service users, carers and the public in how to improve health services, and support wider public involvement in planning and decision making through engagement with consultation structures. There has been much debate as to the preferred models for developing these Forums, particularly around the merits of 'virtual groupings', drawing on existing mechanisms for community engagement. Many at the consultation stage were wary of proposals that did not include definitive arrangements for face-to-face meeting, concerned that public participation would become an administrative exercise.

A new Scottish Health Council (replacing former local health councils) is charged with providing quality assurance as to whether CHPs are effectively involving the public through the Public Partnership Forums. Concerns have been expressed, however, as to the independence and status of this structure and about the lack of provision for advocacy within its remit. The Community Care Forums in particular considered the imposition of the Public Partnership Forums to be an unnecessary duplication of their role but in a form that increased statutory control and reduced local accountability and user and carer direction.

21st Century Social Work Review

The second trigger is the 21st Century Social Work Review, the report of which, *Changing Lives* (Scottish Executive, 2006a), was published after a 12-month period of consultation and examination. A parallel exercise is currently being conducted in England – Options for Excellence – and the Scottish report may well preface elements that emerge from this appraisal. Peppered throughout the report are references to personalisation, a drive to ensure that services assist people to meet their needs and achieve their goals on an individualised basis.

> Personalisation puts the person at the centre as a participant in shaping the services they get, and allows them to work with professionals and their carers to manage risk and resources. (Scottish Executive, 2006b, p 32)

Leadbetter and Lownsbrough (2005, p 4) from Demos develop the argument further:

> Social care in Scotland should be organised around the idea of personalisation: people as active participants in shaping, creating and delivering their care, in conjunction with their paid and unpaid carers, so that it meets their distinctive needs and their hopes for themselves.

Moreover in arguing for a greater capacity for community-based care and in promoting recuperative care programmes, they conclude that 'the line between preventive social work and community development is very thin' (p 27).

Personalised services should be characterised by a greater focus on prevention; partnership across service providers in the public, voluntary and private sectors; flexible service delivery; more empowered users of services; and increased community capacity. Five specific recommendations designed to promote such personalisation are highlighted:

- Social work services must be designed and delivered around the needs of people who use services, their carers and communities.
- Social work services must build individual, family and community capacity to meet their own needs.
- Social work services must play a full and active part in a public sector-wide approach to prevention and earlier intervention.
- Social work services must become an integral part of a whole public sector approach to supporting vulnerable people and promoting social well-being.
- Social work services must recognise and effectively manage the mixed economy of care in the delivery of services.

The second of these recommendations is of particular relevance to the current context. The need to develop community capacity and to increase the role of social work services in building the social economy is detailed. Reference is made to the need to transform the traditionally discrete activity of community social work.

A new approach is now needed, which positions social work services at the heart of communities delivering a combination of individual and community based work alongside education, housing, health and police services. (Leadbetter and Lownsbrough, 2005, p 38)

An initiative by the organisation Communities that Care, which focuses on community capacity building, is cited. For Leith, in Edinburgh, an action plan to respond to poor parental supervision and discipline was developed with workers trained to deliver a responsive programme designed to build resilience. A second example is the implementation of Local Area Coordination for people with learning disabilities, a model originally developed in Australia where it provided shopfront access to advice and support and facilitated the development of both formal and informal support networks.

It is appropriate to characterise current activity around care and communities in Scotland by variants around coordination, collaboration and partnership between different stakeholders and actors within the process. Partnership working in Scotland received particular impetus from *Community Care: A Joint Future*, a report of the Joint Future Group (2000), and a strong central directive with a joint performance assessment framework now propels a programme of joint working between health and social care. In respect of community regeneration and social justice the emphasis is targeted on partnerships with community members, although in health and social care also the role of the user in the co-production of welfare is gathering pace. A preliminary conclusion might be that while the strong tradition of community participation evident in the 1980s has been replaced by both more formalised and more individualised structures, a strong lead has been taken in terms of a partnership agenda.

Capturing the Scottish perspective on care, citizenship and community has a sense of casting around with a butterfly net, seeking to isolate and to pin down specific evidence for difference. Looked at individually, many of the elements cited above could easily slip away out of the net; taken together, however, they start to define a perspective that does indeed allow us to maintain a Scottish identity.

In a review in the *Journal of Social Policy* of a recent volume edited by Ermisch and Wright, *Changing Scotland: Evidence from the British Household Panel Survey* (Bristol, The Policy Press, 2005), Sinclair (2006, p 331) suggests that 'some of the most significant policies "changing Scotland" since devolution have taken place in the processes of government and the institutional landscape rather than in people's lives

---

and values'. There may be marginal differences in demography or in public opinions and preferences, but perhaps what is reflected is a *desire* for a distinct Scottish identity, a need for a sense of community that can be manifest in a series of symbols and artefacts to which individuals can express their allegiance. In this context, what may be interesting to observe is whether, as the personalisation agenda advances, the collective agenda is nonetheless maintained.

References

Audit Scotland (2006) *Community Planning: An Initial Review*, Edinburgh: Audit Scotland.

Barclay Report (1982) *Social Workers: Their Role and Tasks*, London: Bedford Square Press.

Barr, A. (1995) 'Empowering communities – beyond fashionable rhetoric? Some reflections on Scottish experience', *Community Development Journal*, vol 30, no 2, pp 121-32.

Barr, A., Drysdale, J. and Henderson, P. (1997) *Towards Caring Communities*, Brighton: Pavilion Publishing.

Barr, A., Stenhouse, C. and Henderson, P. (2001) *Caring Communities: A Challenge for Social Inclusion*, York: Joseph Rowntree Foundation.

Bell, D. and Bowes, A. (2006) *Financial Care Models in Scotland and the UK*, York: Joseph Rowntree Foundation.

Bell, D., Bowes, A., Dawson, A. and Roberts, E. (2006) *Establishing the Evidence Base for an Evaluation of Free Personal Care in Scotland*, Edinburgh: Scottish Executive Social Research, www.scotland.gov.uk/socialresearch

Bowes, A. and Sim, D. (eds) (1997) *Perspectives on Welfare: The Experience of Minority Ethnic Groups in Scotland*, Aldershot: Ashgate.

Bromley, C., Curtice, J., Hinds, K. and Park, A. (eds) (2003) *Devolution: Scottish Answers to Scottish Questions?*, Edinburgh: Edinburgh University Press.

Burns, D., Flint, J., Forrest, R. and Kearns, A. (2001) *Empowering Communities: The Impact of Housing Associations on Social Capital*, Edinburgh: Scottish Homes.

Care 21 (2006) *The Future of Unpaid Care in Scotland*, Edinburgh: Scottish Executive.

Care Development Group (2001) *Fair Care for Older People*, Edinburgh: Scottish Executive.

Cheetham, J. (2001) 'New Labour, welfare and social work and devolution: a view from Scotland', *British Journal of Social Work*, vol 31, no 4, pp 625-8.

Crosbie, D., Smale, G. and Waterson, J. (1987) *Monitoring and Appraisal of the Scottish Network Development Group: A Pilot Study of Disseminating Community Social Work by Means of a Network*, London: National Institute for Social Work.

Curtice, L. and Fraser, F. (2000) 'The domiciliary care market in Scotland: quasi-markets revisited', *Health and Social Care in the Community*, vol 8, no 4, pp 260-8.

Curtice, J., McCrone, D., Park, A. and Paterson, L. (eds) (2002) *New Scotland, New Society?*, Edinburgh: Polygon.

Curtice, L. and Petch, A. (2002) *How Does the Community Care? Public Attitudes to Community Care in Scotland*, Edinburgh: The Stationery Office.

Darvill, G. and Smale, G. (1990) *Partners in Empowerment: Networks of Innovation in Social Work*, London: National Institute for Social Work.

Dewar, B., Jones, C. and O'May, F. (2004) *Involving Older People: Lessons for Community Planning*, Edinburgh: Scottish Executive Social Research.

Gordon, D. and Donald, S. (1993) *Community Social Work, Older People and Informal Care: A Romantic Illusion*, Aldershot: Avebury.

Haynes, P., Banks, L., Balloch, S. and Hill, M. (2006) *Changes in Communal Provision for Social Care 1991–2001*, York: Joseph Rowntree Foundation.

Hearn, B. and Thomson, B. (1987) *Developing Community Social Work in Teams: A Manual for Practice*, London: National Institute for Social Work.

Hunter, D. and Wistow, G. (1988) 'The Scottish difference: policy and practice in community care', in D. McCrone and A. Brown (eds) *The Scottish Government Yearbook*, Edinburgh: Unit for the Study of Government in Scotland, University of Edinburgh, pp 82-102.

Joint Future Group (2000) *Community Care: A Joint Future*, Edinburgh: Scottish Executive.

Kilbrandon Report (1964) *Children and Young Persons (Scotland)* Edinburgh: HMSO.

Kintrea, K. (1996) 'Whose partnership? Community interests in the regeneration of a Scottish housing scheme', *Housing Studies*, vol 11, no 2, pp 287-306.

Leadbeater, C. and Lownsbrough, H. (2005) *Personalisation and Participation: 'The Future of Social Care in Scotland'*, London: Demos.

Marnoch, G, (2003) 'Scottish devolution: identity and impact and the case of community care for the elderly', *Public Administration*, vol 81, no 2, pp 253-73.

Mooney, G. and Poole, L. (2004) "'A land of milk and honey"? Social policy in Scotland after devolution', *Critical Social Policy*, vol 24, no 4, pp 458-83.

Parry, R. (2002) 'Delivery structure and policy development in post devolution Scotland', *Social Policy and Society*, vol 1, no 4, pp 315-24.

Paterson, L., Brown, A., Curtice, J., Hinds, K., McCrone, D., Park, A., Sproston, K. and Surridge, P. (2001) *New Scotland, New Politics?*, Edinburgh: Edinburgh University Press.

Petch, A. (1999) 'Social care across Great Britain: consolidation or fragmentation', in B. Hudson (ed) *The Changing Role of Social Care*, London: Jessica Kingsley, pp 189-206.

Scottish Executive (1999) *Strategy for Carers in Scotland*, Edinburgh: Scottish Executive.

Scottish Executive (2000) *A Power of Community Initiative: Community Planning: Political Restrictions on Council Employees*, Edinburgh: Scottish Executive.

Scottish Executive (2001) *Report of the Scottish Carers' Legislation Working Group*, Edinburgh: Scottish Executive.

Scottish Executive (2003) *Partnership for Care: Scotland's Health White Paper*, Edinburgh: The Stationery Office.

Scottish Executive (2006a) *Changing Lives: Report of the 21st Century Social Work Review*, Edinburgh: Scottish Executive.

Scottish Executive (2006b) *Response to Care 21 Report: The Future of Unpaid Care in Scotland*, Edinburgh: Scottish Executive.

Scottish Executive (2006c) *Statistics Release: Free Personal and Nursing Care Scotland 2002–2005*, Edinburgh: Scottish Executive.

Scottish Executive (2006d) *Statistics Release: Care Homes Scotland September 2005*, Edinburgh: Scottish Executive.

Scottish Parliament (2006) *Health Committee 10th Report, 2006 (Session 2) Care Inquiry*, Edinburgh: Scottish Parliament.

Sinclair, S. (2006) 'Review of *Changing Scotland: Evidence from the British Household Panel Survey*', *Journal of Social Policy*, vol 35, no 2, pp 331-2.

Smale, G. and Bennett, W. (1989) *Pictures of Practice, Community Social Work in Scotland Volume 1*, London: National Institute of Social Work – Planning and Development Exchange.

Stevenson, R. (2002) *Getting 'under the skin' of Community Planning: Understanding Community Planning at the Community Planning Partnership Level*, Edinburgh: The Stationery Office.

Stewart, J. (2004) *Taking Stock: Scottish Social Welfare after Devolution*, Bristol: The Policy Press.

Part Two
Ethics, care and community

FOUR

Participation, citizenship and a feminist ethic of care

Marian Barnes

Introduction

This chapter proposes a way of thinking about care as a value relevant to contemporary concerns about the way in which we live together and decide together: concerns that are variously conceptualised within policy discourse by reference to community cohesion, social inclusion, community involvement and civil renewal. A particular aim is to offer a critique of policy discourses of civil renewal from an ethic of care perspective. Civil renewal, as elaborated in Home Office publications (particularly those written by David Blunkett when he was Home Secretary), promotes normative notions of the responsibilities of citizenship. Citizens are exhorted to become involved in voluntary action or participatory projects in order to enhance community cohesion and promote the general social good. I want to contrast the way in which responsible citizenship is conceptualised within this discourse with how people speak about their motivations for involvement in groups of service users and citizens seeking to bring about policies capable of achieving social justice for marginalised or disadvantaged groups.

In order to make this comparison I draw on feminist writing on an ethic of care. My argument is that 'care' is usually absent from official discourses of citizenship, participation and civil renewal (see also Balloch, Chapter Two, and Quilgars, Chapter Ten) and, indeed, has also become devalued in the context of those policy areas with which it has been more strongly associated – community or social care. We need to understand why this devaluing has taken place in the context of policies ostensibly and explicitly focused on 'care' and why the notion of care is seen as a somewhat irrelevant if not embarrassing value to appeal to in the context of broader policies concerned with social inclusion and community engagement.

The problem with care

Community care discourse has been profoundly influenced by collective action among those who use social care services (for example, Barnes, 1997; Barnes and Bowl, 2001). The disabled people's movement has had considerable success in gaining recognition of disability as a rights issue (see Campbell and Oliver, 1996). Access to physical environments, to education with non-disabled peers rather than in 'special' environments, to paid work and the capacity to travel within and between social spaces are all seen to have nothing to do with 'care', but to embody everyday human and civil rights. The personal support necessary to enable disabled people to take up such rights has been reconstructed as 'personal assistance' or 'help' (Shakespeare, 2000), as a result of a rejection of the assumed passivity implied by defining such support within a framework of 'care'. Thus, it is not the personal support per se that is rejected, but the notion that the need for such support renders disabled people passive recipients, dependent on care givers. Hence the successful campaign for personal assistance to be available through an employer–employee relationship via the provision of direct payments.

Contemporary with the growth of user movements and the increasing recognition of the agency of those often regarded as lacking capacity for self-determination has been similar action among those who have claimed the identity of 'carers'. One consequence of this has been a tension between claims based precisely in the significance of 'care' and those which reject this as the basis on which support services should be designed. When translated into notions of 'rights', practitioners have been faced with balancing competing rights claims, and policies have assumed that it is possible to distinguish those who are 'carers' and those who are 'users'. The identities of 'care giver' and 'care receiver' are seen to describe distinct groups of people. Perhaps more fundamentally, care itself has become associated with the notion that the world divides into two sets of people: those who are needy and dependent on the good offices of others for their capacity to function on a daily basis, and those who are independent, autonomous and have no need for care. This ignores the fact that the necessity for care is part of the human condition: at different times of life and in different circumstances our needs to receive care are greater (when we are babies, when we are ill, for example) but interdependence is a much more accurate reflection of the human condition throughout the lifespan than is independence.

Feminists have argued that the devaluing of care within the disabled people's movement is associated with a masculinist and materialist prioritisation of individual autonomy at the expense of the relational aspects of both personal and social lives (Hughes et al, 2005). Elsewhere I have argued that a focus on disability as a civil rights issue has contributed to a decoupling of notions of care and justice that are enmeshed in practice within caring relationships (Barnes, 2006). The adoption of an empowerment discourse within social care is intended to challenge the way in which care has come to be associated with confinement, disempowerment and passivity.

Care is also highly gendered. Care is primarily understood as something that takes place almost exclusively within the private sphere, the sphere in which women's lives are lived and which has little to do with the public sphere in which people enact the duties as well as claim the rights of citizenship. The help that disabled people and non-disabled people need in the privacy of their own homes is to prepare them to take part in the public domain where status and value are accorded. There is little intrinsic value accorded to the provision of such support in its own right. The work of care, the washing, dressing, dealing with personal and domestic dirt and damage, is work undertaken primarily by those who are of low social status – women, minority ethnic groups, migrants (for example Ehrenreich and Hochschild, 2002). It is poorly rewarded financially and carried out by those who often have little security or power in relation to employment conditions. This both reflects and reinforces the low value accorded to care:

> [T]he disdain of 'others' who do caring (women, slaves, servants) has been virulent in our culture. This dismissal is inextricably bound up with an attempt to deny the importance of care. Those who are powerful are unwilling to admit their dependence upon those who care for them. To treat care as shabby and unimportant helps to maintain the positions of the powerful vis-à-vis those who do care for them. (Tronto, 1993, p 174)

An alternative perspective

As well as claiming recognition for the significance of the care work undertaken, both unpaid by family members and poorly paid by care workers (see Finch and Groves, 1983), feminist scholars have challenged the notion that care has a lesser value than notions such as rights or justice in the context of social relations. Indeed, many have argued that justice cannot be achieved without care (Sevenhuijsen, 1998; Kittay, 1999). In this chapter I am drawing primarily on the work of Joan Tronto (1993) and Selma Sevenhuijsen (1998, 2000), who have developed an analysis of an ethic of care that promotes care as a political value as well as one that concerns interdependencies between people in their private lives. This perspective challenges the notion of care as a natural expression of women's capabilities, as well as the idea that it is only some people who need care. It argues the necessity of social policies based in an ethic of care as well as offering a framework within which ethical practice can be developed (see Brannelly, Chapter Six). Sevenhuijsen in particular has developed an analysis – Trace – to be used to interrogate social policies from the perspective of ethic of care principles (Sevenhuijsen, 2003). Here I adopt a similar approach to an analysis of policies relating to civil renewal and also to understanding the motivations of those who engage in collective organisation and action among citizens, including disabled people, mental health service users and carers. But first, what is an ethic of care?

A feminist ethic of care

A feminist ethic of care is based in the definition of care offered by Tronto and Fisher:

> On the most general level we suggest that caring can be viewed as a species activity that includes everything we do to maintain, continue and repair our 'world' so that we can live in it as well as possible. That world includes our bodies, ourselves and our environment, all of which we seek to interweave in a complex, life-sustaining web. (Cited in Tronto, 1993, p 103)

Thus, care includes both self-care and care for others; it does not oppose dependence and independence but recognises that we are all givers and receivers of care at some points in our lives; it is not linked to gender or 'women's work'; it acknowledges bodily, spiritual and material aspects of life, the perspectives both of care givers and care receivers, the existence of power and conflict within care, and the moral dimension of care.

Care as a practice recognises the messy moral dilemmas that can only be resolved through moral deliberation; 'muddling through' in particular contexts, rather than by reference to a formal statement of ethical principles intended to guide action in all circumstances. Thus, caring practices are constructed within relationships through processes of narrative that generate understandings of how the moral principles of care need to be applied within these particular contexts (see Barnes, 2006, for a detailed consideration of this in the context of relationships between family care givers and care receivers).

A caring orientation is acquired through engaging in caring practices and reflecting and debating the values and virtues necessary for care. In the public sphere, care as a democratic practice requires the potential for decision-making roles and positions to be open to diverse participants.

Tronto outlined four moral principles of care:

- attentiveness: to recognise and be attentive to others;
- responsibility: to take responsibility for action;
- competence: caring work should be competently performed;
- responsiveness: consider the position of the care receiver from their perspective – it is only possible to know if caring needs have been met by focusing on the experience of receiving care.

Sevenhuijsen added a fifth principle: 'trust'. She argues that trust is always interwoven with power and responsibility and that a willingness to use power in a positive and creative manner is a necessary aspect of care. She sums up as follows:

> The guiding thought of the ethic of care is that people need each other in order to lead a good life and that they can only exist as individuals through and via caring relationships with others. (2003, p 183)

Following this very brief discussion I will apply this perspective to an analysis of official discourses and lay accounts of motivations for public participation.

Civil renewal and social cohesion

New Labour government policy on civil renewal, social cohesion and inclusion and community engagement might be considered consistent with Sevenhuijsen's summary of an ethic of care, because of its emphasis on improving social relationships as a basis from which to achieve social well-being. But I want to suggest that in fact *care* is largely absent from official policy discourses on such issues. I take as my example policy relating to civil renewal. This originated from within the Home Office when David Blunkett was Secretary of State. Following a reorganisation within government in 2006 the Civil Renewal Unit was transferred to the Department for Communities & Local Government.

The focus of the civil renewal agenda is on creating better, more active citizens, and stronger, more cohesive communities:

> There are three ingredients to civil renewal:
>
> - **Active citizens:** people with the motivation, skills and confidence to speak up for their communities and say what improvements are needed
> - **Strengthened communities:** community groups with the capability and resources to bring people together to work out shared solutions
> - **Partnership with public bodies:** public bodies willing and able to work as partners with local people. (http://communities.gov.uk/index.asp?id=1502436)

The philosophical basis for civil renewal was explored in two key papers written by David Blunkett (2003a, 2003b). These express an explicit moral discourse that asserts communitarian values of mutuality, solidarity and common purpose, rather than individualist libertarian values. Blunkett's perspectives on community clearly emanate from Home Office concerns with public order and he identified 'the very basic issues of community life' as 'crime, security, civility and decency' (2003a, p 13). Thus, building community cohesion is seen as closely linked with public order (Home Office, undated). Asking the question 'What is community for?', Blunkett replied:

> We rely on the local community for precisely those things that I have argued the progressive tradition has struggled with – basic social order; decent behaviour; the socialisation of the young into community norms. These are the things that have come most 'unstuck' in disadvantaged communities, whilst those who can afford it buy their way out of collective solutions in gated estates patrolled by private guards. (Blunkett, 2003a, p 14)

The concepts evoked are order, civility, duty and obligation. There is no reference to the relevance of care in this context, no specific indication of the importance of attentiveness to others, nor recognition of the vulnerabilities that mean that most people at some time in their lives require help from others in relationships of unequal power. Indeed, Blunkett argued:

> Political theorists in the tradition I have drawn on in this
> text have argued that a citizen cannot truly be an equal
> member of the community if he or she is reduced to a
> state of permanent dependency on the support of others.
> (Blunkett, 2003a, p 16)

Dependency is understood to refer to financial dependency and is
used to argue the importance of individual asset ownership. But the
underlying message is a familiar one in positing a binary distinction
between dependence (bad) and independence (good), without
acknowledging the essential interdependence of all. A condition of
dependence per se excludes the possibility of citizenship.

Responsibility is key to the conceptualisation of citizenship: 'The ethos
here is one of something for something – of rights and responsibilities
going hand in hand' (Blunkett, 2003b, p 2). Responsibility is treated both
normatively and abstractly as a requirement to conform to obligations
defined by reference to the common good. Responsibility is also key
to the ethic of care – but here the way in which this is conceptualised
is very different. Tronto and Sevenhuijsen argue that responsibility
to act is embedded in a set of implicit cultural practices, rather than
existing as a set of formal rules to be followed. Both distinguish duty
from responsibility. A relational ontology recognises that individuals
can only exist because they are members of networks of care and
responsibility and this has implications for the way in which we think
about our obligations to others: 'the moral subject in the discourse of
care always already lives in a network of relationships in which s/he
has to find balances between different forms of responsibility (for the
self, for others and for the relationships between them)' (Sevenhuijsen,
2000, p 10). This implies that the practical expression of responsibility
for oneself and for those within one's immediate personal and social
networks are necessary and legitimate foci for action to contribute to
the civility at the heart of a cohesive society. Negotiating how such
responsibilities are expressed within particular interpersonal, social and
cultural contexts itself contributes to the development of the moral
awareness necessary for care.

The civil renewal agenda argues that active citizens need to
be developed who have the skills and motivations to take part in
community activities for the benefit of the community as a whole,
rather than for their sole personal benefit, or that of their families. It is
based in the civic republican tradition that identifies the *public realm* as
the 'locus for the highest achievements of the community' (Blunkett,
2003a, p 4). This perspective is echoed in that of political scientists who

explicitly exclude care provided for family members from citizenship activity, because citizenship is defined as something that happens in the public rather than the private sphere. The sense of 'common purpose' (Blunkett, 2003b, p 8) that is evoked is seen as a necessary response to the potential dangers of fragmentation in a culturally diverse society. But by ignoring the private sphere, or by implying that action focused on ensuring the well-being of family members is excluded from a notion of what is required to achieve 'civil renewal', this perspective relegates concern with and action to support vulnerable members of the community to a marginalised and often stigmatised set of practices that have no relevance to the grand social objectives of community cohesion, equality and social justice.

In the civil renewal discourse, the public are citizens who need to be encouraged and supported to become actively engaged in shaping public affairs. They need to be educated in civic virtues, ready to take on the obligations citizenship requires through a direct contribution to the collective political community. The assumption is that there is an absence or insufficiency of such virtues and it is this that creates the need for 'renewal'.

While one objective of active citizenship is social justice (Blunkett, 2003b, p 9), the meaning of this is not elaborated and it appears to exclude those on the wrong end of inequality by virtue of their need for care. Eva Kittay (1999) refers to this as the 'dependency critique' of equality. While I am uncomfortable with her use of the term 'dependants' to describe disabled people and others in need of care, her deliberate strategy of assessing notions of equality and justice against the circumstances of those who cannot live their lives without substantial personal and other support is an important challenge to those who approach issues of citizenship and justice without being attentive to the circumstances of those who are most vulnerable.

At the same time, the civil renewal agenda appears to assume that disabled people, older people and children, people who might most readily be identified as recipients of care, are unlikely to feature as active citizens. The image of active citizens on the front of Blunkett's pamphlet on civil renewal includes no visibly disabled people, older people or children. There is no reference to the action of disabled people's organisations, organisations of mental health service users or other user groups not only in advocating and supporting their members, but also in challenging assumptions about what it is to be disabled, old or to live with a mental health problem, therefore challenging the stigmatising and excluding attitudes and assumptions that create social divisions.

In summary, an analysis of the civil renewal discourse from an ethic of care perspective identifies the following problems:

- It discounts action within the private sphere, when much of the action to support more vulnerable citizens and to challenge their exclusion takes place there.
- It works with an abstract concept of responsibility, rather than recognising the way in which people experience and express their responsibilities within particular socio-cultural contexts.
- It posits a binary distinction between dependence and independence, rather than recognising that we are all interdependent and all have needs to receive care.
- By implication, older and disabled people are viewed as recipients of action through which other people demonstrate their citizenship, rather than active agents contributing to social justice and challenging divisiveness.

Motivations and commitments within community and user groups

In contrast to this perspective we can consider how issues relating to community engagement and its purposes are seen by those engaged in user and community groups. I draw here on research into public participation across a range of policy areas (Barnes et al, 2007), plus other as yet unpublished work that involved interviews with participants in a mental health advocacy group. It is possible to identify a number of different types of commitments that motivate people to take part in such activity and which suggest how 'responsibility' is conceived by citizen participants.

For some, the commitment is to the area in which they live or work. For example, young people involved in a Single Regeneration Budget initiative in an inner-city area with high levels of deprivation saw this as an opportunity to improve the area in which they lived and in which they assumed *their* children would live:

> 'I was brought up in [locality] and have been in [locality] for the last 25 years. I don't see myself moving out so obviously I will probably get married in the next couple of years. I don't want my kids to grow up in an area where I know every corner they turn there is going to be a drug dealer or a really deprived area. If we can change that now, hopefully

when my kids grow up, my family, my friends, they won't have much to worry about.'

Religious commitments providing a value base leading to social action were evident among people involved in a range of participatory initiatives. The following quote is from a man involved in an older people's group in response to a question asking him to describe himself:

'I think trying to be tolerant, trying to understand the other person's point of view, trying to serve, give the benefits of a fairly wide experience in industry and church for that matter. I think that's another thing, bringing something of one's church ... I think it's caring. It's certainly not a preaching role. It's ... you come to be in a way automatically caring.'

Commitments to a specific cause often derived from negative personal experiences which resulted in a desire to improve things for others. In the following example a man involved in a community group campaigning for a Healthy Living Centre talked about his commitment to the cause of health and healthcare:

'Our area where I live is the highest cancer rate in the country ... I have been concerned quite a long time, basically because my family were heavily destroyed by ill-health. Cancers and things. And it always used to fascinate me that a person dying of cancer could go into the likes of the [X] Hospital, and they would be waiting hours just to get a bed.... One particular time with my aunt I became very angry because I was there with her for 14 hours when she broke her hip. And the woman at the time was 76 years of age and we were kept on a trolley in a passageway for 14 hours.'

Some participants explicitly located their motivations in the context of representing 'a people'. For example, a Yemeni man involved in a Senior Citizens' Forum saw his role as ensuring that the voices and experiences of the Yemeni population were heard to improve the lives of older people. A similar perspective was offered by a Nigerian man involved in a social services user group:

'There are a lot of black, old black, people here that have worked all their life in this country, you see, And now so,

> there are problems with things like language and because
> they can't translate, they don't know what is going on.'

A lifelong commitment to causes linked to social justice was evident
among participants engaged in locality-, issue- and identity-based
action. Such people had often been involved in party politics, trades
unions, peace campaigns, women's and community groups. In the words
of one woman involved in an older people's group:

> 'I have – I don't know about all my life, but quite a lot of
> my life felt that things have to be addressed if they're not
> right. If something's not fair you have to do something
> about it.'

For others, commitments originated in experiences of difference,
exclusion or disadvantage. Such experiences included living in poverty,
disability, care giving and differences relating to sexuality, gender or
ethnicity. Involvement was a way of giving voice to such experiences
and to achieve change, if not for themselves then for others in similar
circumstances. A woman involved in a mental health advocacy group
spoke both of her satisfactions in being able to achieve changes for
others, and the support that the group offered her:

> 'It's just nice for people to be heard and I love that. I love
> putting that across. And then when things actually change
> for that person you get terrific satisfaction.
>   I know there is a sympathetic response here [within
> the group] and sometimes that's enough from people here,
> to know that you're not really well but you're coming in
> anyway. I know that I'm going to get all the support here
> and people will help me all they can.'

A disabled woman involved in a social services user group linked her
activism with her sense of personal identity:

> 'I used to describe myself as a disability activist, which I
> suppose underneath I still am.... It is part of my life. I am
> a disabled person. My mum has got this impairment, so I
> was very much aware of it as I grew up. I have brothers
> who have got it. My son has got an impairment. I live very
> much in a disability world. So I am just a natural fighter I
> think. It is naturally part of who I am.'

The way in which people spoke about their motivations and
experiences suggests the importance of understanding how personal

biographies generated a sense of responsibility for action. For these participants responsibility was not an abstract concept but was grounded in relationships with particular others: those living in the same area and sharing in the disadvantages associated with that, or others who shared experiences as disabled people, mental health service users or older people, for example. Those who referred to moral principles deriving from faith or social justice values applied these to action focused on particular others with whom they could identify. The expression of responsibility was related to attentiveness – which can be understood as an openness to understanding the circumstances and needs of others and a preparedness to take action on this basis. Attentiveness to the circumstances of others involved recognition of issues of vulnerability and power and the necessity of giving voice to the perspectives and experiences of those who are often marginalised or stigmatised. The woman active in the mental health advocacy group in particular acknowledged the way in which shared experiences of mental distress enabled attentiveness to the impact of this and led to practical supportive action among group members.

Thus, the sense of responsibility that emerges from these accounts has little to do with a normative notion of citizenship obligation focused on a somewhat abstract 'common good', but rather refers to evident injustices requiring resolution and needs that remain unmet. Whether it be care directed at the environment in which future generations will live, an awareness of the absence of competent care in the way in which health services are provided, or an attentiveness to the way in which different ethnic groups respond to the experience of ageing in an unfamiliar culture, motivations to participate reflected the relational ethics of care.

Deliberating with care

Sevenhuijsen suggests that a care perspective also has implications for the nature of the democratic processes necessary to achieve socially just outcomes. To achieve social justice requires a caring orientation and practice worked out through dialogue that gives recognition to the particular perspectives of those who are disadvantaged and which acknowledges their role as experts in exposing the incivilities within social relations. Interactions within user and community groups exemplify the significance of 'deliberating with care'. Deliberative practices that enable dialogue about different experiences deriving from disadvantage and marginalisation can encourage attentiveness to such experiences and give recognition to them (see Barnes, 2002;

Barnes et al, 2006).The evidence of direct testimony from older people, people with mental health problems and others often regarded as incompetent or lacking in capacity makes it hard to continue to ignore their individual and collective agency.The process of attending to voices expressed in ways other than is usual in official policy contexts and which demand a response because of the injustices they describe can encourage a preparedness to take responsibility to act to ameliorate the situations that are revealed. Such attentiveness also highlights when a lack of competence is evident in the way in which support services are provided, as well as the response of those on the receiving end of services to the nature of the care and support provided.

It is harder to ignore the significance of the moral principles of an ethic of care in circumstances where there is face-to-face dialogue with people whose everyday lives are suffused with the experience of giving and receiving care, although there is also evidence from the practices that exist in some deliberative forums that this cannot be taken for granted (Barnes et al, 2004a).The validity of narrative in expressing a reality to which service providers and policy makers need to respond is not always acknowledged.A care perspective could enhance the capacity of such forums to generate socially just outcomes, assist in developing a vocabulary through which care can be integrated into dialogues about policies and services, as well as encouraging an understanding of the significance of care beyond the context of relations between 'caring' and 'needy' people.

Conclusion

Community cohesion, community involvement and civil renewal are key themes of New Labour social policy and have influenced strategies for neighbourhood renewal, health improvement and public participation pursued by the Home Office, the Office of the Deputy Prime Minister and the Department of Health (Barnes et al, 2004b). Separately, the development of a national strategy for carers (DH, 1999) has given prominence to the role played by lay carers in supporting disabled and older people and the extension of direct payments has been intended to increase service user control over support services, promote 'independence' and enable broader participation in social life. In this context the concept of 'care' is downplayed in favour of rights and empowerment.The relational aspects of care and the significance of care in contributing to social justice are given scant attention in this context.

These policies exist in separate domains: social care policy is seen as the responsibility of the Department of Health (and more recently the Department for Education and Skills in relation to children) and is restricted to a concern with the private lives of needy individuals and those who support them. Civil renewal and community cohesion are the responsibility of the Home Office and the Department for Communities & Local Government, and are focused on action in the public sphere and concerned with public virtues and broader social relations. This chapter has argued that the ethic of care analysis challenges this distinction between private and public virtues and enables connections to be made between care, citizenship and social justice. A care perspective enables a richer notion of justice than is evident in rights claims. It can contribute to an understanding of social cohesion and inclusion as requiring attentiveness to the circumstances and vulnerabilities of others, and taking responsibility to act competently in response to this, based on an understanding of their perspectives and recognising their agency.

A comparison of official and lay discourses of participation suggests that this perspective is more in evidence among citizen participants than in the way in which notions of responsible citizenship are articulated – at least in the context of policies for civil renewal. There is a tendency within government to accept the individualisation thesis, which highlights a decline of responsibility towards others as individuals pursue their own self-interest rather than act for the collective good (Beck and Beck-Gernsheim, 2002). Williams and her colleagues in the Care Values and the Future of Welfare (CAVA) programme have challenged the evidence for this on the basis of extensive research on family life, which reveals the way in which moral reasoning based on care affects decision making about 'doing the right thing' in relation to family (Williams, 2004). My argument in this chapter is that similar moral reasoning based on care is evident in the way in which citizens take responsibility for collective action in the context of user and community groups. A greater preparedness to value care and to support policies and practices based in the moral principles of care should not be understood as reinforcing dependency and denying the citizenship of those in need of support, but rather as a means of seeking just outcomes in conditions of inequality. This is equally relevant to policies focused on personal support for individuals, and to those with objectives relating to community regeneration and civil renewal.

References

Barnes, M. (1997) *Care, Communities and* Citizens, Harlow: Addison Wesley Longman.

Barnes, M. (2002) 'Bringing difference into deliberation: disabled people, survivors and local governance', *Policy & Politics*, vol 30, no 3, pp 355-68.

Barnes, M. (2004) 'Affect, anecdote and diverse debates: user challenges to scientific rationality', in A. Gray and S. Harrison (eds) *Governing Medicine: Theory and Practice*, Maidenhead: McGraw Hill/Open University Press.

Barnes, M. (2006) *Caring and Social Justice*, Basingstoke: Palgrave.

Barnes, M. and Bowl, R. (2001) *Taking Over the Asylum: Empowerment and Mental Health*, Basingstoke: Palgrave.

Barnes, M., Davis, A. and Rogers, H. (2006) 'Women's voices, women's choices: experiences and creativity on consulting women users of mental health services', *Journal of Mental Health*, vol 15, no 3, pp 329-41.

Barnes, M., McCabe, A. and Ross, L. (2004a) 'Public participation in governance: the institutional context', in *Researching Civil Renewal: A Set of Scoping Papers Prepared for the Home Office Civil Renewal Unit*, Birmingham: Civil Renewal Research Centre, University of Birmingham.

Barnes, M., Newman, J. and Sullivan, H. (2007) *Power, Participation and Political Renewal: Case Studies in Public Participation*, Bristol: The Policy Press.

Barnes, M., Knops, A., Newman, J. and Sullivan, H. (2004b) 'The micro politics of deliberation: case studies in public participation', *Contemporary Politics*, vol 10, no 2, pp 93-110.

Beck, U. and Beck-Gernsheim, E. (2002) *Individualization*, London: Sage Publications.

Blunkett, D. (2003a) *Civil Renewal: A New Agenda*, CSV Edith Kahn Memorial Lecture, 11 June, London: Home Office/CSV.

Blunkett, D (2003b) *Active Citizens, Strong Communities: Progressing Civil Renewal*, London: Home Office.

Campbell, J. and Oliver, M. (1996) *Disability Politics: Understanding our Past, Changing our Future*, London: Routledge.

DH (Department of Health) (1999) *Caring about Carers*, London: The Stationery Office.

Ehrenreich, B. and Hochschild, A. R. (eds) (2002) *Global Woman: Nannies, Maids and Sex Workers in the New Economy*, London: Granta Books.

Finch, J. and Groves, D. (eds) (1983) *A Labour of Love: Women, Work and Caring*, London: Routledge and Kegan Paul.

Home Office (undated) *Building Cohesive Communities: A Report of the Ministerial Group on Public Order and Community Cohesion*, London: Home Office.

Hughes, B., McKie, L., Hopkins, D. and Watson, N. (2005) 'Love's labours lost? Feminism, the disabled people's movement and an ethic of care', *Sociology*, vol 39, no 2, pp 259-75.

Kittay, E. F. (1999) *Love's Labor, Essays on Women, Equality and Dependency*, New York and London: Routledge.

Sevenhuijsen, S. (1998) *Citizenship and the Ethics of Care: Feminist Considerations of Justice, Morality and Politics*, New York and London: Routledge.

Sevenhuijsen, S. (2000) 'Caring in the Third Way: the relation between obligation, responsibility and care in Third Way discourse', *Critical Social Policy*, vol 20, no 1, pp 5-37.

Sevenhuijsen, S. (2003) 'Trace: a method for normative policy analysis from the ethic of care', Paper prepared for the seminar 'Gender and Public Policy', Centre for Women's and Gender Research, University of Bergen, 9-11 November.

Shakespeare, T. (2000) *Help*, Birmingham: Venture Press.

Tronto, J. C. (1993) *Moral Boundaries: A Political Argument for an Ethic of Care*, New York and London: Routledge.

Williams, F. (2004) *Rethinking Families*, London: Calouste Gulbenkian Foundation.

FIVE

Ethical dilemmas of front-line regeneration workers

Marjorie Mayo, Paul Hoggett and Chris Miller

Introduction: ethics, ethical dilemmas, the public service ethos and change

Ethics and ethical dilemmas have emerged as issues of increasing interest in the human services. This may reflect wider concerns about increasing individualisation, the demise of community according to communitarians; 'liquid modernity' in Bauman's (2000) terminology. There would seem to be echoes here of the 'Third Way' (Tam, 1998). As Marilyn Taylor (2003, p 21) has pointed out, 'the 'restoring community' theme has been given a new lease of life in recent years by a communitarian movement which draws support from across the political spectrum'.

Accounts of this supposed individualisation include explanations based on the demise of grand theories in the more predominantly post-modernist ideological climate that predominated cultural debates in the final years of the 20th century (Fukuyama, 1989). As a positive spin on this, increasing individualisation has been presented in emancipatory terms, the life politics of identity and choice. With increasing reflexivity, according to Giddens (1994), there is less respect for tradition and more dialogue, including increasingly dialogic relations in personal life. The more tradition loses its hold, Giddens (1994) argues, the more individuals are forced to negotiate lifestyle choices among a diversity of options – although critics have pointed to the limitations on such choices, in practice, for the 'reflexivity losers' (Lash, 1994, p 120), including those more likely to depend on public services, the disadvantaged and the oppressed.

The notion that there has been a reduction in common values has been similarly challenged along with the view that social solidarity has been declining, with the loss of social capital (Putnam, 2000). The underlying causes have been contested, then, along with the extent to which these processes of individualisation have actually been taking place. Anxieties about the impacts of these processes, however, would seem to be more widely shared. This chapter focuses on these concerns in the particular context of human services in general and caring services more specifically.

Is there an identifiable public service ethos, in the current context, then? If so, is this at risk as a result of another key feature of the contemporary context, policies to promote increasing marketisation, 'modernisation' and the New Public Management, the 'New Welfare' associated with the 'New Managerialism?' (Clarke et al, 2000). The meanings of some traditional public service values have been altered, such as a greater focus on results than on process, it has been argued (Kakabadse et al, 2003, p 479). There has been a shift, it has been suggested, away from a collective morality, with a value orientation of community benefits (utilitarian ethics), to a personal-competence morality of individual benefits (egoistic ethics).

In his review of the literature on altruism Julian Le Grand (2003) concluded that there was indeed research evidence that altruistic behaviour still exists in the public sector. People can behave as knights (rather than knaves) and indeed frequently do so even when this is in direct opposition to their personal interests. Public service employees report a greater concern for serving the community and helping others than private sector ones, and this holds true across a range of international contexts. Financial incentives can affect this motivation, however. Commitment to the public sector can be eroded, if professionals feel unable to provide a quality service (Bonoli et al, 2000). Professional motivation can be further undermined by excessive regulation, feeling undervalued and feeling mistrusted. The public service ethos may still be alive, then, but its continuing survival is not to be taken for granted. Professional ethics have themselves been changing, in any case. As Banks (1995) has argued in her study of ethics and values in social work, the traditional Kantian approach, based on the categorical imperative of the absolute value of the self-determining individual and how that individual should be treated, came under increasing challenge in the 1970s for its inadequacy in the face of structural issues of inequality and oppression. Utilitarian approaches, on the other hand, although seen as more relevant in the context of increasing pressure for rationing scarce resources, have their limitations, too, as the basis for professional ethics. Utilitarian approaches have their own contradictions in the contemporary context of increasing concerns with the rights of the individual consumer.

Banks concludes that Wittgenstein's approach has relevance here – the view that people's actions and choices need to be understood within a public context of rule-governed behaviour, taking account of the wider social context. Ethical behaviours need to take account of the inter-relationships between the individual and their social context, as these relationships change over time. As Hugman and Smith (1995) have argued, moral principles are rooted in particular societies and so need to be constantly disputed. Professional ethics, by implication, need to be continuously re-evaluated.

Banks goes on to distinguish between ethical issues and ethical dilemmas. Ethical dilemmas involve a choice between two equally unwelcome alternatives that may involve a conflict of moral principle and it is not clear which choice will be the right one (Banks, 1995, p 12). This leaves the worker with feelings of anxiety and possibly guilt, whatever choice is finally made. While this is a useful theoretical distinction, however, in practice workers may be left with uncomfortable feelings even when the choice that they make seems relatively clear cut. As we shall suggest, subsequently, whether working with ethical issues or working with ethical dilemmas, or both, professionals find themselves engaged emotionally; front-line work necessarily involves emotional labour.

In the current context, professional social workers, like youth and community workers (Banks, 1999) and other front-line professionals, may expect to face increasing ethical issues and dilemmas, as professional ethics come under pressure from:

- increasing marketisation and the New Public Management, increasing pressures for consumer rights and user/community-determined priorities on the one hand and the requirements for rationing scarce resources on the other;
- increasing decentralisation of responsibilities without accompanying powers and resources;
- increasing centralised pressures for social control;
- increasing pressures to work across professional boundaries, involving varying codes and practice;
- increasing distancing, in many contexts, between those performing front-line roles, working directly with individual service users and communities, and those tasked with the management of staff and other resources.

Faced with all these, it has been argued, professionals need more knowledge and critical understanding of ethical issues, time for reflection and professional support. These are in addition to the resources that they themselves bring due to their own personal history, upbringing and cultural mores, and the self-awareness of their own values, motivations and identities. Such self-awareness has already been identified as essential for professionals in the caring services. These resources, both external and internal, should help them to cope most effectively with these increasing pressures and dilemmas, and with the least anxiety and guilt (Bailey and Schwartzberg, 1995). But without these coping mechanisms, it has been suggested that professionals are at increasing risk of burn-out.

This was the starting point for our research. How are front-line professionals coping in this context of increasing ethical uncertainty, shifting professional boundaries and increasing pressures from modernising/New Public Management agendas? How do they hold on to their professional ethics, avoiding total moral relativism, disengagement and/or terminal burn-out? While our study explored the dilemmas as these were experienced by front-line professionals working with communities around regeneration, there may be common issues as well as differences with the experiences of other professionals concerned with care, citizenship and communities more generally. This may be the case whether or not those concerned necessarily define themselves as 'professionals', which is a potentially problematic and contested term.

A study of ethical dilemmas in contested communities

Our study concerns ethical dilemmas in contested communities. It is a psycho-social study of front-line regeneration workers, the ways in which they identify ethical dilemmas and the resources they draw upon to address these. It adopted a psycho-social approach to explore the personal as well as the social factors involved. We focused on front-line professionals working around regeneration issues, professionals at the front line where the public sector meets the private, voluntary and community sectors, working across professional boundaries. Front-line regeneration professionals typically lack shared professional frameworks (most of our sample came from other professional formations such as youth work, community work, health promotion, housing management and education, for example). Together they face the dilemmas inherent in current policies to promote decentralisation and user-determined rather than professionally determined priorities, but within the framework of centrally defined targets and resources. While our study was not focused on caring per se, there would seem to be a number of underlying issues of potentially common concern, in the current policy context. These include issues related to working across professional boundaries, as well as issues related to New Public Management more broadly.

Our study started with a series of interviews with 30 front-line professionals (typically six interviews with each respondent) to explore their personal biographies, how they came to be doing this work, their motivations and values. This led into the discussion of their dilemmas and their coping mechanisms and sources of support. These individual interviews were followed up with small group discussions, leading to a joint seminar to share perspectives on the findings and their implications for policy and practice – including their implications for professional training and professional support. The interviews were conducted in two urban areas, both areas where there were pools of very experienced staff as well as those who were newer to this type of front-line work. This was in order to compare and contrast experiences and perspectives over time. Both areas also included a number of black and minority ethnic workers.

From the first interviews, in which participants focused on their biographies, a wealth of material emerged about respondents' motivations and values. In some cases early experiences had been problematic, including domestic violence, family breakdown and experiences of abuse. Others had experienced loss through migration, including the experience of becoming a refugee. There was an identifiable group of respondents who expressed their commitment to working in the human services as a form of 'reparation'. This was about being for others the supportive caring person who was there for them, or, in other cases, being the person that they would like to have had as a support in childhood and/or adolescence.

For others, their commitment seemed more evidently rooted in the strength of the values surrounding them in early life, from religious faith, for example, and/or from political, trade union and labour movement commitments. Others added the importance of subsequent experiences, getting involved in mobilisations around particular contemporary issues. Despite the differences overall, there were common strands here – personal histories that were invoked to explain the strength of respondents' commitments. Although many, if not all, of the respondents had come into their present jobs by happenstance rather than by design, their current occupations were by no means random professional outcomes.

On the contrary, respondents spoke, often passionately, about their values and how these were central to their professional identities. 'I'd like to say that I've contributed to my community', 'I want to be part of something that's going to be positive' (experienced community and youth worker). 'There is something to be done in terms of serving people here in this job', 'I'm idealistic' (regeneration worker – a relative newcomer to this area of work). However articulated, these basic values, together with the satisfaction gained from aspects of the job, sustained professionals' motivation. Without a set of beliefs about things, it was suggested, 'I don't think you could do this kind of work ... something's going to have to carry you through.' It was noteworthy, in fact, that several had consciously rejected opportunities for promotion precisely because this would have taken them away from front-line work with individuals and communities.

Does this mean that there are no grounds for concern about the future of the public service ethos, then? Not necessarily. Our sample was by no means random. Those who were interested in participating in the study were, perhaps, almost by definition, likely to be those most committed to the ethical issues in question. Nor do expressions of values and commitment in principle necessarily translate effectively into practice. And even among our sample, there seemed to be potentially significant differences. Front-line professionals may continue to make powerful emotional investments in their work, but these may be based on differing perspectives and values. We are certainly not suggesting that front-line professionals are necessarily heroic, nor that they are, by definition, effective champions throughout their careers. The risks of burn-out are not to be discounted either.

Some of these potential differences of perspective began to emerge when we analysed the varying ways in which front-line professionals were identifying dilemmas and addressing these. The following section summarises the types of issues that emerged. Not all of these constituted dilemmas in the full sense, as defined by Banks (1995), however. Some of these were effectively ethical issues (as defined by Banks) rather than ethical dilemmas in the full sense of that term. Situations that involve ethical issues may still leave professionals with feelings of disquiet, however, even if the scope for professional judgement and action is relatively circumscribed in such cases. Considerable emotional labour may be involved here, even if the 'right' outcome is relatively clear, as set out by the relevant procedures. The workers may or may not identify with the outcomes in these types of cases, if the result was procedurally correct, but ethically more complex. Professionals may be left with feelings of deep discomfort in such situations, including situations in which they feel that they have little or no scope for making personal choices, as a result of increasing bureaucratisation and/or increasing central control. And one person's dilemma is not, of course, necessarily another's.

Dilemmas that emerged from the interviews and group discussions

These dilemmas were categorised into two groups, those that seemed to be inherent in this type of front-line professional role and those that seemed to be increasing, specifically linked to the current policy context. In summary, these dilemmas were as follows:

Ongoing dilemmas inherent in front-line work with communities

- Dilemmas identified as being inherent in this occupational space – being both an insider within service structures and an outsider working with service users and communities. There were dilemmas inherent in this 'sandwich position' between service providers, service users and communities, and between civil society, the state and the market more generally.
- Dilemmas about professional boundaries and formal procedures more particularly, including the specific dilemmas that may be posed when 'ex users' and/or community activists who have become staff/volunteers break the rules and/or push the boundaries.
- Dilemmas of when to intervene, and when not to intervene: when to enable individuals and groups to find the space to develop their own strategies and to make their own 'mistakes'.
- Dilemmas inherent in maintaining reasonable and sustainable boundaries between the pressures of the work and the worker's own personal life, safeguarding the space for personal and family relationships and children.
- Dilemmas inherent in working across the boundaries of class, race, gender and personal experience, and feeling at least relatively comfortable working across these differences. Professionals from working-class backgrounds expressed tensions and dilemmas in working with middle-class professionals in management positions for example, exemplifying some of the hidden and continuing injuries of class, as described so vividly by Sennett and Cobb (1972).

Dilemmas that seemed to be becoming more acute in the current context

- Dilemmas associated with working with people's cynicism, disillusion and mistrust in local areas where there had been a series of regeneration initiatives in recent years. Professionals experienced dilemmas associated with the requirements of their roles, to encourage people to participate, despite this scepticism, only to experience further let-downs and disappointments subsequently (an experience that caused considerable pain and some 'soul searching', as illustrated from our research).
- Dilemmas associated with finding oneself the butt of pent-up anger, taking the flak for decisions and/or lack of action taken or indeed not taken elsewhere. In these types of situation the workers needed to maintain professional and organisational loyalties and procedures while enabling communities to find ways forward, and without taking their expressions of anger personally.
- Dilemmas involved in working at different levels; working with local issues and feeling rooted and confident in speaking for the locality versus working at more strategic levels. Professionals who left the 'front line' expressed anxieties about possibly losing the sense of local rootedness, in the process of moving up and out of the 'front line', even if they felt that they might be more effective at a more strategic level.
- Dilemmas inherent in working with conflicts within and between different groupings and interests within the voluntary and community sectors, including the specific dilemmas associated with increasing competition for scarce resources. This emerged as a particularly sharp issue towards the end of the research, as the funding for a number of special regeneration programmes was due to expire shortly.
- Dilemmas associated with issues of representation – who may legitimately claim to speak on behalf of whom, and what to do if 'representatives' appear to be failing to represent their constituents' interests democratically and/or inclusively.
- These dilemmas were experienced as being particularly acute when issues around ethnicity, race and racism were involved. Such dilemmas could be exacerbated if management structures failed to provide support, being fearful of addressing issues around racism at all, in the view of some of our participants.
- Dilemmas inherent in short-term policy interventions and time-limited programmes, evaluated on the basis of top-down targets. The professionals experienced pressures and dilemmas in meeting

these requirements, while recognising the need for longer-term interventions to develop trust, agree locally relevant priorities and work towards sustainable outcomes.

• More specifically, dilemmas arising from government policies towards young people, what was described as the increasing criminalisation of young people and the pressure to represent young people as 'problems' in order to convince funders of the case for funding initiatives and projects to meet their needs.

This list provides a summary of the key themes that emerged from the interviews and group discussions. Despite considerable differences in the local contexts, in fact, in terms of political cultures and local community histories, there was broad agreement on the nature of the dilemmas experienced by professionals. There were increasing pressures, including the particular dilemmas involved in working with conflicts in multicultural contexts. There was also broad agreement around the range of coping strategies employed.

Overall, the joint discussions between participants from the two different areas gave some emphasis to the ways in which the roles themselves and the work situations were dilemmatic. Inevitably, the role involved tensions, and workers needed to understand these and work with them, rather than taking the flak personally, from whichever direction this came. These situations typically involved ethical issues even if the professionals involved were clear about how to proceed; ethical issues in Bank's (1995) terminology rather than ethical dilemmas in the full sense of that term.

While participants were acutely aware of the 'New Managerialism' as it impacted on their particular work situations, this also seemed to generate more issues than dilemmas in the full sense. Centrally imposed targets simply had to be met. From some of the interviews there was evidence that targets were actually welcomed in some instances, where workers believed that these would lead to improvements in service delivery. The sophistication of the joint discussions about centrally determined targets was impressive. But this did leave us with questions about the impact of the resulting pressures on front-line professionals, already pressured enough, it might be supposed, from the tensions inherent in their roles.

One particular aspect emerged from some of the group discussions and more explicitly from the joint discussions between participants from the two different areas. This was the question of whether there may be differences between the patterns of dilemmas identified by the more experienced workers in comparison to those being identified by

—

more recently recruited professionals. Were there shifts about where to draw the ethical bottom line?

The more experienced professionals considered that such shifts were indeed taking place. Professionals in both Inquiry Groups made some similar comments about this potential 'generation gap'. The more experienced professionals were in no doubt about the 'next generation's' motivation. These were by no means 'Thatcher's children' in terms of motivation. But the more experienced professionals did express reservations about the 'next generation's' perceptions of themselves as professionals and their perceptions of their roles and boundaries. As the voluntary and community sectors had become more professionalised, it was suggested, workers expected to move around from one job to another on a career trajectory. This pattern fitted with the more casualised nature of employment more generally. Ironically, then, becoming more professionalised involved adapting to more casualised employment. There was some 'loss of passion', it was suggested, and perhaps some shifts of vision. Professionals may be becoming more detached and more circumscribed in their approach to what might be achieved.

It should be emphasised that these trends were not necessarily being recognised by those who were newer to this field, in our sample. They would, nevertheless, be consistent with trends identified by Sennett (1999), for example. His study of the impact of more flexible ways of working included consideration of their impact on an individual's personal character and sense of commitment. This increased sense of detachment was viewed with mixed emotions in some cases; accepting that some distancing was essential in order to survive, professionally, while simultaneously expressing some sense of loss. There are potentially significant implications here for the caring professions more generally.

There are resonances again here too with the work of Sennett. In his study of respect (Sennett, 2003), he reflects on the strategies employed by his mother, a social worker, giving clients space as a way of showing them respect, as distinct from more traditional approaches based on more charitable impulses. While Sennett clearly understood and valued his mother's stance on boundaries, he also reflects on the tensions associated with these processes of boundary drawing – 'caring for others without compassion' (Sennett, 2003, p 140). He describes his own experiences with a medical professional following an injury to his hand. This was an injury of enormous significance in his life, as he had been pursuing a career as a professional musician, a musical career that was abruptly ended at this point. While accepting the reasons for professional distancing, he reflected that he had actually wanted human empathy: 'I wanted it to matter to the doctor' (Sennett, 2003, p 141). These are, of course, tensions inherent in professional relationships in the caring services. The question is whether the delicate balance between professional empathy and professional distance might be shifting too far, in the current policy context.

The more experienced professionals also identified ways in which their roles and responsibilities were becoming more and more complex and more and more challenging. Partnership working was identified as an example of this. Involving resident representatives as members of partnership boards entailed its own particular dilemmas (including the dilemmas associated with representation and democratic accountability). The dilemmas as well as the potential benefits of partnership working have already been identified and explored as issues in public policy more generally (Balloch and Taylor, 2001; Glendinning et al, 2002). Increasing inter-professional working, as in the new Children's Centres, may also be expected to involve pressures and professional dilemmas as well as benefits.

In summary, then, ethical issues and ethical dilemmas were seen to be increasing, in the contemporary context, although this was not necessarily being perceived by the next generation of professionals, coming into the field. While there were indeed examples of ethical dilemmas, however, some of the most stressful situations included those in which the professional had relatively limited scope for the exercise of discretion. The ethical issues and tensions were inherent in the professional role, the insider/outsider interpreting across sectors and structures. This involved taking the flak from all sides on occasion, striving to square the circle of centralised targets and locally relevant priorities. The procedures may have been clear but the emotional labour involved in carrying them out, in such contexts, may have been no less painful.

Coping strategies and support/lack of support

So how were these professionals coping; with what support systems and structures? In summary, there were examples of professionals who referred to the excellent support that they enjoyed from their line managers. But these were very much in the minority. Most professionals were coping as best they could, by themselves. Typically they were constructing their own personal support systems through informal networks of colleagues, former colleagues and trusted friends. The value of good supervision was very much recognised, however.

It was noteworthy that two professionals were actually paying for non-managerial supervision themselves, personally. This was because they recognised its value, but had been unable to obtain it in their work settings. In addition, a number referred to very personal ways of unwinding at the end of a particularly stressful day: going to the pub with friends, running, playing football, listening to music, playing computer games, a variety of ways of taking their minds off the day's dilemmas.

In some cases, professionals were not just feeling unsupported by the formal structures. There were examples of instances where they had felt positively undermined by lack of management support. In one case, for example, management simply shied away from dealing with a staffing issue, leaving the professional who had raised this out on a limb, totally unsupported, on their own.

Both more experienced professionals and those who were newer to the role expressed strong views about the importance of space for reflection. The interview process for our research was time-consuming but even very busy professionals expressed appreciation of the time and space for reflecting in these ways. Clearly this was a significant gap in their normal working lives. Since then, seminar programmes have been developed in one of the local universities, specifically designed to address this gap. The aim is to provide a safe space within which front-line professionals can reflect on current policy debates and the implications of current developments for their professional identities, values and practice. These seminars have the additional advantage that students on relevant professional programmes can share in these discussions and reflect on their experiences on placements, in preparation for their future roles at work.

More generally, however, we reflected that the most important coping strategies were far less specific. These professionals were coping by drawing on their own inner resources, qualities of resilience, flexibility and creativity. These resources were rooted in their own personal biographies, values and identities, bringing these to the situations in hand. The qualities of resilience and flexibility were particularly relevant in coping with the more generalised pressures associated with ethical issues. These were the situations in which ethical considerations were indeed involved, but where the professionals themselves were not faced with unbearable choices for the moment. As it has already been suggested, in such situations, professionals may have had relatively limited scope for the exercise of ethical judgement, perhaps, but they were, nevertheless experiencing the range of conflicting pressures and emotions inherent in their roles.

Potential implications

In summary, there would seem to be potential implications at different levels. There would seem to be a number of implications for professional education and training, to equip professionals with the knowledge (including self-knowledge and self-awareness) and critical understanding to cope with ethical issues and dilemmas. This would seem essential if professionals are to hold on to professional values as these develop in changing contexts.

In addition, there would seem to be important implications for supporting professionals on a continuing basis. Realistically, as one of the local policy makers interviewed commented, resources for management support are likely to continue to be limited, at least for the foreseeable future, let alone resources for non-managerial supervision and support. This makes it all the more important to ensure the provision of safe spaces for reflection and mutual support.

Last and by no means least, there would seem to be potentially important implications for public policy. The new localism may in fact exacerbate rather than resolve a number of the tensions inherent in public policies: to promote increasing marketisation and individual consumer choice with services to be delivered in increasingly business-like fashion, top down, while promoting user involvement, community participation and active citizenship. To what extent might such a policy context be contributing to the erosion of the public service ethos?

The research provided evidence to document the strength of so many professionals' values. But there were indications of more disturbing trends under way. The next generation of professionals may be redefining their boundaries. Increasing polarisation might be exacerbated perhaps, if professionals were to become more even more distanced with front-line services increasingly delivered by less qualified staff. How might such scenarios impact on the strength or otherwise of the public service ethos, and what might be the impact on care, citizenship and communities more generally?

References

Bailey, D. and Schwartzberg, S. (1995) *Ethical and Legal Dilemmas in Occupational Therapy*, Philadelphia, PA: Davis.

Balloch, S. and Taylor, M. (eds) (2001) *Partnership Working: Policy and Practice*, Bristol: The Policy Press.

Banks, S. (1995) *Ethics and Values in Social Work*, London: Macmillan.

Banks, S. (ed) (1999) *Ethical Issues in Youth Work*, London: Routledge.

Bauman, Z. (2000) *Liquid Modernity*, Cambridge: Polity Press.

Clarke, J., Gewirtz, S. and McLaughlin, E. (eds) (2000) *New Managerialism: New Welfare?*, London: Sage Publications.

Fukuyama, F. (1989) 'The end of history', *The National Interest*, no 19, pp 3-18.

Giddens, A. (1994) 'Living in a post-traditional society', in U. Beck, A. Giddens and S. Lash (eds) *Reflexive Modernization*, Cambridge: Polity Press, pp 56-109.

Glendinning, C., Powell, M. and Rummery, K. (eds) (2002) *Partnerships, New Labour and the Governance of Welfare*, Bristol: The Policy Press.

Hugman, R. and Smith, D. (1995) *Ethical Issues in Social Work*, London: Routledge.

Kakabadse, A., Korac-Kakabadse, N. and Kouzmin, A. (2003) 'Ethics, values and behaviours: comparison of three case studies examining the paucity of leadership in government', *Public Administration*, vol 81, no 3, pp 477-508.

Lash, S. (1994) 'Reflexivity and its doubles', in U. Beck, A. Giddens and S. Lash (eds) *Reflexive Modernization*, Cambridge: Polity Press, pp 110-73.

Le Grand, J. (2003) *Motivation, Agency and Public Policy*, Oxford: Oxford University Press.

Putnam, R. (2000) *Bowling Alone*, New York: Simon and Schuster.

Sennett, R. (1999) *The Corrosion of Character*, New York and London: W.W. Norton.

Sennett, R. (2003) *Respect*, London: Penguin.

Sennett, R. and Cobb, J. (1972) *The Hidden Injuries of Class*, New York: Knopf.

Tam, H. (1998) *Communitarianism*, London: Palgrave.

Taylor, M. (2003) *Public Policy in the Community*, Basingstoke: Macmillan.

SIX

Citizenship and care for people with dementia: values and approaches

Tula Brannelly

Introduction

People with dementia require help and support to remain living in their communities, and by far the most common form of care that people with dementia receive is lay care. It is estimated that there are 750,000 people diagnosed with dementia in the UK, of whom 18,500 are under 65 years old (Alzheimer's Society, 2003). Policy has for many years been encouraging community-based services in preference to institutionally based services (DH, 2001), and the majority of older people prefer to stay in their own homes. Because of the nature of dementia, balancing the needs of people involved in providing care with the needs and preferences of a person with dementia often presents dilemmas for all involved.

The incidence of dementia increases with age, and the fact that people are living longer in the UK and other 'developed' countries, means that more people in the future will develop dementia. Table 6.1 illustrates the increases in the incidence of cognitive impairment by age in England, and the expected population rises.

By these figures, there were 61,950 people aged 65-74 with dementia in 2002, and this figure will have risen to 83,745 by 2026, with a larger increase for the over 85s. In 2002 there were 131,928 people

Table 6.1: Number of people with dementia by age in England

Age group	65–74	75–84	85+	85–94	95+
% with severe cognitive impairment	1.5	3.1		13.8	40.2
Population size (thousands) by age (2002)	4,130	2,805	956		
Population size (thousands) by age (2026)	5,583	4,232	1,775		

Sources: DH (2002); Wanless (2006, pp 43-4)

with dementia over the age of 85, and this figure will have risen to 244,950 by 2026. These are conservative estimates calculated at the lower percentage of 13.8% for 85- to 94-year-olds. In addition, people with learning disabilities are also living longer and experience a high incidence of dementia, usually at a younger age. Developing dementia results in a return to institutional life for some, admission to an institution for others or a change of institution as services are ill-equipped to provide the specialist help that people with learning disabilities, and their carers, require (Hatzidimitriadou and Milne, 2005, p 353; Wilkinson et al, 2005).

The numbers of people with dementia living in communities is difficult to fathom. It is estimated that 5% of people with dementia live in specialised dementia residential and nursing homes. There are many people with dementia living in non-specialist residential homes, perhaps without diagnosis or any treatment or other interventions. In a study in the West Midlands area by Haynes et al (2006) the number of available residential placements decreased by 9.9% between 1991 and 2001, and both nurses and social workers discussed the difficulty of accessing resources, in particular residential placements for which competition was fierce. This provided an additional aspect of complexity when responding to what people with dementia and carers required or requested.

Previous assumptions of the burden of older people on younger people are now challenged as largely unfounded (Browning et al, 2005, p 67), as much care given and received by older people is interdependent – older people care for each other. It is when this relationship is not available that others step in to help out, be they other family members, friends or neighbours. Carers of older people do face care-giving stress, and services are required to acknowledge and consider this in the way that services are provided. Notably, some services that have been developed such as institutional respite are not popular with care givers or receivers, and so are less successful than anticipated (Nolan et al, 2002). It appears that at least part of the reason for this is that services fail to understand the biography of the persons they are trying to help, or indeed the relationships in which care is achieved (Barnes, 2006, p 20). There is a general reluctance to accept services due to their lack of suitability, and this was borne out in the present study.

Care needs change substantially as dementia progresses. People with dementia and carers experience loss and grief with the progression of dementia, which influences how carers and the person with dementia are able to meet caring needs together. Carers learn how to care and adapt to new needs faced by the person with dementia, so that caring itself is a constant negotiation (see Nolan and Dellasega, 2000).

The newer paradigm in researching care giving incorporates both the benefits of providing care as well as the difficulties encountered (Murphy et al, 1997; Wells and Kendig, 1997; Barnes 2006). This is the evidence that services need to consider in relation to how care happens with people with dementia and carers. The author suggests that the following are significant in offering care that meets the needs of people with dementia and their carers:

- an understanding of the relationship between the person with dementia and carers, including recognition of the biography of how care has happened in these relationships in the past;
- leading from this, an understanding of the needs of both to achieve care;
- lay carer employment and other care responsibilities, including care for self;
- design of services that complement rather than disrupt care giving.

This chapter presents findings from a study examining how care is negotiated between people with dementia, their lay carers and professional carers, namely community psychiatric nurses (CPNs) and social workers. An ethic of care framework (Tronto, 1993) was used to analyse care as it can be used to examine different occupational groups and provides principles to influence good care.

An ethic of care

An ethic of care is a political argument for the de-gendering and de-privatisation of care (Sevenhuijsen, 2003a), and has set out ethical practice on which good care can be established (see Chapter Four). It has been used to analyse the content of social policies (Sevenhuijsen, 2003a), what caring means to lay carers (Barnes, 2006), as well as the changing nature of caring responsibilities within and outside family networks resulting from the reorganisation of family and work (Williams, 2001; Sevenhuijsen, 2003b). Here, it is used to analyse the practices of social workers and CPNs for the way that ethics influence practice and consider the ethics of the care provided (Brannelly, 2004).

This research was conducted with 50 people with dementia, their carers (when present) and the CPNs and social workers involved in their care, who were observed for 14 months to decipher how decisions were made about care outcomes, especially placements in nursing and residential homes. Observations occurred in people's homes, day centres, hospitals, residential and nursing homes. The participants with dementia ranged in age from 38 to 101 years old. Literal fieldnotes were produced and shared with practitioners and were the starting point for discussion within the in-depth interviews. The analysis utilised an ethic of care (Gilligan, 1982; Tronto, 1993; Sevenhuijsen, 1998), chosen specifically because it has a starting point of inclusion of all care givers and receivers. The four principles of 'integrity of care' (Tronto, 1993) allow analysis of practitioners' values and approaches to people with dementia and their carers. This discussion focuses on interactions between people with dementia, their carers and practitioners, particularly when people were removed from their communities, here referenced by removal from locality and social networks. It also reflects on current policy.

Table 6.2 shows the outcomes of care at the times of the interviews with practitioners. Ten of the 50 people with dementia were placed in residential and nursing homes; of these, five did not want or accept the placement.

Table 6.2: Care outcomes for people with dementia

Care outcome	Number of people seen by CPNs	Number of people seen by social workers
Residential placement	2	6
Nursing home placement	0	2
At home with care package	24	6
In general hospital – to return home	3	0
In psychiatric hospital – sectioned	1	0
Continuing residential/nursing home placement	2	2
Unknown	0	1 (duty case)
Other	0	3 (deaths)
Total	32	20

Note: Two people were seen by both a CPN and a social worker.

Living in the community

Of the 50 participants, 32 continued living at home with varying levels of help, usually with carer support, and community services, some of whom had substantial difficulties. Two people relied solely on the help of their carer, and in both situations it was the carer who had barred any additional services as they did not want them because they thought they were too distressing for the person with dementia. For example, carers ruled out day centres where they saw distressed people with dementia; or would not accept personal care being carried out by strangers. Alternatives were not available to them. Two people did not have a family carer, and both were admitted to residential care, and not in the way that had been previously agreed with them (discussed further below). In terms of high levels of service provision, a 101-year-old woman was receiving seven health and social calls a day as well as two family calls. Her family and CPN requested assessment for placement in residential care (her family had cared for her for more than 30 years and her main carer, her daughter, had become unwell), but the social worker had refused to make an application as she thought it would be refused considering the high levels of community support the woman received.

Concerned about the safety of people with dementia, practitioners often tried to find solutions that meant that the person could stay at home. For example, an elderly woman had been escorted home by the police in the middle of the night dressed in her nightdress on two occasions in the previous four weeks. In discussions with the woman, who wanted to remain at home, the police and the woman's carer, her nephew, it was decided that the solution was to lock the woman in the house at night. She had a lodger who agreed to let her out in the event of an emergency. Although reluctant, it was agreed and her nephew called every evening to check on her and lock the doors. Although restrictive, this met the needs of the woman, the carer and practitioners and meant that the woman stayed in her own home.

Practitioners referred to 'tweaking' service provision, such as introducing personal, day or respite care so that the needs of all were met. Where people with dementia and carers were reticent, some practitioners supported them by attending the service with them and agreeing to discontinue it if it was not acceptable. In other circumstances people with dementia were evidently not enjoying services, becoming very distressed while they were there and were visibly upset on their return home and practitioners dismissed this as a symptom of dementia and told carers that nothing could be done about it. In some circumstances, the biography of a person with dementia ruled out trying certain services. An example would be where an agoraphobic woman was terminally ill but nursed at home so that she did not have to experience the acute anxiety of leaving her home. For another woman who did not enjoy socialising, individual rather than group care was organised.

Moving out of the community

Encouraging people to accept a small level of service put concerned others, such as carers or the general practitioner, at ease and averted the need for people to move out of their home. The significance of accepting such services was not explained to people with dementia; but practitioners would discuss that if a person did not accept a relatively minor service, such as delivered meals, there was a need for compulsory detention. It was apparent that services were not explained to carers either, and despite practitioners focusing on how the carer coped with caring, they had not offered any kind of practical support to enable them to care. As a result, when carers found physical caring too difficult the emphasis shifted straight to admission into residential care. Two of the practitioners assumed that carers were aware of services that were available and that they would let them know what services they needed at any given time. Most frequently, admission occurred when the carer experienced difficulty providing care, often due to the physical disabilities caused by dementia, and the person with dementia did not disagree to the placement.

Practitioners felt the need to encourage admission into residential care when faced with external influences. A social worker encouraged a woman reluctant to leave her home to move into residential care, as there was a risk that the agreed funding would be lost if she refused the care, and that her decision might influence future decisions regarding funding for her care. She had lived in sheltered housing, and was keeping the warden awake through the night by using the emergency buzzer when unable to do things for herself.

The most restrictive of circumstances was when people with dementia did not want to leave home and admission was compulsory. On one occasion a 76-year-old man with no carer was admitted to a residential home and then not allowed to leave, and his capacity was questioned when he found the home unacceptable because they had removed his belongings and forcibly bathed him. Another man without a carer had planned his admission with his CPN but was urgently admitted after cooking sausages in his kettle and from the admission unit was transferred into a residential placement that was not of his choice. One social work practitioner assumed that carers did not want to continue caring and so did not attempt community services but admitted the person with dementia into residential placement. She did this with both the people with dementia whom she was working with. She did not ask the carer about their preference and commented that caring for people with dementia was too much of a burden for carers to carry.

For one of these people, the diagnosis of dementia and assessment of capacity were questionable (for more detail, see Brannelly, 2006).

These examples of people leaving their communities are provided for two reasons. The first is to discuss how care within communities would be better supported if practitioners adopted the inclusive ethic of care approach. Second, policy does not currently engage adequately with the issues that are involved in making decisions about removing a person with dementia from their community and providing enough support to carers and people with dementia.

An ethic of care analysis

The purpose of using an ethic of care as the analytical framework is threefold. First, it enables discussion of interdependence, in this case how carers and people with dementia cared for each other as well as receiving care from the practitioner. Second, the focus of care becomes apparent through negotiations to work out how care should happen. Third, it provides a different lens for looking at how to care for people inclusively, people who may previously have been marginalised.

For many people with dementia in this study there was a constant negotiation of care with careful consideration of needs, resulting in acceptable care until, for some, care eventually broke down and the person with dementia moved into a residential placement. This is an anxious time, with 'exceptionally high emotional content' for which dementia is noted (Phillips et al, 2006). Experiences such as admission to psychiatric hospital and care homes hold many fears and challenges.

Attentiveness

If the needs of the person requiring care are not recognised by those providing care then care cannot happen. Throughout the incidents above there were elements of attentiveness. Practitioners met their statutory duties and provided empowering care for carers and people with dementia, while carers and people with dementia responded to practitioners and allowed them to provide care, particularly where those needs could be met more easily in the earlier stages of care. In order to provide collaborative and negotiated care, the relationship between those involved needs to be honest and trusting enough for this to occur.

Attentiveness was demonstrated by all needs being met adequately during the first phase of care when people with dementia remained at home. Fear about safety at home prompted placements at day centres, but this was with everyone's agreement and met everyone's needs. For carers this meant that anxiety levels were reduced during the day, the practitioner was able to support carers' care giving and people with dementia had company and activity during the day. There were many moments of very skilled and sensitive interventions between people with dementia and practitioners, such as when a practitioner worked with a person with dementia to remind her of the previous day's oncology consultation, and the treatment she might receive for her cancer.

There is no doubt that times of heightened stress are testing times for relationships, and that placement in psychiatric hospital for people with dementia who have no history of previous mental ill-health is often a very stressful event. Both people with dementia and carers require substantial support at this time, and extended involvement by the community practitioners may well meet this need better than 'handing over' to ward staff.

People with dementia recognised carers' needs also, by accepting placements at day centres or accepting respite care to allow the carer to rest. In contrast, it could be said that practitioners were inattentive when people with dementia were moved to residential placements in which there was no involvement in the decision. Practitioners' biographic knowledge of people with dementia and their carers needs to be accepted by other professionals as a guide for providing attentive care.

Responsibility

Responsibility refers to personal motivations for care and the preparedness to take the action necessary to ensure care is provided. It is expected that in kin relationships caring motivations relate in part to reciprocity. Professional motivations are considered rather differently. Professionals are encouraged to maintain distance in relationships so that they do not become too involved or, indeed, maternalistic/paternalistic to those they care for. This emphasis on questioning the motivations of practitioners, or expectation that involvement leads to the corruption of a relationship, can result in denial of personal involvement and can be unhelpful.

Practitioners who I observed having friendly chats with people with dementia and their carers, and exchanging stories of each others' families, suggested that such action would be viewed as '*un*professional'. But these exchanges were seen as positive events, clearly enjoyed by people with dementia and enabled establishment of trust. They allowed people with dementia and their carers to see what kind of person was offering care, and they could judge whether they would be cared for. They were able to get a 'feel' for the practitioner, even if they did not know what their role was and what help they may be able to provide.

Practitioners do not demonstrate responsibility when they use distance as a source of coping in order to make decisions that are unpalatable to the people they care for. The clearest example of this was when a practitioner described the process of final placement in residential care as 'bureaucratic', signalling the end of the practitioner's personal involvement.

Competence

Competent care refers to good care outcomes, and this was evident at different stages of accepting care. People with dementia accepted care because carers and practitioners explained why the care was required. People with dementia responded positively to this by accepting alternative non-familial care. Practitioners were also competent when attempting to get other professionals to collaborate in an attempt to ensure that needs were met. Unfortunately, this was not always possible, and contributed to placement decisions without the involvement of the person with dementia.

Responsiveness

Practitioners need to listen to the care receiver to assess the quality of care provided. Carers and people with dementia were both care givers and receivers. To be responsive, care givers are attentive to the needs of care receivers, provide good care that meets needs, tweaking it when required, and then listening to care receivers to establish whether the care provided has achieved what was intended, again reviewing and changing any interventions as necessary. Responsiveness was demonstrated in some situations such as practitioners abandoning residential placements when the person with dementia did not like it. Most care provision was acceptable to people with dementia. When people with dementia found placements disagreeable, it was an indication that the suitability and quality of the placement was inadequate and therefore responsive practitioners would review and possibly change the placement.

Policy and legislation

People with dementia who are incapacitated to make decisions about their future (called global incapacity and often used in practice) according to a physician are not protected under mental health or human rights law, but by common law doctrines of best interests and duty of care. In other words, any action that can be justified under these doctrines need never be reviewed or revisited, the minimalist protections that other law affords. In this situation policy becomes all important, and the *National Service Framework for Older People* (DH, 2001) was welcomed by interested groups, particularly as it recognised ageism and called for measures to tackle it in policy and practice.

The *National Service Framework for Older People* can be challenged for its lack of guidance for carers, people with dementia and practitioners when difficult decisions need to be faced because a person with dementia is no longer able to be supported in the community. Emphasis on carer involvement and community provision does not help practitioners provide suitable good care in these difficult times. Care based on an ethic of care would enable practitioners to ensure their practice was ethically sound.

In this study CPNs tended to have longer-term involvement with people with dementia and their carers, while social workers were called in when the more difficult, hard-end decisions about placements needed to be made. Hence, the CPNs tended to see more people at home, whose needs may be less pressing than the people with dementia seen by the social workers. Having built intimate knowledge of and relationships with people with dementia and their carers, CPNs 'handed over' care to social workers, and did not work collaboratively to influence care. Only two of the 50 participants with dementia had both a social worker and a CPN involved in their care.

Conclusions

Viewing care as interdependent and an essential element of human relationships rightly challenges the 'burden and heroine' (Barnes, 2006, p 177) discourse often associated with carers and the cared for. The intent here was to show how people with dementia, although requiring high levels of care, are also able to provide care for their carers, especially when supported to do so. People with dementia are typically constructed as incapable and incapacitated. Care has to be worked at, but the foundations for building good care are more likely

---

to be established in relationships where people have cared for each other over years of interdependence.

An ethic of care:

- acknowledges the interdependency of care givers and receivers, including people with dementia, lay carers and practitioners;
- encompasses a range of agendas in a situated context to facilitate negotiated care outcomes;
- encourages participation in collaborative care with other practitioners, lay carers and people with dementia;
- ensures that the emphasis of the quality of care is considered from a service user perspective.

The roles of community practitioners such as social workers and CPNs could better support people with dementia and their carers by seeing as strengths the aspects that each brings that fit with an ethic of care. Nurses are often involved long term and accumulate a great knowledge of the biographies and preferences of both the person with dementia and their carers, but withdraw when the most difficult decisions have to be made. Social workers are involved at these most difficult times but do not have the benefit of this knowledge. This is likely to produce care that is not as well suited to the person with dementia and their carers as it could be.

Likewise, when admissions to hospital or other placements happen, practitioners previously involved need to continue their involvement to provide some continuity for the person with dementia and their carers, but also to guide other practitioners so that the care provided is suitable and fitting to the needs of the person with dementia and their carers. Understanding the key role of carers in meeting needs is something that, in particular, nurses have not attended well to previously, but adopting an ethic of care centralises the work of carers.

Multidisciplinarity has resulted in working practices where professionals guard their roles. The focus of concern can shift from providing care to protecting boundaries, which is unhelpful for service users. The dichotomy exists about the importance of relationship building and establishing trust with care receivers, and professional agendas dominating care outcomes. Professional care givers need to prioritise the agenda of care receivers to collaborate to meet those aims. This requires meaningful relationships, where practitioners are able to become involved in order to care. The author would argue that an ethic of care provides a set of principles that can help practitioners to maintain the balance of interpersonal involvement and care.

Citizenship and dementia may at first appear to be odd bedfellows. Dementia gradually takes from the person; it takes independence, communication and abilities, but it does not take the human. Relationships that aim to preserve citizenship can do so by remembering the person and using biography to guide care. This is best achieved by people with dementia being surrounded by places and people they know and who know them so that they remain within their communities in which they are themselves. Alternatives are difficult to contemplate, and even harder to endure and so need to be restricted to when they are absolutely necessary, if at all. Care based on the ethic of care enables negotiations that are inclusive and therefore ensures that potentially marginalised voices are heard and responded to.

References

Alzheimer's Society (2003) *What is Dementia?*, Alzheimer's Society Information Sheet, www.alzheimers.org.uk/Facts_about_dementia/ PDF/400_WhatIsDementia.pdf

Barnes, M. (2006) *Caring and Social Justice*, Basingstoke: Palgrave.

Brannelly, P. (2004) 'Citizenship and care for people with dementia', PhD thesis, University of Birmingham.

Brannelly, T. (2006) 'Negotiating ethics in dementia care: an analysis of an ethic of care in practice', *Dementia, The International Journal of Social Research and Practice*, vol 5, no 2, pp 197-212.

Browning, C., Wells, Y. and Joyce, A. (2005) 'The experience of ageing: influences on mental health and well-being', in V. Minichello and I. Coulson (eds) *Contemporary Issues in Gerontology: Promoting Positive Ageing*, London: Routledge, pp 53-77.

DH (2001) *National Service Framework for Older People*, www.dh.gov. uk/assetRoot/04/07/12/83/04071283.pdf

DH (2002) *Health Survey for England 2000: The Health of Older People*, London: DH.

Gilligan, C. (1982) *In a Different Voice: Psychological Theory and Women's Development*, London: Harvard University Press.

Hatzidimitriadou, E. and Milne, A. (2005) 'Planning ahead: meeting the needs of older people with intellectual disabilities in the United Kingdom', *Dementia, The International Journal of Social Research and Practice*, vol 4, no 3, pp 341-59.

Haynes, P., Banks, L., Balloch, S. and Hill, M. (2006) 'Public policy and private provisions: changes in residential care from 1991 to 2001', *Health and Social Care in the Community*, vol 14, no 6, pp 499-507.

Murphy, B., Schofield, H., Nankervis, J., Bloch, S., Herman, H. and Singh, B. (1997) 'Women with multiple roles: the emotional impact of caring for ageing parents', *Ageing and Society*, vol 17, pp 277-91.

Nolan, M., Ingram, P. and Watson, R. (2002) 'Working with family carers of people with dementia: "negotiated" coping as an essential outcome', *Dementia, The International Journal of Social Research and Practice*, vol 1, no 1, pp 75-93.

Nolan, M. R. and Dellasega, C. (2000) '"I really feel I've let him down": supporting family carers during long-term care placement for elders', *Journal of Advanced Nursing*, vol 31, no 4, pp 759-67.

Phillips, J., Ray, M. and Marshall, M. (2006) *Social Work with Older People* (4th edition), Basingstoke: Palgrave.

Sevenhuijsen, S. (1998) *Citizenship and the Ethics of Care: Feminist Considerations on Justice, Morality and Politics*, London: Routledge.

Sevenhuijsen, S. (2003a) 'Trace: a method for normative policy analysis from an ethic of care', Paper prepared for the seminar 'Gender and Public Policy', Centre for Women's and Gender Research, University of Bergen, 9-11 November.

Sevenhuijsen, S. (2003b) 'The place of care: the relevance of the feminist ethic of care for social policy', *Feminist Theory*, vol 4, no 2, pp 179-97.

Tronto, J. C. (1993) *Moral Boundaries: A Political Argument for an Ethic of Care*, London: Routledge.

Wanless, D. (2006) *Wanless Social Care Review: Securing Good Care for Older People, Taking a Long Term View*, London: King's Fund.

Wells, Y. and Kendig, H. L. (1997) 'Health and wellbeing of spouse caregivers and the widowed', *Gerontologist*, vol 37, pp 666-74.

Wilkinson, H., Kerr, D. and Cunningham, C. (2005) 'Equipping staff to support people with an intellectual disability and dementia in care home settings', *Dementia, The International Journal of Social Research and Practice*, vol 4, no 3, pp 387-400.

Williams, F. (2001) 'In and beyond New Labour: towards a new political ethics of care', *Critical Social Policy*, vol 21, no 4, pp 467-93.

Part Three
Bridging the gaps:
a practice-based approach

Rough justice, enforcement or support: young people and their families in the community

Dawn E. Stephen and Peter Squires

Introduction

In recent years the issue of anti-social behaviour and the policies for its control, or management, have seen a rapid rise to prominence. There has been a sequence of waves of serious political investment into the problem, very much led from the centre by Tony Blair himself (for an overview, see Squires, 2006a). Beginning with ambitions to 'strengthen communities' and 'nip youth crime in the bud' and 'enforce' more effectively the obligations of parents in the 1998 Crime and Disorder Act (and the new youth justice system emerging from this) the anti-social behaviour agenda grew and grew, prompting at least one commentator to question whether in 'inventing anti-social behaviour' to draw some attention away from the wider crime problem, the government had not fashioned an even bigger rod for its own back (Tonry, 2004).

Next came the *Respect and Responsibility* White Paper (Home Office, 2003) reasserting the contractual model of citizenship, much beloved of New Labour, which tied the government's social inclusion agenda (SEU, 1998, 2000) to its broader 'responsibilisation' strategy (Levitas, 1996; Garland, 2001), leading to the 2003 Anti-Social Behaviour Act. A year later came the first Annual Report of the Home Office-sponsored campaign *Together: Tackling Anti-Social Behaviour*, which, on page one, confidently asserted: 'as crime has fallen, anti-social behaviour has become a major cause of concern in communities across the country' (Home Office, 2004a). The implication was fairly clear, crime was supposedly falling, and the lesser problems of nuisance and anti-social behaviour were now coming to preoccupy people instead. By the summer of 2004, addressing anti-social behaviour formed a central plank of the new Home Office five-year strategic plan (Home Office, 2004b).

Finally and forcibly reasserting the, at first glance, common-sense but also deeply ideological, core to the government's anti-social behaviour message, the Prime Minister launched the *Respect Action Plan* in January 2006 (Home Office, 2006). This document was punctuated by a series of seemingly homespun motivational slogans:

> The only person who can start the cycle of respect is you.
>
> Give respect – Get respect.
>
> The future depends upon unlocking the positive potential of young people.
>
> There is no greater responsibility than raising the next generation.
>
> Respect cannot be learned, purchased or acquired, it can only be earned.

The behavioural and contractual assumption implicit in the slogans was that such respect and disrespect issues and the behaviour to which they were related were constructed almost entirely as questions of choice and personal motivation. The situated social question of anti-social behaviour, notwithstanding complex dilemmas about the very variable perceptions of behaviour construed as anti-social, was reframed as a type of 12-step programme that the virtuous or committed might choose to ascend (albeit, at times prompted by the threat of enforcement sanctions). Perhaps it goes without saying, but our existing work on this issue (Squires and Stephen, 2005a, 2005b; Squires, 2006a; Stephen, 2006) has entirely sought to reject this interpretation of anti-social behaviour. Here, we would argue (a point we return to later in the chapter) about the need to create opportunities for people to earn respect and acquire and demonstrate responsibilities.

Nevertheless, notwithstanding the broader sociological and criminological engagement we have generally sought with this issue, as the anti-social behaviour agenda grew and developed as indicated above, a number of more immediate issues, often directly related to questions of policy implementation, practice and partnership working, have also arisen. In this chapter, and still working from our existing perspective, we turn to consider these questions, both as they arose in our original research and as they have surfaced in subsequent anti-social behaviour debates. These questions concern: first, the balance or, more properly, the relationships between enforcement and support in anti-social behaviour management work (very much an echo of the much older care versus control debate in social welfare history); second, the extent to which anti-social behaviour enforcement action is a genuinely 'last' resort of community safety practitioners (there being much national political rhetoric surrounding the alleged need for many Crime and Disorder Reduction Partnerships to 'raise their game' on the anti-social behaviour enforcement front, and seek more Anti-Social Behaviour Orders (ASBOs) as earlier interventions, see Squires, 2006a, pp 144-5); third, there is the question of the position and perspective of the 'victim' in anti-social behaviour management work. Here, not least, lies the further question of how we might conceive of the status of 'victimhood' in relation to anti-social behaviour (Walklate, 2006). Finally, coming full circle, there are questions about 'outcomes' at the level of real neighbourhoods and communities and the processes and relationships of citizenship (forms of social capital) established and sustained (or not) within them.

From the outset we have to acknowledge that in social and public policy discourses, the language of community has tended to serve a number of purposes. Thus, notions of 'community' tend to exercise a legitimating function for policy arrangements (Lacey and Zedner, 1995), implying a degree of naturalness, informality, inclusiveness, equity and spontaneity regarding localised human relationships and purposes. In this light, selected 'community values' can acquire an aura of legitimacy, which, rather than *creating* them in the first instance, policy interventions are seen merely as protecting and preserving. However, recent developments in community policy making, collectively understood as elements in a broader strategy of 'responsibilisation' (Garland, 2001), have tended to bring communities *within* the processes of governing rather than have them as the objects of governing. In other words, communities have become increasingly 'governmentalised' wherein recent notions of 'stronger communities' require some reassessment: Stronger for whom? Stronger against whom? Community safety, as we have recently argued (Squires, 2006b), is not necessarily a positive sum relationship. With this in mind it becomes necessary to consider, in detail, how the implementation of community policies impact on the quality of citizenship and levels of well-being enjoyed by all members.

At first sight and given our avowedly critical stance towards existing anti-social behaviour measures (Squires and Stephen, 2005a) it might seem somewhat contradictory to engage in a discussion of these issues. We consider it possible, however, to continue a sustained critique of these policies at a number of levels, especially in terms of what we have described as a 'politics of injustice' (Stephen and Squires, 2004; Squires, 2006a; Stephen, 2006), while also offering suggestions for the adoption of some more humane practices within this fast-developing policy field. Our earlier fieldwork threw up one particular area where we can confidently offer some optimism and this concerns the positive impact that individual enforcement practitioners might have on those subject to anti-social behaviour or youth justice interventions (Smith, 2003: chapter 4). One of our interviewees commented:

> It was like a friendship contract … I felt I'd been dumped when it was over. I appreciate everything that's been done for me on this contract.… As a parent I will defend mine to the end, but this contract has made me realise things, that I need to see both sides, it's not nice to be told the truth. I'm quite sad it's over, wouldn't mind if he went back on a contract again. I liked the impersonality [sic], it was nice, quite touching to get that sort of response from absolute strangers [names police and community safety officers] … made me think.… My God, I'm responsible for these monsters.… They've been there.… It's like the ambulance service, you never need an ambulance, but you know it's there … I know if I want to speak to [community safety officer] she's there. They're like the fourth emergency service. I feel quite grateful to them … it was all positive, nothing but positive, they broke the barrier down I had in dealing with people … the contract saved us a job and helped us, it made life easier for us. (Stephen and Squires, 2003, pp 57–8)

Although this mother reported that her initial feelings about the Acceptable Behaviour Contract (ABC) had been entirely negative and confrontational, she now welcomed the supportive relations with the community safety and police officers. As shown above, this mother had wished the supportive relationship to continue on a more formal basis when the contract was completed. Arising from her family's earlier experiences with enforcement agencies (her oldest son was in prison), her initial expectations of any workable relationship had been extremely low.

This issue of expectation proved to be one of our key findings. At the most basic level, where expectations of the supportive relationship had been low or non-existent among families, the highest levels of satisfaction were expressed. Correspondingly, when expectations that long-standing support needs would begin to be addressed (for example, the children's special educational needs or mental health problems), implicit in the families' understanding of the mutual obligations associated with the term 'contract' (and not least in view of the contractual discourse within which New Labour had originally framed the question of anti-social behaviour: Squires, 2006a), then evaluations were least favourable, if not highly critical of the ABC process, as reflected in the following remark:

> I feel it's very one-sided....The council don't offer anything in the contract, they ask them [the young person] to sign that they'll not do all these things, but they're giving nothing in return. (Stephen and Squires, 2003, p 78)

To be fair, this was an issue recognised by many of the community safety project team staff we interviewed. It raises a question regarding the very place and nature of this 'contract' in relation to the wider partnership that the community safety team represented. The community safety team members very much saw themselves as something of a catalyst for the new ways of inter-professional and partnership working that the local authority as a whole needed to embrace. On the other hand they expressed a sense of dismay that other service areas were not as effective or responsive as they needed to be. There was a tangible sense of frustration that the community safety team staff had to do all the chasing up of correspondence, documents and decisions, filling the communication and implementation gaps appearing in other existing services areas. One of our community safety team staff interviewees made the point:

> 'Oh I know they are all overworked, we're all overworked, but it is frustrating when you have to chase them up to do everything yourself. I know we're here to make a difference, get people working differently and that will involve a lot of firefighting in the early days, and knocking heads together, but if we are still doing this in 10 years' time, than we'll have failed to bring about the changes that are needed.' (Fieldwork interview with community team staff member)

Implicit in this comment is the notion of community safety teams engaging in and facilitating new forms of joined-up working. That is, community safety teams were to be 'joined up' rather than 'added on'.

What also emerged strongly from our research fieldwork was the recognition that community safety can only be achieved if families are themselves enabled within the ABC process. Somewhat ironically, the families with whom we worked recognised that, while ABCs are very much located within an enforcement paradigm, if employed in an anti-oppressive manner, they can offer new opportunities for empowerment that encourage reflexivity and accountability. More significantly, the contractual relationship could begin to challenge the structured inequalities that characterised the families' lives, if only through opening up opportunities to rebalance power relationships with agency personnel. This would certainly appear to be what the mother in the extract on page 108 appreciated most about the ABC process. It was what the majority of families believed was wanting in their own ABC experiences. Community safety practitioners are in a strong position to work with families to challenge the aspects of their own and their families' progressive marginalisation to date. As lead agents in the Community Safety Partnership (provided community safety, as opposed to simple enforcement, priorities are forwarded within the Partnerships), community safety practitioners are in many respects well placed to tap into wider networks and resources to enable families to begin to alter the circumstances within which their children's anti-social behaviour develops. However, as the second mother above (p 109) bemoaned, this must be set in motion in the early stages of the ABC process to help families recognise that they are receiving something of significance to their real expressed needs in return for their efforts.

Regardless of the families' evaluations of their experience, one key factor dominated accounts: positive accounts of the individual community safety officers. This finding that 'one good worker can make all the difference' (Millie et al, 2005, p 36) therefore provides the impetus for the remainder of this chapter. The greatest irony is that, through the practice of community safety, those practitioners involved in enforcement appeared to be beginning to provide the kinds of support the families reported they had been seeking for years, but as one mother reflected ,'they're limited in what they can do ... they are only allowed to do so much' (Stephen and Squires, 2003, p 74). The families' concerns were to be supported in two of the priorities identified by one youth worker who worked closely with the community safety team. These were the need:

- to look at the young people's situations holistically;
- for empowering support for the families.

Enabling families

> Enforcement tactics may contain their misbehaviour in the short term, but for the longer term, enforcement clearly needs to be balanced with inclusionary measures. (Millie et al, 2005, p 36)

The rhetoric and practices of responsibilisation associated with anti-social behaviour enforcement essentialises individuals and their problems. Constructions of 'yobs', 'thugs', 'hoodies' and 'neighbours from hell' in politicians' speeches wholly disregard 'parenting as an embedded, situated process, amenable to change only through social and material circumstances' (Gillies, 2005, p 87). The wider social context within which this anti-social agency develops and proceeds includes, for example, poor educational provision or inadequate mental health support for special learning needs and behavioural problems, enabling individualised ABCs and ASBOs to be imposed without providing the resources for individuals and their families to address their deeper problems and thus pursue 'law-abiding' lives. In their structuring as 'abandoned citizens' (Clarke, 2005, pp 452-53), the process of enforcement is also heavily reliant on stigmatisation, not least in terms of public naming and shaming, yet this is utterly counterproductive (Jamieson, 2005; Squires and Stephen, 2005a). If the aims of this activity are to 'normalise' individuals' agency within their communities and promote community inclusion, very basic sociological lessons point to quite contrary outcomes:

> Stigmatisation appears to be both a powerful mechanism for controlling the flow of social resources and an enormous hindrance to social justice. It is part of a social process from the identification and marking of people of 'low social value' through to the acts of discrimination and social exclusion that are the end points of the process. (Reidpath et al, 2005, p 479)

The advent of Individual Support Orders to 'tackle the underlying causes of a young person's anti-social behaviour' (YJB, 2006, p 4) for 10- to 17-year-olds was a very welcome shift in the government's approach. Unfortunately, such support is highly conditional, it is not universal, assessment is based on the managerialist risk-focused imperatives (entirely characteristic of the 'new youth justice': Squires and Measor, 2005) and it is typified by an abject anti-humanism: 'any intervention matrix will have to be based on the premise that the most intensive/prolonged intervention will be reserved only for the most serious cases with very high *Asset* scores' (YJB, 2006, p 6).

The launch of the *Respect Action Plan* (Home Office, 2006) trumpeted additional means by which the government aims to support families, and increase activities for young people and reduce their truancy. Nonetheless, however positive the move to provide greater resources for young people and support for families through greater roles for welfare professionals may be, the continuing focus on blaming 'problem families' (Jamieson, 2005) and tightening enforcement through increased summary powers further underlines the government's rather superficial commitment to tackling underlying 'causes'. Our concerns are expressed no more clearly than in this conclusion:

> [D]espite a rhetoric of empowerment and investment, the current emphasis on support represents a top-down projection of values and standards on families, thereby 'supporting' conformity rather than promoting access to parenting resources. (Gillies, 2005, p 70)

While appreciating these fundamental, and indeed worrying, deficiencies there still appears scope to capitalise on opportunities for meaningful change. Given such institutional constraints on individual community safety practitioners there is much to be gleaned from our first mother's description of the support being 'like the fourth emergency service'. Community safety officers' roles appeared to have very fluid edges and, from our discussions with practitioners themselves, it was clear that they certainly offered more support to the families than might have been expected (including, as we have seen already, establishing vital communication links between other local service agencies). Significantly, the extent to which they were able to empathise with the families' situations was very apparent and they seemed to be able to balance the enforcement/support line in a highly commendable manner. In developing these highly positive aspects of their role, community safety practitioners can learn much from anti-oppressive social work developments (Braye and Preston-Shoot, 1995; Pinkney, 2000; Dominelli, 2002) and, indeed, what has been learned about practitioner 'conceit' in appropriating service users' knowledge and expertise to reinforce oppression (Wilson and Beresford, 2000, p 554). Social workers have long balanced role tensions inherent in their statutory responsibilities (Wilson and Beresford, 2000) and have formulated creative means by which oppressive constructs and stigmatisation can be challenged through anti-oppressive relationships with clients:

An anti-oppressive framework seeks to de-individualise clients' problems in order to see them within the wider social context of their lives. In addition, this framework attempts to move away from an 'expert' model of service delivery towards one that is more inclusive of clients' experiences and that incorporates recognition of coping and resistance to oppression. Central to the anti-oppressive approach is a commitment towards changing social relationships and institutions that perpetuate the exclusion of marginalized groups of people. (Pollack, 2004, p 694)

A key aspect of this literature is a concern with the ways through which 'wider socio-economic structures produce personal troubles' (Heron, 2005, p 343) and, while practitioners are limited in their ability to tackle these 'troubles' directly, they can work to challenge the relations of power that exist with their clients, and act as a vital gatekeeper to resources previously denied to the families through their structured position of powerlessness. For one of our mothers this 'broke down the barriers' she had previously held with figures of authority, and enabled her to ask for support (although, of course, not everyone is likely to feel so). Further, in line with government policy, this enabled her to appreciate the need to accept some responsibility for the behaviour of her children. This negotiation of 'mutual recognition' (Sennett, 2004, p 260) within her individual interactions with the community safety and police officers appeared to provide vital potential for germinating seeds of inclusion through the fostering of opportunities for her own and her children's self- and social development (see Sennett, 2004). Accordingly, in considering how community safety practitioners can maximise their own potential, among the illuminating social work literature one particularly helpful paper stands out in highlighting means by which anti-oppressive practice can be developed with offenders (Pollack, 2004). Pollack advocates six principles in programme development, which will be discussed in turn:

(1) All individuals possess strengths and abilities.
(2) The process of service development is as crucial as the outcomes.
(3) Interventions must address a current need identified by participants themselves.
(4) Social justice themes must be integrated throughout the service/programme.

(5)   Participants must have real and tangible mechanisms through which they contribute skills, knowledge and decision making.
(6)   Community links must be facilitated. (Pollack, 2004, p 705)

All individuals possess strengths and abilities

Our work with 'anti-social families' uncovered the rich resourcefulness parents held. Most commonly this resourcefulness related to thick folders of correspondence that the parents had sent to try to secure relevant educational support for their children through appeals to education authorities, social services and local politicians. Two mothers had also tried to set up local Attention Deficit Hyperactivity Disorder (ADHD) support groups only to be thwarted by their lack of professional training, or health and safety considerations. Even the youngest children interviewed (9 and 10 years old) offered concrete solutions to the problems on their estates, such as developing youth facilities in which they could occupy themselves and expend energies. The fact that the families were generally not successful in their attempts to effect change for their children further reinforced their sense of powerlessness and exclusion. This resourcefulness should be acknowledged and supported through effective dialogue and concrete action on the part of community safety practitioners and, as we have noted earlier, through opportunities to gain respect and assume and demonstrate responsibilities. This would also serve to work towards meeting Pollack's fifth point above.

The process of service development is as crucial as the outcomes

The biggest complaint from families was that the ABC was presented to them very much as a fait accompli. They had generally received no warning, and most of the terms of the contract had been drafted by the community safety team prior to the first meeting. The second most common complaint related to the mismatch between managerialist outputs, that is, contracts were deemed to have been concluded successfully by the community safety team when, in fact, children had simply learned to control (or conceal) 'problem' behaviour until they returned to the privacy of the family home, thereby placing their families at greater risk. Alternatively, some children had been placed under long periods of virtual house arrest simply to keep them off the streets. The qualitative outcomes parents had expected were usually not delivered, and the contracts had generally been regarded by them as unsuccessful. This problem was rooted in the failure of other members of the Community Safety Partnership to engage. Terms of contracts must be negotiated mutually with all parties outlining their obligations and aspirations for a successful outcome with these terms being reviewed by all involved throughout the period of contract imposition.

Interventions must address a current need identified by participants themselves

The children and their families complied with the terms of contracts because of the threat of eviction, which added considerable stress to their already strained circumstances. It is incongruous to require individuals to meet the terms of contracts without offering sustainable means of achieving this. As suggested above, the children and their families need to be listened to and their expressed needs addressed. Other partner agencies, such as education, health and social services, must, therefore, be more involved in the drafting of contracts and the formulation of action plans. Children and their families should be encouraged to feel that they are full partners in relationships of mutuality and respect. This would also serve to work towards meeting point (5) above.

Social justice themes must be integrated throughout the service/programme

If the simple suggestions above are followed, perpetrators and their families will derive a sense of justice and inclusion, rather than the abject sense of injustice and objectification that permeated their accounts. The families felt they were being punished for situations beyond their control, and for which they had been fighting for support for some years. Community safety practitioners need to acknowledge the situated context for both behaviour and understandings of that behaviour, and this necessarily involves practitioners adopting a much more critical approach to their work akin to social work critical practice: 'a refusal of/an opposition to the interlocking relations of power that pervade ... encounters with clients' (Heron, 2005, p 341). In recognising the need to look at social, not criminal justice, solutions to the clients with whom they work, community safety practitioners can identify the part they could play in resisting prevailing discourses of exclusion associated with anti-social behaviour.

Community links must be facilitated

This was a key recommendation forthcoming from the families with whom we worked. They could not understand why mediation with neighbours had not been attempted before the contracts were imposed. Once contracts are concluded families have to continue living alongside neighbours who initially reported them but, without mediation to foster their reintegration into the community, they will remain excluded from the social and cultural resources of the neighbourhood. By virtue of their key position as lead agents in the Community Safety Partnership, creative forms of restorative justice that meet the needs of all parties should be developed. The contrast between anti-social behaviour *enforcement* action and interventions informed by mediation practice and the principles of restorative justice could not be more clear cut. Community safety discourses often make direct reference to the restorative principles implied by the ideas of 'naming and shaming', especially so in some more politically inflected contributions of the debate. More pragmatically, however, other commentators refer to 'naming and shaming' simply in terms of giving effect to the enforcement action – neighbours need to know who is being so targeted in order to 'police' the behaviour of those subject to court orders (Stone, 2003). This seems a far cry from Braithwaite's (1989) original formulation of the notion of shaming and reintegration. There seems a world of difference between shaming to reintegrate and shaming in order to more effectively exclude.

In formulating support programmes along these rather simple lines, the obligations of the 2004 Children Act and the related aspirations of *Every Child Matters* can begin to be addressed, especially 'listening to children, young people and their families when assessing and planning service provision, as well as in face-to-face delivery' (DfES, 2004, p 4).

If deficiencies are apparent in strategic planning for trust and respect (Williams, 2004, p 410), even within this purportedly 'radical' child-focused programme (DfES, 2004), how much more does this criticism apply to anti-social behaviour enforcement? Earlier work has argued that young people have, for so long and in an increasing number of ways, become 'the Achilles heel of community safety planning' (Measor and Squires, 2000, p 257). But, by contrast, in this chapter we have sought to argue that anti-oppressive working with families and young people can begin to foster the foundations for mutual relations of respect for young people and their families. Furthermore, working in this way might help to cultivate opportunities for young people and families to be listened to and appropriate support, based on their expressed needs, set in place to enable the terms of ABCs and ASBOs to be more realistically met. The benefits of individual practitioners' interventions in mediating between youth justice system clients and policy within a multi-agency partnership, underpinned by a welfare ethos, have been demonstrated with authors concluding 'that these new collaborative arrangements have begun to realize positive changes' (Burnett and Appleton, 2004, p 51). If an ethos of genuine anti-oppressive partnership working can be realised as suggested above, this respectful 'exchange' has been shown to provide 'the social principle which animates the character of someone who gives back to a community' (Sennett, 2004, p 64). With such relationships in place it might then be possible to speak of sustainable community safety for all citizens and citizenship values and an ethic of citizenship that is open, achievable and enjoyable by everyone. This suggests a new take on a familiar political slogan: not so much 'tough on crime and tough on the causes of crime' as 'committed to citizenship values and committed to ensuring the contexts and conditions for the equal enjoyment of citizenship values', perhaps.

References

Braithwaite, J. (1989) *Crime, Shame and Reintegration*, Cambridge: Cambridge University Press.

Braye, S. and Preston-Shoot, M. (1995) *Empowering Practice in Health and Social Care*, Buckingham: Open University Press.

Burnett, R. and Appleton, C. (2004) 'Joined-up services to reduce youth crime', *British Journal of Criminology*, vol 44, no 1, pp 34-54.

Clarke, J. (2005) 'New Labour's citizens: activated, empowered, responsibilized, abandoned', *Critical Social Policy*, vol 25, no 4, pp 447-63.

DfES (Department for Education and Skills) (2004) *Every Child Matters: Change for Children*, DfES/1081/2004, Nottingham: DfES Publications.

Dominelli, L. (2002) 'Anti-oppressive practice in context', in R. Adams, L. Dominelli and M. Payne (eds) *Social Work: Themes, Issues and Critical Debates* (2nd edn), London: Macmillan, pp 3-29.

Garland, D. (2001) *The Culture of Control*, Oxford: Oxford University Press.

Gillies, V. (2005) 'Meeting parents needs? Discourses of "support" and "inclusion" in family policy', *Critical Social Policy*, vol 25, no 1, pp 70-90.

Heron, B. (2005) 'Self-reflection in critical social work practice: subjectivity and the possibilities of resistance', *Reflective Practice*, vol 6, no 3, pp 341-51.

Home Office (2003) *Respect and Responsibility: Taking a Stand Against Anti-social Behaviour*, London: Home Office.

Home Office (2004a) *Together: Tackling Anti-social Behaviour: One Year On*, London: Home Office.

Home Office (2004b) *Confident Communities in a Secure Britain: The Home Office Strategic Plan 2004–2008*, Cm 6287, London: The Stationery Office.

Home Office (2006) *Respect Action Plan*, London: Home Office Respect Taskforce.

Jamieson, J. (2005) 'New Labour, youth justice, and the question of "Respect"', *Youth Justice*, vol 5, no 3, pp 180-93.

Lacey, H. and Zedner, L. (1995) 'Discourses of community in criminal justice', *Journal of Law and Society*, vol 23, no 3, pp 301-25.

Levitas, R. (1996) 'The concept of social exclusion and the new Durkheimian hegemony', *Critical Social Policy*, vol 16, no 46, pp 5-20.

Measor, L. and Squires, P. (2000) *Young People and Community Safety: Inclusion, Risk, Tolerance and Disorder*, Aldershot: Ashgate.

Millie, A., Jacobson, J., McDonald, E. and Hough, M. (2005) *Anti-social Behaviour Strategies: Finding a Balance*, Bristol: The Policy Press.

Pinkney, S. (2000) 'Anti-oppressive theory and practice in social work', in C. Davies, L. Finlay and A. Bullman (eds) *Changing Practice in Health and Social Care*, London: Sage Publications.

Pollack, S. (2004) 'Anti-oppressive social work practice with women in prison: discursive reconstructions and alternative practices', *British Journal of Social Work*, vol 34, no 5, pp 693-707.

Reidpath, D. D., Chan, K.Y., Gifford, S. M. and Allotey, P. (2005) '"He hath the French pox": stigma, social value and social exclusion', *Sociology of Health and Illness*, vol 27, no 4, pp 468-89.

Sennett, R. (2004) *Respect: The Formation of Character in an Age of Inequality*, London: Penguin.

SEU (Social Exclusion Unit) (1998) *Bringing Britain Together: A National Strategy for Neighbourhood Renewal*, London: HMSO.

SEU (2000) *Policy Action Team Report 8: Anti-social Behaviour*, London: ODPM.

Smith, R. (2003) *Youth Justice: Ideas, Policy, Practice*, Cullompton: Willan Publishing.

Squires, P. (2006a) 'New Labour and the politics of anti-social behaviour', *Critical Social Policy*, vol 26, no 1, pp 144-68.

Squires, P. (ed) (2006b) *Community Safety: Critical Perspectives on Policy and Practice*, Bristol: The Policy Press.

Squires, P. and Measor, L. (2005) 'Below decks on the youth justice flagship: evaluating youth justice', in D. Taylor and S. Balloch (eds) *The Politics of Evaluation*, Bristol: The Policy Press, pp 21-40.

Squires, P. and Stephen, D. E. (2005a) *Rougher Justice: Young People and Anti-social Behaviour*, Cullompton: Willan Publishing.

Squires, P. and Stephen, D. E. (2005b) 'Rethinking ASBOs', *Critical Social Policy*, vol 25, no 4, pp 517-28.

Stephen, D. E. (2006) 'Community safety and young people: twenty-first century *homo sacer* and the politics of injustice', in P. Squires (ed) *Community Safety: Critical Perspectives on Policy and Practice*, Bristol: The Policy Press, pp 219-36.

Stephen, D. E. and Squires, P. (2003) *Community Safety, Enforcement and Acceptable Behaviour Contracts*, Brighton: HSPRC, University of Brighton.

Stephen, D. E. and Squires, P. (2004) '"They're still children and entitled to be children": problematising the institutionalised mistrust of marginalised youth in Britain', *Journal of Youth Studies*, vol 7, no 3, pp 351-69.

Stone, N. (2003) 'Legal commentary: anti-social behaviour orders: naming juveniles', *Youth Justice*, vol 2, no 3, pp 163-9.

Tonry, M. (2004) *Punishment and Politics: Evidence and Emulation in the Making of English Crime Control Policy*, Cullompton: Willan Publishing.

Walklate, S. (2006) 'Community safety and victims: who is the victim of community safety?', in P. Squires (ed) *Community Safety: Critical Perspectives on Policy and Practice*, Bristol: The Policy Press, pp 169-80.

Williams, F. (2004) 'What matters is who works: why every child matters to New Labour: commentary on the DfES Green Paper *Every Child Matters*', *Critical Social Policy*, vol 24, no 3, pp 406-27.

Wilson, A. and Beresford, P. (2000) '"Anti-oppressive practice": emancipation or appropriation?', *British Journal of Social Work*, vol 30, no 5, pp 553-73.

YJB (Youth Justice Board) (2006) *Individual Support Orders Procedure: A Protocol to be Used and Adapted by YOTs when Managing ISOs*, London: YJB.

EIGHT

Survivors of domestic violence, community and care

Paula Wilcox

Introduction

Domestic violence involves a pattern of coercive behaviours ranging from verbal abuse/threats, coercion, manipulation, and physical and sexual violence, to rape and homicide. On an individual level, therefore, experiencing domestic violence entails immense interpersonal struggles invoking honour, pride and shame. Such individual struggles are, however, set in a context of abstract (but very real) social structures and long-term social processes that construct gendered lives such that men in general are dominant over women. Wider community knowledge[1] supports the research evidence, which consistently finds that the majority of domestic violence in heterosexual relationships is perpetrated by men against women (for recent figures see, for example, Walby and Allen, 2004; Home Office, 2005). When I refer to domestic violence in this chapter, therefore, I refer to male violence against female intimate partners and ex-partners.[2]

In the mid-1990s my doctoral research programme involved qualitative action research with a local area-based domestic violence forum in a northern city. An important outcome of this research was a community-based project to provide support and services for women (Wilcox, 1996, 2000a, 2006a). Today, the city has four community-based domestic abuse projects (including the project I worked with), which provide essential support to women and children experiencing or recovering from domestic abuse. These community-based projects have not been without their problems but recent analysis of the benefits to statutory services of their provision in the voluntary sector has included reduced costs to health services, reduced risk of harm to children and an increase in the number of successful prosecutions. There are some other examples of organisations working along similar lines (see Hague et al, 2003; Hague, 2005) but when we look at the national picture this situation is not replicated.

Indeed, domestic violence is rarely addressed at the level of the local community although we know that it impacts on all communities, irrespective of 'race', gender, class, religion or cultural make-up. Moreover, gender-based violence is now recognised as a global phenomenon (WHO, 2002). And while there have been some positive shifts in awareness and attitudes among the professions that deal with domestic violence (although still more needs to be done) the turn to community is notably absent where domestic violence is concerned, as Walklate (2002) points out. I am interested in looking at why this should be the case and why it is that, despite the growth of user movements since the early 1990s, domestic violence survivors are rarely seen as a user or community group.

Elsewhere (Wilcox, 2006b) I have argued that the lack of attention to domestic violence in community contexts is likely to relate partly to (mis)understandings of domestic violence and partly to a focus on agency/state responses. Gendered discourses, through which women construct their social identities as caring, and which assume women's continuing availability as carers, may also underpin the relative neglect of informal and community support for women experiencing domestic violence.

At the same time research on formal agency service provision for survivors of domestic violence has revealed its extreme variability and inconsistency (Humphreys et al, 2000). Access to services is a lottery for those involved, provision is geographically patchy and varies greatly in quality in individual organisations (Humphreys et al, 2000). Many organisations have contact with domestic violence, but few record it systematically, have explicit policies or know which other agencies are involved (Kelly, 1996; Stark and Flitcraft, 1996; BMA, 1998; Crisp and Stanko, 2000). This too may be partly due to a continuing failure on the part of agencies to acknowledge and record domestic violence survivors as a user group.[3]

This chapter draws on empirical research carried out in 2005 and 2006 with survivors in the south of England, extending earlier discussion on communities and their responsiveness to domestic violence survivors (Wilcox, 2006b). In order to do this the chapter will look at how dominant definitions of domestic violence have tended to exclude community considerations. It will examine state-sponsored policies and their influences on work against domestic violence. From this point the chapter will address the need to approach work in the community with a gendered and raced lens, moving on to explore domestic violence survivors' different motivations for involvement in community groups, in contrast to dominant ideas about responsible citizenship used in public discourse. Lastly, the chapter will look at the links between traditionally gendered discourses of caring and their impact on the hidden nature of domestic violence survivors. The chapter concludes by arguing that there is a duty of care to address the support of domestic violence survivors in communities.

Dominant definitions of domestic violence

One aspect of explaining the scarcity of community-based work against domestic violence is the way it has been defined. Dominant definitions have tended to focus on the intimate, heterosexual couple, hiding the way in which involvement in, and impacts of, such violence ripple outwards affecting children, other members of the family, members of friendship groups and members of the wider community, such as neighbours. Moreover, the urgent need to act on extreme incidents of physical violence (which threaten women and children's physical safety) has led to the widespread perception of domestic violence as discrete *incidents* rather than as an ongoing process. This dominant understanding has hidden the effects of domestic violence over time, the cumulative impact on women and children of, what may seem from the outside, 'minor' infringements of their emotional and physical integrity.

At the same time, the dominant understanding of domestic violence as extreme incidents of mainly physical violence has led to a prioritisation of work with formal social agencies. Designed to act on exceptional incidents, social agencies can work intensively with individuals in crisis[4] but only for relatively limited periods of time (Kelly, 1999). Accepting that domestic violence is a process over time with seemingly 'lower-level' ongoing infringements problematises an over-reliance on agency response. Moreover, agencies such as the criminal justice system 'do not always effectively address the individual needs of women' (Kelly, 1999, p 120).

The women's refuge movement has, by and large, not adopted dominant definitions, taking the latter view that domestic violence is a process over time, which involves emotional, sexual and financial abuses as well as physical violence, where 'low-key' behaviours can be very threatening within the overall pattern of behaviour:

> Domestic violence is not a 'one-off event' or incident but part of an on-going pattern of controlling behaviour. Often very subtle signals can be extremely threatening: violence does not have to be overt to achieve its ends. (Harwin and Barron, 2000, p 206)

There are practical reasons why the refuge movement has rarely been able to become involved with community-based work. The refuge movement has always prioritised the provision of shelter and services to safeguard women's and children's safety. The funding of refuges has been, and remains, insecure and pitifully small, placing severe restrictions on what can be achieved beyond this core essential mission. Indeed, funding has been so insecure and limited that even the core provision of safety is often under threat. Preventive work with the wider community and work around raising survivors' voices has, therefore, of necessity been strictly limited.

The funding of research on domestic violence is also limited and there has been an understandable tendency here too to focus on researching formal agency support rather than community-based work. The funding of services to domestic violence survivors as well as research on domestic violence is very much affected by wider public discourse on domestic violence and hence state-sponsored policies.

State-sponsored policies

The focus and direction of state-sponsored policies and research have been influential in shaping the lack of community-based work against domestic violence. The first important point of note is that once domestic violence was finally recognised as a serious social problem it was largely conceptualised as a discrete and specialised topic. Hence, in recent years there has been *Safety and Justice: The Government's Proposals on Domestic Violence* (Home Office, 2003); an inter-ministerial group on domestic violence, based in the Office of the Deputy Prime Minister, concerned with housing-related support; the introduction of the Supporting People Programme (ODPM, 2005); the Home Office initiative (2000-03) to fund a range of projects focusing on violence against women (Crime Reduction Programme 2000-03); Crime and Disorder Reduction Partnerships being encouraged to identify domestic violence as a priority for action; and, most recently, the 2004 Domestic Violence, Crime and Victims Act.

This flurry of policy development is clearly welcome and has raised the level of public discourse around, and awareness of, domestic violence. The establishment of domestic violence as a *discrete* social problem has been essential in putting it on the public agenda. However, the problem now is about making the links between domestic violence and the constellation of social dimensions it impacts on for women (and children): their safety, health, pregnancy, employment, poverty, housing, education, lone parenthood, general well-being and so forth.

Not infrequently researchers in areas that are key for understanding domestic violence have completely neglected it. Research and literature on employment, poverty, lone parenthood and community work, for example, rarely if at all take account of domestic violence, thus revealing a significant lack of joined-up thinking!

This has been the case in recent UK policy developments, 'which have revived concepts of community and citizenship within the context of care' (Balloch, Chapter Two, this volume). The National Strategy Action Plan *A New Commitment to Neighbourhood Renewal*, published by the Social Exclusion Unit (SEU) in 2001, which focuses on impoverished areas, for example, makes no mention at all of domestic violence, yet all the research that is available points to complex linkages of domestic violence with women's impoverishment and poor work prospects (see, for example Kirkwood, 1993; Tolman and Raphael, 2000; Wilcox, 2000b, 2006a; Humphreys and Thiara, 2002; Lyon, 2002; Meisel et al, 2003). In the US there has been more attention to the adverse impacts of domestic violence on women's employment (see Shepard and Pence, 1988; Murphy, 1993; Lloyd, 1997) whereas in the UK research on women's employment tends to overlook domestic violence as a factor; Kingsmill's review *Women's Employment and Pay* (2003) is a recent example. This factor has contributed to the continuing hidden nature of domestic violence survivors as a group.

The White Paper *Modernising Social Services* (DH, 1998) also fails to identify domestic violence survivors as a group; although there is a mention in this document of such violence being an aspect of *child protection*:

> [M]ost families who become caught up in the child protection system are at high risk of social exclusion. The SSI report, *Child Protection: Messages From Research*, shows that many have multiple problems – poverty, family breakdown, mental health problems, **domestic violence**, alcohol and drug misuse – which need careful assessment and targeted intervention by local authorities to ensure that children are not put at risk. (DH, 1998, ch 3, para 3.9; author's emphasis)

These (and other) areas of state-sponsored work have had the potential to bring about a stronger emphasis on community-based action against domestic violence but thus far have had a rather limited impact: for example, community safety policies and neighbourhood renewal.

Community safety policies and practice might have represented an alternative *additional*[5] community-based approach towards tackling domestic violence but also largely failed in this respect. First of all the programme represented only a tiny proportion of the criminal justice system as a whole (in 1993/94 community safety activities formed just over 1% of the annual criminal justice budget; Crawford, 1998, p 63) and second, within this tiny budget social issues, such as domestic violence, had an extremely low profile as compared with property crimes or crimes in public places.

One reason for this low profile was the reliance of community safety approaches on rational choice theory, which ignores differently gendered identities and practices. A gender-neutral approach tends to perpetuate the status quo in terms of structural inequalities. The theory and practice of community safety continued to orient attention towards 'crime on the streets' – 'the community in public' – and away from 'crime behind closed doors' (Walklate, 2002). However, a very small number of domestic violence projects were funded via the community safety approach; for example the community-based project the author was involved in received funding for two years from the police Community Initiative Programme (1994-95).

Neighbourhood renewal is another area of community-based work that holds out the promise of community-based work against domestic violence. The Neighbourhood Renewal Unit website is unusual for highlighting gender as a key issue and having six neighbourhood renewal advisors specialising in gender issues: 'Gender refers to both men and women and it is important to understand the differing forms of disadvantage experienced by both sexes in the context of deprivation' (NRU, 2005). Moreover, their website refers to the fact that '81% of victims of domestic violence are women', and takes a potentially integrated approach pointing out that:

> All the neighbourhood renewal priorities and services
> – employment, education, crime, housing, health and
> liveability (which means making public spaces greener, safer
> and cleaner) – have different impacts on men and women.
> (NRU, 2005)

There is at least one example of a Domestic Violence Project in Walsall's New Deal for Communities. This has a Crisis Intervention Service, which provides ongoing support to victims following referral by the police; training programmes for professional workers; 'Learning in Schools' to raise awareness in young people about bullying, domestic violence and the right to feel safe; and 'Stopping Aggression in the Family Environment (SAFE)', which offers support for people who want to stop being abusive to their partners, and two 24-hour helplines staffed by volunteers, one of which offers a multilingual service in Punjabi, Urdu, Hindi, Bengali and Gujarati (Walsall Council, 2006). How well this project has worked in practice is difficult to say without further research but, by and large, neighbourhood renewal has not resulted in significant gains in terms of work against domestic violence in the community or the involvement of survivors in terms of practice or policy development.

Domestic violence may now be more firmly on the policy agenda but it is rare for survivors of domestic violence to be consulted or involved in developing policies and/or evaluating the services that are so vital to their survival.

> [A]bused women survivors have rarely self-organised to participate in service and policy development. They have never been thought of as a service user group in their own right or viewed as part of the service user movement in general. (Hague, 2005, p 194)

Continued exclusion from this role contributes to the continuing dominant perception of domestic violence as a privatised and stigmatised issue. And while it is true that there are many survivors working in paid and unpaid roles, in the domestic violence and other allied fields, their own experiences and identities as survivors are usually hidden; at the same time, we do not yet fully understand survivors' reasons as to whether and why they may, or may not, wish to participate, how participation might happen and what kinds of support they might need. So we have a situation where, unlike many other service users, domestic violence survivors remain largely unheard and unseen.

Clearly, state-sponsored policies, while important in terms of the symbolic message they give that domestic violence is a crime and no longer behaviour that women (or anyone) should have to endure, have been less effective in terms of being translated into action and practice at the community level. The author now turns to look at the notion of 'community' and some of the reasons why communities may be less responsive to domestic violence survivors than might be expected.

Community, gender and domestic violence

One fundamental problem with 'community' is its multiple meanings (recognised by Hillery as early as 1955)[6] and hence the deep ambiguity around this concept. The normative subtext of 'community' is that it is a good thing (as in Etzioni's [1995] communitarianism), it has a warmth and relative closeness to us all as compared with the state, and as Raymond Williams pointed out, this assumed 'good' can seemingly be applied to any set of relationships (1976, p 76).

However, other analyses of 'community' have pointed up the negative side of 'community' inasmuch as it can be a narrow, inward-looking phenomenon in which stereotyping and prejudice lurk large. Moreover, 'community' can be used to refer to a geographical location and/or a community of interest, for example the 'gay community', 'minority ethnic community' and so forth. However, such categorisations can themselves be harmful when they impose a singular identity on, for example, minority ethnic communities (Patel, 2000, p 168). Implicit, for example, in a localised approach is the extent to which this implies a mixture of people/s and, in the case of domestic violence in heterosexual relationships, men and women.

As has been pointed out by Barnes and others (see, for example, Barnes, 1997; Barnes and Bowl, 2001), the collective action of users of social care services has deeply influenced community care discourse; a good example of this would be the disability rights movement. In the case of domestic violence this has not been the case. For domestic violence survivors, family and the local community are likely to be the very context women are *forcibly restricted to* by their violent male partner, excluding them from wider roles in the public sphere (Wilcox, 2000b, 2006a). And in relation to social care services in the community, women experiencing domestic violence largely see these as represented by social services ('the social').

This study found that survivors' fear about the role of social service workers in relation to domestic violence continues to be strong and the vast majority of comments survivors made about social services were negative. Fear of losing children was paramount in their minds and two of the research participants had indeed had their children taken into care.

> Interviewer: 'What about social services? Have any of you had any experiences?'
>
> Interviewee:
> 'I don't even want to go into them.'
>
> 'I have had terrible, terrible experiences with social services, from London and Brighton.'
>
> 'I hate them.'
>
> 'I'm sorry, social services. All that … they really piss me off. I don't even want to go there with my experience with them because I feel like going down and blowing them up.'

'I have always had this big thing of being very scared of social services. I wouldn't want to go near them.'

Male perpetrators of domestic violence often threaten their female partners that 'the social' will take their children away, thus increasing women's intense fears about this aspect of social work (McWilliams and McKiernan, 1993; McGee, 2000). As Warner and Pantling (2002, p 123) reveal, minoritised communities are at even greater risk from outside agency intervention as there are higher rates of black and minority children than majority ethnic children taken into care. Using a gendered and raced lens in the context of domestic violence demonstrates that the notions and practices of community and community care are not only different for women as compared to men but that they also differ between majority ethnic and minority ethnic women.

As has been argued elsewhere, we need to critically interpret romanticised notions of 'community'. The idea that they may be more open, democratic and less subject to inequitable power relations (for example, of dominant masculinity) is simply misleading. As Kelly (1996, p 71; author's emphasis) argues, 'the stress on similarity in definitions of community means that variable experiences of social life that accrue by virtue of gender, class, race, age and sexuality *cannot be acknowledged*, let alone studied'.

Given the potentially ambiguous nature of support for survivors is it possible that they would wish to become involved in any way in groups in the community? It is important to point out that such groups in this research were groups based around a community of interest rather than area-based groups.

Survivors' motivations for involvement in community groups

Marian Barnes (Chapter Four) has contrasted the way in which responsible citizenship is conceptualised within public discourse around community cohesion/social inclusion with the way in which people speak about their motivations for involvement in groups. She argues that '... "care" is usually absent from official discourses of citizenship, participation and civil renewal ... and, indeed, has also become devalued in the context of those policy areas with which it has been more strongly associated – community or social care' (p 59). People speaking about their motivations and commitments within community and user groups reveal very different perspectives on commitment and responsibility.

This was also the case in the present study carried out in Brighton and Hove with survivors who were involved in different ways with specialist outreach domestic violence services. In many cases, as below, a woman's commitment developed as a result of 'negative personal experiences, which resulted in a desire to improve things for others' (Barnes, Chapter Four, p 68).

> Interviewer: 'Do you think if you went to a domestic violence forum meeting … whether you would feel it would be of benefit to you?'
>
> Interviewee: 'It might not be of benefit to us but it might of benefit to women in the future.'

Another aspect of commitment was more personally motivated since hearing another woman's narrative about her similar experiences was usually found to be supportive to other women. This motivates commitment because not only is it about hearing what others have to say, it is also an encouragement to others to break the stigma that inhibits many women from talking about their experiences of domestic violence. These motivations are especially important in more informal drop-in groups:

> Interviewee: 'I think it is because then you can hear other women's views as well because sometimes you think it is just you and you think, my god, I'm going mad and it's just me … so it's like, to hear it from other women as well.'
>
> Interviewer: 'What encouraged you to come along?
>
> Interviewee: 'I don't know because I've never been to one before or anything I just thought it would be nice to give my views on stuff so, give my ideas and stuff … I suppose sometimes it's hard to talk about it as well and I suppose I thought as well sometimes it helps you to talk about it and also to, like you, hear what other people say as well.'

For domestic violence survivors to engage in such groups (drop-ins, local forums, city-wide forums) it is essential to think extremely carefully about the safety of group members, the nature of the group, how many people will attend, what security measures are in place and what support will be needed:

> 'One, because I used to enjoy the forum meetings that was at [name of location] the drop-in place. And two, because

I just admire you lot and what you do and all that and I thought a meeting would be interesting and see what other women have to say. It was a bit nerve-racking because I haven't been to one of these meetings for ages and I hadn't had the form with me and I thought, oh my god, what am I going to say. You know, like, if there is a huge lot of people there, I'm not going to speak.'

'Just let people know that it's safe and ... like a relaxed atmosphere. We ought to have maybe some of the workers from [name of organisation]. If someone just said something back to you and really upset you and you wanted to run out and burst into tears, you can. Knowing that you know someone else there probably makes you feel a bit better.'

In public policy discourse on civil renewal the concepts drawn on are 'order, civility, duty and obligation'; care, support and friendship are ignored in this context, and there is 'no specific indication of the importance of attentiveness to others, nor recognition of the vulnerabilities that mean that most people at some time in their lives require help from others in relationships of unequal power' (Barnes, Chapter Four, p 64). Attentiveness to others is a key facet of an ethics of care approach and this is often found in domestic violence survivor groups, as the quote below demonstrates:

'I cried so many times in that drop-in – they must think I am a right prat but ... I know they don't think like that because they've pulled me up and said [name] you're not a prat or anything like that, you're allowed to cry and I know you're not laughing it's just I feel silly crying in front of a lot of other women, and they said, that's what we're here for.'

This powerful level of attentiveness is all the more remarkable when it is considered that the survivors in this group are themselves going through a complex and lengthy process in trying to survive.

Domestic violence survivors: care givers in need of care

Dichotomous thinking forms the basis of traditionally gendered discourse on caring. This discourse has been, and continues to be, relevant in the construction of responses to domestic violence. First, relations that exist outside the market, such as caring, are less visible in western societies as the hegemony of neoliberal discourse gives primacy to economic relations. In an era of 'globalising democracies and diminishing welfare states', relations of caring are also becoming more fragile (McDaniel, 2002). Moreover, gendered discourses that construct caring as women's work, and through which women construct their social identities as caring, tend to assume women's continuing availability as carers (Twigg, 1990; Ungerson, 1990). The responsibility for caring and support, whether as labour, as part of a normative framework of obligations and responsibilities or as an activity that carries financial and emotional costs (Daly and Lewis, 2000, cited in Williams, 2001) remains primarily with women[7] and especially minoritised women. One of the effects of these traditional discourses on caring is that adult, non-disabled women are far less likely to be seen as deserving targets of care and support.

Women survivors of domestic violence, therefore, find themselves in a contradictory social location. As women they are expected to individually manage the care of their family, while the impact of living with domestic violence means that they need care and support for themselves (as well as for their children). This is an almost impossible tightrope that women experiencing domestic violence have to walk, since to admit to the latter (the need for care) may be seen as jeopardising their ability to carry out the former (giving care to their children), perhaps especially in the eyes of professional workers. Indeed, the extent to which domestic violence undermines women's ability to care for their children is hotly contested in the literature. In practice, stigma continues to be attached to adult heterosexual women who are experiencing/have experienced domestic violence as they are seen by others, as well as themselves, to have failed to manage their relationship. Professionals may well also see them as ultimately failing to protect their children.

My own research in the 1990s and 2005-06 supports the view that women's efforts to resist abuse and to protect their children are often underestimated (Radford and Hester, 2001). Survivors experiencing domestic violence and severe material deprivation nevertheless maintained agent stances, actively pursuing safety for themselves and their children (Wilcox, 2006a). This does not mean, however, that survivors are not in need of care and support for themselves during and after leaving the violent husband/partner.

There were many instances where the external structural context, as well as individual responses to women from potential informal and formal supporters, was less than helpful in the process of gaining safety;

indeed, 'the breakdown of resettlement is often linked to the absence of support' (Kelly and Humphreys, 2001, p 270). Unhelpful responses tended to deny or minimise the violence and to blame the woman for staying in the relationship and the losses endured after ending the relationship. Here, the characterisation of such women as survivors, while positive in many ways, is also partially problematic in that it tends to hide the likelihood of damage and women's ongoing need for care and support.

The feminist literature at times also deals in dichotomies; for instance, distinguishing between caring for dependent persons who are not able to care for themselves and caring for those who can manage well on their own (Leira and Saraceno, 2002, p 62). While this conceptualisation distinguishes between women caring for non-disabled husbands, who could well look after themselves, as opposed to caring for children, it also polarises those who are dependent from those who are seemingly independent, failing to recognise the levels of interdependence that exist for all human beings: we will all have periods of dependency from time to time. Following the logic of this conceptualisation, dependence for the adult woman is likely to be seen as negative and demeaning and this raises problems in thinking through supporting women who are survivors of domestic violence. Hague et al (2003), for example, argue that abused women should not be seen as dependent, saying that 'abused women continue to be viewed as dependent, just as they were probably treated during the abuse' (2003, p 16).

An approach that reflects a concept of interdependence would argue that, while survivors should not be characterised as solely dependent, nor should they be characterised as entirely independent (since this would imply a lack of harm from experiencing domestic violence). Williams (2001, p 481) has discussed this issue in relation to disability, arguing that the task is to redefine the concept of independence 'to fit with a notion of interdependence'. It seems clear that women who survive male violence are in need of a range of forms of support, help and care that are largely lacking at present. Moreover, as I have argued, varying degrees of need for care and support *will* exist over varying lengths of time for different women. This is neither something women should be ashamed of nor something to be viewed unfavourably by professionals. At times of transition, trying to stop the violence from occurring, or having to end a violent relationship, when the need for care and support is considerably heightened, women often have severely depleted support networks. Seeking care and support in these circumstances should therefore be viewed as a strong and positive step by all those involved.

Conclusion

The chapter began by noting the relative lack of community-based work against domestic violence in the UK partly due to dominant definitions of domestic violence diverting attention from the impacts of domestic violence in the community more widely due to their focus on heterosexual couples. A focus on domestic violence as comprising discrete incidents rather than being an ongoing process has encouraged a concentration on formal agency support, hiding the extent to which informal support may be helpful, as well as the intersection between formal and informal support (Wilcox, 2006a). A review of state-sponsored policies suggests that while these are of symbolic importance in condemning domestic violence, and have raised public awareness of this serious social problem, they have had limited impact in fostering projects and activism to decrease the incidence of domestic violence at the level of the community.

Academic and policy research in the UK on social factors of critical importance to survivors of domestic violence, such as employment, poverty, lone parenthood and community work rarely, if ever, examines the impact of domestic violence in these fields. Similarly, work on social exclusion, a key target of New Labour policy, has tended to ignore or sideline domestic violence. So while the fact that domestic violence is now on the public agenda is to be welcomed, the current focus and direction of state-sponsored policies and research are contributing towards the continuing invisibility of domestic violence survivors as a group and the concomitant scarcity of community-based work against domestic violence.

As previously mentioned, domestic violence continues to be stigmatised and survivors are seen by others (as well as themselves) as having failed to manage their relationship and ultimately as having failed to protect their children. Women survivors of domestic violence are therefore in the contradictory situation of being simultaneously care givers (to their children/family) and not infrequently being blamed for allowing the situation to continue, while being in need of care themselves. Our task here must be to work against dichotomous thinking that perceives individuals as either independent (not needing care) or dependent (needing care) and rather see how we can develop notions of 'interdependence' (Williams, 2001). This is particularly vital work for domestic violence survivors who are mothers.

Despite currently disempowering contexts – it seems clear that women who survive male violence need a range of forms of support, help and care that are largely lacking at present – there are survivors of domestic violence who are able to give each other mutual support. The absence and indeed devaluation of 'care' in official discourses of citizenship, participation and civil renewal contrast sharply with the ways in which such survivors of domestic violence talk about their motivation and involvement in groups and drop-ins arising out of negative personal experiences but also a desire to support others with similar experiences.

This research has revealed that there are survivors who want to have their voices heard and who are willing to be involved in different ways, such as through drop-in facilities, through support or self-help groups, provided such forms of participation are thought through with the utmost care to address their needs for safety.

Notes

[1] This data was gained by observations and informal conversations in a range of community settings over the last 10 years.

[2] This is not to deny that some heterosexual men experience domestic violence from their female partners nor to detract from research and work on domestic violence in same-sex relationships.

[3] Hopefully, this situation will change for the better with the gender equality duty for public bodies coming into force in April 2007, since organisations now have to show 'fair treatment' of women and men in policy and service delivery as well as employment (EOC, 2006).

[4] Crisis theory postulates that in an emergency routine coping strategies break down. The crisis is a time of great risk but also provides the possibility of change since people are more open to, and in need of, help from outside (Kelly, 1999).

[5] I say 'additional' as this chapter does not aim to undermine in any way the vital services provided by formal agencies, such as the police.

[6] George Hillery analysed 94 sociological definitions of the term 'community' and identified 16 different definitional concepts within this sample (1955, pp 111, 115).

[7] Time use studies in Britain reveal that distributions of domestic work remain largely traditionally gendered. For example, women spend two hours 18 minutes a day as compared to men's 45 minutes a day on cooking and routine housework; and on caring for and playing with their children, women spend

36 minutes a day as compared to men's 13 minutes a day (ONS, 1999, Table 6.1, Time use by gender).

References

Barnes, M. (1997) *Care, Communities and Citizens*, Harlow: Addison Wesley Longman.

Barnes, M. and Bowl, R. (2001) *Taking Over the Asylum: Empowerment and Mental Health*, Basingstoke: Palgrave.

BMA (British Medical Association) (1998) *Domestic Violence: A Health Care Issue?*, London: Chameleon Press.

Crawford, A. (1998) *Crime Prevention and Community Safety: Politics, Policies and Practices*, London and New York: Longman.

Crisp, D. and Stanko, E. (2001) 'Monitoring costs and evaluating needs', in J. Taylor-Browne (ed) *What Works in Reducing Domestic Violence? A Comprehensive Guide for Professionals*, London: Whiting and Birch, pp 335-58.

DH (Department of Health) (1998) *Modernising Social Services*, London: The Stationery Office, www.archive.official-documents.co.uk/ document/cm41/4169/4169.htm

Domestic Violence, Crime and Victims Act 2004, www.opsi.gov.uk/ ACTS/acts2004/20040028.htm

EOC (Equal Opportunities Commission) (2006) *The Gender Equality Duty*, Manchester: EOC, www.eoc.org.uk

Etzioni, A. (1995) *The Spirit of Community: Rights, Responsibilities and the Communitarian Agenda*, London: Fontana.

Hague, G. (2005) 'Domestic violence survivors' forums in the UK: experiments in involving abused women in domestic violence services and policy-making', *Journal of Gender Studies*, vol 14, no 3, pp 191-203.

Hague, G., Mullender, A. and Aris, R. (2003) *Is Anyone Listening? Accountability and Women Survivors of Domestic Violence*, London and New York: Routledge.

Harwin, N. and Barron, J. (2000) 'Domestic violence and social policy: perspectives from Women's Aid', in J. Hanmer and C. Itzin (eds) *Home Truths about Domestic Violence: Feminist Influences on Policy and Practice: A Reader*, London and New York: Routledge, pp 205-27.

Hillery, G. A. (1955) 'Definitions of community: areas of agreement', *Rural Sociology*, no 20, pp 111-23, cited in R. B. Hamman (undated) *Computer Networks Linking Network Communities: Effects of AOL Use upon Pre-Existing Communities*, www.socio.demon.co.uk/ cybersociety/

Home Office (2003) *Safety and Justice: The Government's Proposals on Domestic Violence*, London: Home Office.

Home Office (2005) *Domestic Violence: A National Report*, London: Home Office.

Humphreys, C. and Thiara, R. (2002) *Routes to Safety*, Bristol: WAFE.

Humphreys, C., Hester, M., Hague, G., Mullender, A., Abrahams, H. and Lowe, P. (2000) *From Good Intentions to Good Practice: Mapping Services Working with Families where there is Domestic Violence*, Bristol/York: The Policy Press/Joseph Rowntree Foundation.

Kelly, L. (1996) 'Tensions and possibilities: enhancing informal responses to domestic violence', in J. L. Edleson and Z. C. Eisikovits (eds) *Future Interventions with Battered Women and their Families*, Thousand Oaks, CA, London and New Delhi: Sage Publications.

Kelly, L. (1999) *Domestic Violence Matters: An Evaluation of a Development Project*, Home Office Research Study 193, London: HMSO.

Kelly, L. and Humphreys, C. (2001) 'Supporting women and children in their communities: outreach and advocacy approaches to domestic violence', in J. Taylor-Browne (ed) *What Works in Reducing Domestic Violence? A Comprehensive Guide for Professionals*, London: Whiting and Birch.

Kingsmill, D. (2003) *Women's Employment and Pay*, www.kingsmillreview.gov.uk

Kirkwood, C. (1993) *Leaving Abusive Partners: From the Scars of Survival to the Wisdom for Change*, London: Sage.

Leira, A. and Saraceno, C. (2002) 'Care: actors, relationships and contexts', in B. Hobson, J. Lewis and B. Siim (eds) *Contested Concepts in Gender and Social Politics*, Cheltenham: Edward Elgar, pp 55-83.

Lloyd, S. (1997) 'The effects of domestic violence on female employment', *Law and Policy*, vol 19, no 2, pp 139-67.

Lyon, E. (2002) *Welfare and Domestic Violence Against Women: Lessons from Research*, Pennsylvania, PA: National Resource Center on Domestic Violence.

McDaniel, S. A. (2002) 'Women's changing relations to the state and citizenship: caring and intergenerational relations in globalizing Western democracies', *The Canadian Review of Sociology and Anthropology*, vol 39, no 2, pp 125-51.

McGee, C. (2000) *Childhood Experiences of Domestic Violence*, London: Jessica Kingsley.

McWilliams, M. and McKiernan, J. (1993) *Bringing it Out in the Open: Domestic Violence in Northern Ireland*, Belfast: HMSO.

Meisel, J., Chandler, D. and Menees Rienzi, B. (2003) *Domestic Violence Prevalence and Effects on Employment in two California TANF Populations*, California, CA: California Institute of Mental Health.

Murphy, P. (1993) *Making the Connections: Women, Work, and Abuse*, Orlando, FL: Deutsch.

NRU (Neighbourhood Renewal Unit) (2005), www.neighbourhood. gov.uk

ODPM (Office of the Deputy Prime Minister) (2005) *Creating Sustainable Communities: Supporting Independence*, London: ODPM, www.spkweb.org.uk/

ONS (Office for National Statistics) (1999) *Omnibus Survey, May 1999* London: The Stationery Office.

Patel, P. (2000) 'Southall Black Sisters: domestic violence campaigns and alliances across the divisions of race, gender and class', in J. Hanmer and C. Itzin (eds) *Home Truths about Domestic Violence: Feminist Influences on Policy and Practice: A Reader*, London and New York: Routledge.

Radford, L. and Hester, M. (2001) 'Overcoming mother blaming? Future directions for research on mothering and domestic violence', in S. A. Graham–Bermann and J. L. Edleson (eds) *Future Directions for Research on Mothering and Domestic Violence*, Washington, DC: American Psychological Association, pp 135-55.

SEU (Social Exclusion Unit) (2001) *A New Commitment to Neighbourhood Renewal*, London: SEU.

Shepard, M. and Pence, E. (1988) 'The effect of battering on the employment status of women', *Affilia*, vol 3, no 2, pp 55-61.

Stark, E. and Flitcraft, A. (1996) *Women at Risk: Domestic Violence and Women's Health*, California, CA: Sage Publications.

Tolman, R. M. and Raphael, J. (2000) 'A review of research on welfare and domestic violence', *Journal of Social Issues*, vol 56, no 4, pp 655-82.

Twigg, J. (1990) 'Models of carers: how do social care agencies conceptualise their relationship with informal carers?', *Journal of Social Policy*, vol 18, no 1, pp 53-66.

Ungerson, C. (ed) (1990) *Gender and Caring: Work and Welfare in Britain and Scandinavia*, Hemel Hempstead: Harvester Wheatsheaf.

Walby, S. and Allen, J. (2004) *Domestic Violence, Sexual Assault and Stalking: Findings from the British Crime Survey*, Home Office Research Study 276, London: Home Office Research, Development and Statistics Directorate.

Walklate, S. (2002) 'Gendering crime prevention: exploring the tensions between policy and process', in G. Hughes, E. McLaughlin and J. Muncie (eds) *Crime Prevention and Community Safety: New Directions*, London, Thousand Oaks, CA, and New Delhi: Sage Publications, pp 58-76.

Walsall Council (2006) *Agencies Join Together in Walsall to Tackle Domestic Violence*, www.walsall.gov.uk/print/news/

Warner, S. and Pantling, K. (2002) 'Minoritisation and motherhood: women, children and domestic violence', in J. Batsleer, E. Burman, K. Chantler, H. S. McIntosh, K. Pantling, S. Smailes and S. Warner (eds) *Domestic Violence and Minoritisation: Supporting Women to Independence*, Manchester: Women's Studies Research Centre.

WHO (World Health Organization) (2002) *World Report on Violence and Health*, Geneva: WHO.

Wilcox, P. (1996) 'Social support and women leaving violent relationships', Unpublished doctoral thesis, University of Bradford.

Wilcox, P. (2000a) 'Researching in the community: power and control in a study on domestic violence in England', *Research in Community Sociology*, vol X, pp 141-64.

Wilcox, P. (2000b) '"Me mother's bank and me nanan's, you know, support": women who left domestic violence in England and issues of informal support', *Women's Studies International Forum*, vol 23, no 1, pp 1-13.

Wilcox, P. (2006a) *Surviving Domestic Violence: Gender, Poverty and Agency*, Basingstoke: Palgrave/Macmillan.

Wilcox, P. (2006b) 'Communities, care and domestic violence, *Critical Social Policy*, vol 26, no 4, pp 722-47.

Williams, F. (2001) 'In and beyond New Labour: towards a new political ethic of care', *Critical Social Policy*, vol 21, no 4, pp 467-93.

Williams, R. (1976) *Keywords*, London: Fontana.

NINE

Promoting choice and control: black and minority ethnic communities' experience of social care in Britain

Jabeer Butt

The racist murder of Stephen Lawrence and the eventual report (Macpherson, 1999) into the handling of the investigation by the Metropolitan Police is likely to be viewed by social scientists as a watershed in the way public services work with, and for, Britain's black and minority ethnic communities. Those of us involved in promoting race equality at that time are likely to testify to widespread debate as to what is to be done among both front-line practitioners and senior managers in social care (although not always between senior managers and practitioners). But beyond generating pieces of paper from 44,000 public bodies attempting to meet the requirements of the 'duty' to promote race equality by publishing a race equality plan or scheme imposed by the 2000 Race Relations Amendment Act, it is tempting to ask whether there has been any discernable change in the experience of those who need support from black and minority ethnic communities.

This chapter will consider some of the evidence on the experience of social care of black and minority ethnic people. It will suggest that there has been identifiable change in the support available to and taken up by these communities. However, the chapter will also show that this support is often patchy in its coverage and only rarely promotes choice and control for these communities. It will then consider why this situation persists, examining various aspects of both policy and practice. The chapter will conclude with a brief examination of the role of black and minority ethnic-led voluntary organisations in providing support that is particularly valued by service users, and suggests that perhaps it is the adoption of a community development approach that makes these organisations more successful than others.

Background

The often-quoted conclusion of the Association of Directors of Social Services and Commission for Race Equality in 1978 is worth repeating here:

> Our conclusion is that the response of social services departments to the existence of multi-racial communities has been patchy, piecemeal, and lacking in strategy.... (ADSS/CRE, 1978, p 14)

A number of studies since have demonstrated the persistence of this picture. Butt et al in 1991 noted:

> Our survey shows that, while most SSDs [social services departments] have made some commitment and a few appear to have made some headway in progressing equality, many have adopted a piecemeal or haphazard approach that makes it difficult to answer the question whether or not the services they provide are equally fair. (Butt et al, 1991, p 3)

Towards the end of the 1990s the Audit Commission and the now defunct Social Services Inspectorate concluded:

> Many councils are not responding effectively to diverse communities. It is worrying that in three-quarters of councils reviewed to date, less than one-third of respondents felt that matters of religion, race or culture were taken into account....
>
> Users and carers for minority communities, not surprisingly therefore, are less satisfied with the services they get than those who describe themselves as 'white European'. (SSI/Audit Commission, 1999)

The Audit Commission (Audit Commission and SSI, 2004) returned to the subject in 2004 and lamented the 'disappointing' progress made by these departments. The Commission for Social Care Inspection in 2006 published the results of its performance rating exercise for social services in England, noting that among the five 'areas' that social services needed to improve most were taking account of the needs of 'minority groups' and providing 'Services that reflect the community, promote equality and comply with relevant legislation' (CSCI, 2006, p 6).

The constancy of this picture has not stopped the debate about why we should promote equality from evolving. Much of the early impetus focused on the moral imperative, while more recently attention has been paid to the 'business case' for delivering equality and this has been, on occasion, replaced with notions of the rights of citizens or taxpayers (Phillips et al, 2006, captures some of this). Interestingly, rarely in the debates on promoting the rights of citizens do we see much discussion of why the experience of British black and minority ethnic communities, who often possess British citizenship, has so many parallels with minority communities in Western Europe, who often do not possess citizenship.

Exploring evidence of needs

These overall assessments are accompanied by growth in evidence for particular 'client groups'. So, for example, data from the 2001 Census show that, when standardised for age, around 16% of men and around 15% of women of the 'White British' ethnic group have a long-term limiting illness or a disability that restricts daily activities for a variety of ethnic groups (ONS, 2004). In comparison, the figures are nearer 17% for 'Indian' men and almost 20% for 'Indian' women. For 'Black Caribbean' men the figures are nearer 18% and over 19% for 'Black Caribbean' women. The greatest contrast is with Pakistani women (over 25%) and Bangladeshi women (25%). Importantly, these patterns reflect these communities' self-assessment of their health in responding to the Health Survey of England in 1999 (ONS, 2004).

The 2001 Census data suggest that there is some difference between black and minority ethnic groups, and between men and women from these groups. But the data also suggests that black and minority ethnic people have higher rates of 'disability' than their 'White British' counterparts when standardised for age. In addition, this same data show that black and minority ethnic women are more likely than men to have a 'disability' that restricts their daily activities. This, again, contrasts with the pattern for the 'White British' ethnic group, where the Census records higher rates for men than women. The Chinese group is the one black and minority ethnic group for whom these conclusions do not apply: the Census records comparatively lower levels of 'disability' for them.

Significantly, the Census data also suggest that if we disaggregate the 'White' community, there is evidence of higher rates of disability and long-term limiting illness for some of the Irish community.

These data on higher rates of disability and long-term limiting illness are accompanied by evidence of continuing discrimination and disadvantage. So, for example, black and minority ethnic disabled people are at greater risk of experiencing unemployment and lower incomes than other disabled people (Smith and Twomey, 2002). Also they are more likely to live in private rented accommodation (the sector with the poorest quality of housing) and in 'non-decent homes' than other black and minority ethnic people (ODPM, 2003). At the same time they share two of the characteristics of those who have benefited least from the post-1997 attack on social exclusion: disability and coming from a 'minority ethnic community' (SEU, 2004).

The point here is not that there is much to be done, but to explore why progress has been so limited.

Why does this situation persist?

It could be argued that perhaps this situation persists because of the paucity of evidence on the experience of social care of black and minority ethnic communities (Butt and O'Neill, 2004). While it is undoubtedly true that there is much to be done in the systematic recording of this experience, and understanding its implications for policy and practice, it is nevertheless the case that a significant body of evidence exists that at the very least demonstrates need. The experience of black and minority ethnic older people is one example. This experience has been explored at a local level (for example, Qureshi, 1998) and increasingly at a national level (for example, Berthoud, 1998; Moriarty and Butt, 2004). This has been accompanied by increasingly sophisticated studies, with Evandrou (2000), for example, combining six years of data from the General Household Survey to examine income and health, while Butt et al (2003) have carried out in-depth interviews using a nationally representative sample derived from the Family Resources Survey.

The picture painted by these, and other studies, shows that black and minority ethnic older people, like many other older people in the UK, have significant support and care needs; also, that these needs are not necessarily being met appropriately or adequately by their families or service providers (see the review by Butt and Mirza, 1996). This picture is confirmed by the Social Services Inspectorate in their inspection of community care services for older people in general (Murray and Brown, 1998) and by Qureshi (1998) for the Bangladeshi community and Kam Yu (2000) for the Chinese community.

However, this evidence of age-related discrimination is only part of the picture. Many of these studies also show the experience of 'direct' and 'institutional' racism by black and minority ethnic older people. Therefore the evidence on income and wealth detailed by Berthoud

(1998) shows that some older people from these communities have income that is similar to the 'better-off' older people in the UK. However, for the majority (including Indian and Caribbean older people) their income levels are lower than those of their white counterparts. This is particularly so for Pakistani and Bangladeshi older people. Furthermore, the increased frailty that often leads to needing support and care among older people in general appears to occur in black and minority ethnic older people at a younger age (Evandrou, 2000, is the latest to confirm this). While some of this increased frailty at a younger age can be explained by genetic differences, much of it can only be explained by the material consequences of racism such as poor working conditions, higher rates of unemployment, poor housing and inadequate access to health and other support services (Butt et al, 1999).

Another 'client' group that has seen a significant growth in evidence is black and minority ethnic disabled people. The complexity of the impact of impairment on the lives of disabled people (Grewal et al, 2002) including their housing needs (Beresford and Oldman, 2002) would suggest that we need to be careful in drawing out cross-cutting messages from this evidence. Nevertheless, there are some consistent messages.

Most studies suggest that black and minority disabled ethnic people express the same needs, wants and desires as their non-disabled counterparts, whether this is to have access to information for those with visual impairments (Johnson and Scare, 2000), the chance to laugh and cry with friends (Bignall and Butt, 2000) or whether it is to have a home with appropriate aids and adaptations (Molloy et al, 2003). At the same time there is evidence that some black and minority ethnic disabled people are active in shaping their lives (Shaping Our Lives, 2003).

Studies often also highlight that black and minority ethnic disabled people require support to exercise choice and control in their lives (Vernon, 2002). Sometimes this support is provided by their family or friends as part of a reciprocal relationship where black and minority ethnic disabled people provide support too (Jones et al, 2002). As is the case for all disabled people, many black and minority ethnic disabled people emphasise the value of these social and support networks and often place any discussion about independence in the context of wanting to maintain support from their families (Bignall and Butt, 2000). Furthermore, families and carers are reported as the principal source of information for disabled and D/deaf people about the impairment, as well as other areas such as the receipt of benefits (Ahmad et al, 1998).

However, these same relationships can be a source of stress for some black and minority ethnic disabled people, with some feeling undervalued or trapped (Bignall and Butt, 2000), and with others highlighting some of the prejudices and discrimination they have experienced from their family, friends or community (Hussain et al, 2001). Furthermore, D/deaf young people who use British Sign Language report a lack of a common language in which they can communicate with their families (Ahmad et al, 1998).

A number of studies report lack of choice and control in areas such as accessing education (Bignall and Butt, 2000), managing money (Ahmad et al, 1998), housing (Molloy et al, 2003), opportunities to socialise (Darr et al, 1997), practising religion (Ahmad et al, 1998), employment opportunities (Vernon, 2002) and accessing information (Johnson and Scase, 2000) and services in general (Roberts and Harris, 2002). Some of these projects suggest that choice and control is often poorer (or perceived to be poorer) for disabled and D/deaf black and minority ethnic communities than for other disabled and D/deaf people (Chamba et al, 1999). However, comparative information is not always available.

In similar fashion to black and minority ethnic disabled people, their carers report barriers to having their needs met and being able to provide support effectively (Katbamna et al, 2003) including when children and young people are providing support to their parents (Jones et al, 2002). Barriers that are reported include lack of accessible information about support available (Katbamna et al, 1997; Johnson and Scase, 2000) as well as poor housing (Hatton et al, 2004) and inadequate income (Chamba et al, 1999).

There is some evidence of using and valuing black and minority ethnic voluntary organisations and the services they provide (Butt, 1994; Watters, 1996) as well as 'peer' support groups (Bignall and Butt, 2002). In addition, some studies have identified the importance of black and minority ethnic workers (Rai-Atkins et al, 2002). However, a consistent message is of poor support provided by formal services (Chamba et al, 1999). At the same time, studies warn that a low take-up of services is not an indication of low levels of need (Flynn, 2002). Furthermore, while family support exists and is valued, so, for example, appropriate and accessible housing is often only accepted by black and minority ethnic disabled people when it is in an area that allows the maintenance of social and support networks (Butt and Dhaliwall, 2005). However, there is no evidence for service providers to conclude that a lack of take-up of services is because 'they look after their own'.

As noted above, the evidence base is not as rich for all social care 'clients' from black and minority ethnic groups. But neither is it the case that we have few studies that demonstrate the existence of need, or its complexity as was argued in the early 1990s (Williams, 1990).

Legislative and policy framework

If it is not necessarily an issue of evidence then perhaps there are shortcomings in the legislative and policy framework.

The government proposal to establish a single commission for equality and human rights in Britain is the latest step in a series of legislative and government changes since 1997. These changes have included the enactment of various aspects of the Disability Discrimination Act, which although passed in 1995 began to come into force some time after. Over the same period there has been the enactment of the 2000 Race Relations Amendment Act. Most recently there has been the passing of the 2004 Carers (Equal Opportunities) Act and the 2005 Disability Discrimination Amendment Act, which among other changes will see the imposition of a new duty on the public sector to promote disability equality.

The 2000 Race Relations Amendment Act increased the scope of duties upon 'public bodies' to cover both a general duty and a specific duty. In terms of their general duty, these 'public bodies' are obliged to do three things when they develop policies, provide services, or in their employment practice. They are required to eliminate unlawful discrimination (direct and indirect discrimination as well as victimisation), promote equality of opportunity and promote good race relations.

In promoting race equality, public bodies are required to be proactive by both consulting minority ethnic communities about proposed services and policies as well as anticipating, assessing and monitoring the impact of their policies and practices on minority ethnic communities. This includes the delivery of a range of services but also includes an obligation to ensure that minority ethnic communities are able to gain equal access to information about the services, policies and procedures of these agencies. The general and specific duties under the 2000 Race Relations Amendment Act have now been incorporated as part of the Best Value Performance Indicators assessed by the Audit Commission.

As noted previously, the 2000 Race Relations Amendment Act also requires public bodies to produce both a Race Equality Scheme and an Action Plan detailing how they intend to implement and continue to monitor their general duties. The Commission for Racial Equality assessment of these plans has suggested that it has not produced the universal engagement with the promotion of race equality hoped for (CRE, 2004). However, the requirement for public bodies to consult the 'public' on their plans and show how these have been taken on board is still a potentially powerful tool for change.

Further, an examination of the recent White Papers on adult social care, and the future of community health and social care, shows that the attention to equality persists (DH, 2005). While there has been much criticism of the proposals for the establishment of the single equalities commission because of the potential loss of focus on race equality and the failure to support it with a single equalities Act (www.equalitydiversityforum.org.uk), it is nevertheless the case that the limited attention to equalities in the 1980s and 1990s no longer persists (REU, 1989).

It would be interesting to assess how this legislative framework promotes the rights of citizens as opposed to establishing bureaucratic procedures that may ultimately bear little fruit. Nevertheless, it is clear that the government believes that this is the mission that they are on (Home Office, 2005).

Practice

If there have been significant strides in terms of the legislative and policy framework, perhaps the reason for the limited change in the experience of social care of black and minority ethnic communities is the lack of change in practice.

The implementation of the Single Assessment Process as part of the National Service Framework for Older People (Phillip, 2006) is the latest attempt by the Department of Health to encourage social care providers to take a wider view of the needs of older people in carrying out assessments. Most attempts to define a good model for assessment have tried to encourage this wider view of the problems potential services users may face, for example the Learning Materials on Mental Health (1996). However, it is perhaps an indication of the limited impact of these attempts that the Department of Health has had to revisit guidance on effective assessment and is now requiring all those who provide support to older people to collaborate in carrying out these assessments.

One attempt to develop this wider view in relation to Britain's black and minority ethnic communities is by Dutt and Ferns (1998). Applying their holistic model to assessment with black and minority ethnic older people means taking into account a range of factors, including:

- social factors (such as the organisation of care in families);
- economic factors (such as the experience of poverty);
- political factors (such as racialised immigration policies that hinder black and minority ethnic people from reforming their families after immigration);
- psychological factors (such as the onset of depression with the recognition by some black and minority ethnic older people that they are unlikely to be able to 'return' to their birth country).

In addition, assessment of individual need seeks to identify discriminatory barriers in order to remove them.

Adopting this model requires practitioners to look specifically at the variety of ways in which black and minority ethnic individuals and communities utilise informal support to cope with living in Britain. An example of this is the church or Mosque or temple-based support services that have sprung up in the places where black and minority ethnic people live.

Potentially, there are several barriers to carrying out effective assessments with black and minority ethnic older people. These barriers include:

- lack of knowledge of social care among black and minority ethnic communities;
- care workers' lack of knowledge or stereotypical views of the lives of black and minority ethnic older people;
- failure to take into account the experience of racism;
- failure to adopt a holistic model of assessment.

A particular manifestation of these barriers is the adoption of an ethnocentric value base. Social care provision is informed by values, many of which are promoted by the government and agencies, but some are influenced by the values of workers. While multiculturalism is a value that is often promoted, how we translate this into action is less clear. In this context there is the potential for an ethnocentric model of assessment becoming dominant (sometimes the term Eurocentric is used). This means that the values of one ethnic group begin to be seen as natural or normal and assessment and actions are then influenced by this.

So, for example, the focus on individuals as opposed to communities may be seen to be the result of the importance attached to individualism in West European society. Care would need to be taken not to develop stereotypes (for example, all black people are the same). However, being aware that an ethnocentric model poses the problem of seeing one ethnic group's lifestyles as normal is also essential.

As noted above, the evidence of continuing failure properly to assess the needs of black and minority ethnic service users is that they continue to report a lack of satisfaction with services (Audit Commission and SSI, 2004) and are not able to exercise choice and control in their lives. Therefore, an element of future action is to ensure that the requirements of the Single Assessment Process to take a wider view or holistic approach to assessment does mean developing practice that engages black and minority ethnic service users and does not result in them continuing to be seen in stereotypical terms or made to fit in to services designed for others. In this context, it is worth repeating the Commission for Social Care Inspection's (CSCI, 2006) emphasis on the need to improve the commissioning of care services so that they meet the needs of minority ethnic groups.

A point worth noting here is that often this debate about appropriate assessment surfaces another debate: who is best suited to carry out these assessments and provide the service identified? Often the conclusion to these questions is black and minority ethnic workers. While a research gap persists in understanding the contribution of black and minority ethnic workers to better practice (Butt and Davey, 1997), it is possible to argue that we need to be careful not to come to essentialist conclusions – suggesting that you have to be black to work effectively with black workers – but instead explore the skills (such as keeping users informed [Thoburn et al, 1995]) and knowledge base that these workers bring to the relationship with service users.

An important step is to consider existing solutions. For example, there is now significant practice-based experience of the use of ethnic matching in the provision of home help and home care services. Some social services departments have developed specific home care services for the Bangladeshi and Chinese communities, and others have recruited black and minority ethnic home carers into their mainstream service (Mussenden and Yee, 1998).

Another starting point for the development of services may be to adapt or refashion existing services, as in the case of Milton House, a residential home run by Bradford Social Services Department. Butt et al (1999) document how a wing of this residential centre was set aside for use with Asian older people. Staff with the right skills were recruited. A change in policy was also instituted: they would accept any older Asian person who was referred to the service. There was also to be a mix of service, some of it day care, some of it residential.

However, the evidence also suggests that for the most part this form of appropriate provision is limited in its availability, and that mainstream provision is still struggling. As a result, it is likely that the provision of support may involve considerable negotiation of existing services and may encounter some difficulties in meeting care needs.

Voluntary and community organisations

Another starting point may be to learn from the black and minority ethnic-led voluntary and community organisations. Interest in any evidence of 'supportive services' has increasingly focused on these organisations (Butt and Box, 1997). There is some evidence of mainstream services being described as supportive (Murray and Brown, 1998). Often, however, it has been black and minority ethnic voluntary organisations that have been said to be providing supportive services. An example is Yee and Mussenden (1998) who detail the home care service provided by a voluntary organisation in Wandsworth. Butt and Box (1997) record the day care and befriending services provided by another organisation in Leeds.

This evidence of supportive services provided by black and minority ethnic voluntary organisations has meant that there has been some attention paid to these organisations since the early 1990s (Butt, 1994). Those who advocated for black and minority ethnic organisations, and some of their users, pointed to a number of factors contributing to their success in providing support to black and minority ethnic older people factors, such as these organisations' 'practice', the trust and confidence their users have in them, the employment of black and minority ethnic workers, their ability to communicate effectively and their geographical locations. Importantly, the consultation process that has informed the Joseph Rowntree Foundation's call for proposals once again saw black and minority ethnic older people highlight groups such as SubCo in East London, the Pepperpot Club in West London, Leeds Black Elders Association and the Merseyside Chinese Association as examples of groups that provided supportive services.

Yet there is little systematic information available to support these views. For some of these organisations there is little information on the make-up of older people who use their services. Furthermore, like many other social care agencies, black and minority ethnic voluntary organisations also struggle with the question of how effective their services are. Sometimes this has resulted in funders using financial management as the principal factor in deciding whether a group receives support, rather than the effectiveness of the service they provide (Butt, 1994). Also there is little information on what, if anything, these groups are doing to evaluate the effectiveness of their services. While funding organisations are increasingly demanding that these organisations collect and produce this information, there is little evidence to suggest that these organisations are doing any better than their counterparts in health and social care (Butt and Box, 1997).

Nevertheless, their black and minority ethnic users continue to identify them as supportive and valued. Further, beyond the social capital sometimes available to these communities in the form of families and friends, it appears that black and minority ethnic voluntary and community organisations appear to be an important element of this social capital. Worryingly, the lessons for other organisations who work with black and minority ethnic services appear to be trapped within these organisations as there seems to be little in the way of systematic knowledge transfer.

Conclusion

The power of appropriate support provided when people require it can transform the opportunities and quality of life of those in need. However, when choice and control is limited or undermined by racist stereotypes or a failure to engage users in identifying needs and how they can be effectively met, then social care perpetuates discrimination and disadvantage. A review of the evidence would suggest that for the majority of black and minority ethnic people approaching social care providers in 2007, their experience will be different from what would have happened in 1987 and certainly different from 1977. The improvement over these time periods is likely to be greatest if support is now being sought from black and minority ethnic-led voluntary organisations. In part, this is because these organisations appear to be better able to engage black and minority ethnic people in identifying their needs and agreeing what support is needed and how it is best provided. In part, it is also because these organisations are more likely to exist in sufficient scale for people to know of their existence.

However, the overall prospects for black and minority ethnic service users still remain patchy and, for a significant number, poor. Importantly, the evidence for this picture is not only provided by small-scale studies, but emerges from large-scale datasets, as well as inspection reports, of many of the regulators involved in the field of social care. The fact that this picture repeats that which emerged 20 and 30 years ago may not be surprising but certainly should be shocking. The shocking value of this picture is not because mainstream provision has 'improved', while services to black and minority ethnic communities have not, but a result of the constancy of this picture. We have known for some time about the limitations of support provided and the existence of needs, yet have failed to transform social care to ensure that it increases choice and control for all those who need support. Worryingly, because of the piecemeal nature of changes that have taken place, it sometimes appears that significant improvement is as far away as ever. Also, the piecemeal nature means that the changes that have taken place have not had the impact that they may otherwise have done.

Evidence that a holistic approach to understanding needs of these communities, and the comparative success of voluntary and community organisations in securing positive approval from black and minority ethnic people, does hold out the possibility that improvements are feasible. Whether this means that we all have to adopt a community development approach in social care is not something that can be argued for on the evidence presented here. However, it can be argued that for those who are experiencing discrimination and disadvantage, this seems a more productive approach. An approach that learns to work with the social capital in these communities (whether it is the way individuals and families organise themselves in the face of limited support from mainstream agencies, or whether it is the comparative success of voluntary and community organisations) certainly deserves greater attention. This also has the possibility that change in policy and practice impacts not only on black and minority ethnic communities, but on all communities. It is perhaps, also, when we will see the new emphasis on citizenship move from rhetoric to reality.

Finally, a note of concern must be recorded. The new managerialism with its focus on targets and efficiency that appears to 'win' the battle in social care may mitigate against a community development approach where we still appear to be working out what is a target and how we know when it has been met. Without engaging in this debate about targets and their measurement, we will not be able to engage in the thornier debate as to what is cost-effective in providing support.

References

ADSS/CRE (Association of Directors of Social Services/Commission for Racial Equality) (1978) *Multi-racial Britain: The Social Services Response*, London: CRE.

Ahmad, W. I. U. and Atkin, K. (eds) (1996) *'Race' and Community Care*, Milton Keynes: Open University Press.

Ahmad, W. I. U., Darr, A., Jones, L. and Nisar, G. (1998) *Deafness and Ethnicity: Services, Policy and Politics*, Bristol/York: The Policy Press/ Joseph Rowntree Foundation.

Audit Commission and SSI (Social Services Inspectorate) (2004) *Old Virtues, New Virtues: An Overview of the Changes in Social Care Services over the Seven Years of Joint Reviews in England 1996–2003*, London: Audit Commission.

Beresford, B. and Oldman, C. (2002) *Housing Matters: National Evidence Relating to Disabled Children and their Housing*, Bristol: The Policy Press.

Berthoud, R. (1998) *The Incomes of Ethnic Minorities*, ISER Report 98-1, Colchester: Institute for Social and Economic Research, University of Essex.

Bignall, T. and Butt, J. (2000) *Between Ambition and Achievement: Young Black Disabled People's Views and Experiences of Independence and Independent Living*, Bristol: The Policy Press.

Bignall, T., Butt, J. and Pagarani, D. (2002) *Something to Do: The Development of Peer Support Groups for Young Black Disabled People*, Bristol: The Policy Press.

Butt, J. (1994) *Same Service or Equal Service? The Second Report on Social Services Departments' Development, Implementation and Monitoring of Services for the Black and Minority Ethnic Community*, London: HMSO.

Butt, J. and Box, L. (1997) *Supportive Services, Effective Strategies: The Views of Black-led Organisations and Social Care Agencies on the Future of Social Care for Black Communities*, London: Race Equality Unit.

Butt, J. and Davey, B. (1997) 'The experience of black workers in the social care workforce', in M. May, E. Brunsden and G. Craig (eds) *Social Policy Review 9*, London: Social Policy Association, pp 141-61.

Butt, J. and Dhaliwall, S. (2005) *Different Paths: Challenging Services: A Study of the Housing Experiences of Black and Minority Ethnic Disabled and Deaf People*, London: Habinteg Housing Association.

Butt, J. and Mirza, K. (1996) *Social Care and Black Communities: A Review of Recent Research Studies*, London: HMSO.

Butt, J. and O'Neill, A. (2004) *'Let's Move On': Black and Minority Ethnic Older People's Views on Research Findings*, York: York Publishing Services.

Butt, J., Box, L. and Lyn Cook, S. (1999) *Respect: Learning Materials for Social Staff Working with Black and Minority Ethnic Older People*, London: REU.

Butt, J., Gorbach, P. and Ahmad, B. (1991) *Equally Fair? A Report on Social Services Departments' Development, Implementation and Monitoring of Services for the Black and Minority Ethnic Community*, London: HMSO.

Butt, J., Moriarty, J., Brockmann, M., Sin, C. H. and Fisher, M. (2003) *Quality of Life and Social Support Among Older People from Different Ethnic Groups*, Growing Older Findings, no 23, Swindon: ESRC.

Chamba, R., Ahmad, W. I. U., Hirst, M., Lawton, D. and Beresford, B. (1999) *On the Edge: Minority Ethnic Families Caring for a Severely Disabled Child*, Bristol: The Policy Press.

CRE (Commission for Race Equality) (2004) *The Commission for Racial Equality and Human Rights*, London: CRE.

CSCI (Commission for Social Care Inspection) (2006) *Performance Ratings for Social Services (England) 2005*, London: CSCI.

Darr, A., Jones, L., Ahmad, W. I. U. and Nisar, G. (1997) *A Directory of Projects and Initiatives with Deaf People from Minority Ethnic Communities*, Bradford: Social Policy Research Unit, University of Bradford.

DH (Department of Health) (2005) *Independence, Well-being and Choice*, Social Care Green Paper, London: DH.

Dutt, R. and Ferns, P. (1998) *Letting through Light*, London: Race Equality Unit.

Evandrou, M. (2000) 'Ethnic inequalities in health in later life', *Health Statistics Quarterly*, no 8, pp 20-8.

Flynn, R. (2002) *Short Breaks: Providing Better Access to and More Choice for Black Disabled People and their Families*, Bristol/York: The Policy Press/Joseph Rowntree Foundation.

Grewal, I., Joy, S., Lewis, J., Swales, K. and Woodfield, K. (2002) *Disabled for Life? Attitudes Towards, and Experiences of, Disability in Britain*, DWP Research Report 173, London: DWP.

Hatton, C., Akram, Y., Shah, R., Robertson, J. and Emerson, E. (2004) *Supporting South Asian Families with a Child with Severe Disabilities*, London: Jessica Kingsley.

Home Office (2005) *Improving Opportunity, Strengthening Society*, Press Release, London: Home Office, http://press.homeoffice.gov.uk/press-releases/Improving_Opportunity,_Strengthe?version=1

Hussain, Y., Atkin, K. and Ahmad, W. I. U. (2001) *South Asian Disabled Young People and Their Families*, York: Centre for Research in Primary Care/Joseph Rowntree Foundation.

Johnson, R. D. and Scase, M. O. (2000) *Ethnic Minorities and Visual Impairment: A Research Review*, Seacole Research Paper 1, Leicester: De Montfort University.

Jones, A., Jeyasingham, D. and Rajasooriya, S. (2002) *Invisible Families: The Strengths and Needs of Black Families in which Young People Have Caring Responsibilities*, Bristol/York: The Policy Press/Joseph Rowntree Foundation.

Kam Yu, W. (2000) *Chinese Older People: A Need for Social Inclusion in Two Communities*, Bristol/York: The Policy Press/Joseph Rowntree Foundation.

Katbamna, S., Baker, R., Ahmad, W. I. U., Bhakta, P. and Parker, G. (1997) *The Needs of Asian Carers*, Leicester: Nuffield Community Care Studies Unit, University of Leicester.

Katbamna, S., Baker, R., Ahmad, W. I. U., Bhakta, P. and Parker, G. (2003) 'Do they look after their own? Informal support for South Asian Carers', *Health and Social Care in the Community*, vol 12, no 5, pp 398-406.

Hatton, C., Akram, Y., Shah, R., Robertson, J. and Emerson, E. (2004) *Supporting South Asian Families with a Child with Severe Disabilities*, London: Jessica Kingsley,

Macpherson of Cluny, Sir W. (1999) *The Stephen Lawrence Inquiry*, London: The Stationery Office.

Molloy, D., Knight, T. and Woodfield, K. (2003*) Diversity in Disability: Exploring the Interactions between Disability, Ethnicity, Age, Gender And Sexuality*, DWP Research Report 188, London: DWP.

Moriarty, J. and Butt, J. (2004) 'Inequalities in quality of life among older people from different ethnic groups', *Ageing and Society*, vol 24, no 5, pp 729-53.

Murray, U. and Brown, D. (1998) *They Look After their Own Don't They? An Inspection of Community Care Services for Black and Minority Ethnic People*, London: Social Services Inspectorate/Department of Health.

Mussenden, B. and Yee, L. (1998) *Developing Services for Black and Minority Ethnic Older People*, Wandsworth: Wandsworth Social Services.

ODPM (Office of the Deputy Prime Minister) (2003) *English House Condition Survey: Main Report*, London: ODPM.

ONS (Office for National Statistics) (2004) *Focus on Ethnicity and Identity*, London: ONS.

Phillip, I. (2006) *A New Ambition for Old Age: Next Steps in Implementing the National Service Framework for Older People*, London: Department of Health.

Phillips, T. (2006) The *Equalities Review: Interim Report for Consultation*, www.theequalitiesreview.org.uk/upload/assets/www.theequalitiesreview.org.uk/interim_report.pdf

Qureshi, T. (1998) *Living in Britain: Growing Old in Britain: A Study of Bangladeshi Elders in London*, CPA Report 22, London: Centre for Policy on Ageing.

Rai-Atkins, A., in association with Ali Jama, A., Wright, N., Scott, V., Perring, C., Craig, G. and Katbamna, S. (2002) *Best Practice in Mental Health: Advocacy for African, Caribbean and South Asian Communities*, Bristol/York: The Policy Press/Joseph Rowntree Foundation.

REU (Race Equality Unit) (1989) *The Griffiths Task Force Recommendations on Community Care*, London: REU.

Roberts, K. and Harris, J. (2002) *Disabled People in Refugee and Asylum Seeking Communities*, Bristol/York: The Policy Press/Joseph Rowntree Rowntree Foundation.

SEU (Social Exclusion Unit) (2004) *Breaking the Cycle: Taking Stock of Progress and Priorities for the Future*, London: ODPM.

Shaping Our Lives (2003) *From Outset to Outcome: Report of Four Development Projects on User Defined Outcomes*, York: Joseph Rowntree Foundation.

Smith, A. and Twomey, B. (2002) 'Labour market expectations of people with disabilities', *Labour Market Trends*, August, pp 415-27.

SSI (Social Services Inspectorate)/Audit Commission (1999) *Making Connections: Learning the Lessons from Joint Reviews of Social Services*, SSI/Audit Commission.

Thoburn, J., Lewis, A. and Shemmings, D. (1995) *Paternalism or Partnership: Family Involvement in the Child Protection Process*, London: Department of Health.

Vernon, A. (2002) *User-Defined Outcomes of Community Care for Asian Disabled People*, Bristol: The Policy Press.

Watters, C. (1996) 'Representations and realities: black people, community care and mental illness', in W. I. U. Ahmad and K. Atkin (eds) (1996) *'Race' and Community Care*, Milton Keynes: Open University Press, pp 105-23.

Williams, J. (1990) 'Black and minority ethnic elders', in I. Sinclair (1990) *The Kaleidoscope of Care: Review of Research on Welfare Provision for Elderly People*, London: National Institute for Social Work, pp 107-34.

TEN

Community care development: developing the capacity of local communities to respond to their own support and care needs

Deborah Quilgars

Introduction

This chapter evaluates the successes and challenges experienced in developing a Community Care Development Project. In recognition of the lack of joint work on 'community care' and 'community development', a three-year pilot project was established in Hull in 1999 by a partnership of local statutory and voluntary sector agencies to find out whether the community sector could be supported in addressing unmet low-level support and care needs. The chapter begins by outlining the national and local background to the project, before moving on to document the approach taken. The extent to which the project had a measurable impact on communities is then considered, and, in particular, the extent to which it met the community care needs of local communities.

Policy background: why a 'community care development' project?

Community care has, for the most part, been narrowly defined. In the 1990s, central government policy on community care encouraged limited statutory resources to be increasingly targeted on those with the highest level of health and social care needs; and away from lower-level, often preventative, services (Audit Commission, 1998). At the same time, the numbers of people with support needs living within the community in ordinary housing increased (Burrows, 1997). However, the importance of low-level and preventative support for both traditional community care users and for a much wider group of 'vulnerable' people (for example, homeless people) was re-acknowledged by the end of the decade (Quilgars, 2000). In particular, the Supporting People programme, launched in April 2003, provides housing-related support to 1.2 million vulnerable people to help them live more independently.

The government recently identified how Supporting People works with three needs groups: people who are also in receipt of care services, people living independently with support only, and people experiencing or at risk of social exclusion (ODPM, 2005a). However, connections between Supporting People and Department of Health agendas have remained limited (Audit Commission, 2005), while those with social exclusion agendas have been weaker still. Although it has been recognised that 'supporting people to live independent lives is an important element of building better communities' (ODPM, 2005a, p 4), Supporting People continues community care's primarily individualised approach to delivering assistance to people in defined target groups (including a recent suggestion to introduce an individual budget approach).

Despite most caring activity still being undertaken by families and other informal carers, community care has tended to be associated with care in the community; that is, care being delivered in a particular location, rather than as care by the community (Bayley, 1973). Moreover, despite social work's early origins in community work, the wider community as a whole has rarely been involved in formulating policy and delivering social and health services (Barr et al, 2000). Although the *Choosing Health* White Paper (DH, 2004) highlights successful examples of supporting local people to identify their needs in the development of healthy communities, the real impetus for community-based initiatives has been driven through social exclusion agendas, via the new commitment to neighbourhood renewal (SEU, 2001) under the Neighbourhood Renewal Unit in the Department for Communities & Local Government (DCLG). Overseeing this, is the government's £38 billion Communities Plan, which focuses on improving people's housing, neighbourhoods and quality of life (ODPM, 2003), which includes a goal to assist vulnerable people in securing and maintaining housing, further expounded in the recent five-year plan in this area (ODPM, 2005b).

The government also has a strong policy interest in the role of volunteering and, more broadly, active citizenship. The Home Office Active Communities Directorate (first set up in 1997) was relaunched in 2002 to support greater participation in society. Recently, its work was moved from the Home Office to the new Office of the Third Sector in the Cabinet Office (along with social exclusion), emphasising its sustained importance from the government's perspective. Research has shown that levels of participation in voluntary and community activities are lower in deprived areas compared with more wealthy areas (Home Office, 2002). The Civil Renewal Unit also has similar interests in participation in society and has also recently been moved to the DCLG, bringing it closer to neighbourhood renewal priorities. It is evident that a number of government departments or offices are responsible for issues that might cross over between care, support and community issues. The DCLG recently became the new lead for the cross-departmental Together We Can campaign, which attempts to link participative opportunities across departments.

Community development, with its roots in community work, has traditionally been the vehicle through which community participation and activity has been encouraged and supported (Craig, 1989). While this term is rarely utilised at the national policy level, allied or sub-approaches have received attention and the government has recently put in place a community 'capacity building' framework (Civil Renewal Unit, 2003; Home Office, 2004), following the seminal work by Putman (2000) identifying the importance of social capital. The full-time equivalent of 20,000 workers are carrying out this type of work across the UK (Taylor, 2006). Community involvement in mainstream service delivery (across areas such as health, crime, employment and housing) in deprived areas has also received recent attention (ODPM, 2005c), as well as more generally being emphasised in new Local Area Agreements.

However, despite a high priority on the role of communities, regeneration planning in practice has largely ignored the specific housing, care and support needs of vulnerable people (Fletcher, 2000). A clear example of this is how Single Regeneration Budget initiatives effectively excluded, although through omission rather than intent, disabled people from community regeneration processes (Edwards, 2001). While community development has always had a concern with nurturing common interests, and a half of community capacity-building projects are focused on particular groups (for example, young people, older people), the potential conflicts of working to universal, generic objectives and targeting specific groups within overall regeneration policy has been highlighted in the past (Brownhill and Darke, 1998).

As a result of the mismatch between community care/support policy and regeneration policy, a number of commentators in the early 2000s argued for bringing these two policy domains closer together (for example, Fletcher, 2000; Edwards, 2001). However, to date, only one key study has focused on both the role of community care and community development: an action research project in Scotland (Barr et al, 2000).

This study demonstrated a range of benefits to taking a community development approach to the formulation of community care policy; and of incorporating a community care perspective into social inclusion agendas. The study reported on here represents the first evaluation of an English Community Care Development Project.

The Community Care Development Project: definitions and approach

The starting point for the development of the Community Care Development Project in Hull was recognition by both the local authority and voluntary sector providers that tightening eligibility criteria for statutory community care services meant that an increasing level of lower-intensity care and support needs were going unmet in the community. The local Council for Voluntary Service approached social services with a suggestion about exploring the untapped potential of the less formal voluntary and community sector:

> 'The one thing that was missing from community care had always been communities themselves. What community care actually meant was established voluntary organisations (or newly established voluntary organisations) and social services and health moving to extend more provision into non-institutionalised care – what had never happened was social services or anybody going to talk to communities about the care that they provided and the potential for communities to become more caring.' (Voluntary sector representative)

A successful Joint Finance bid (for £94,000) led to the establishment of a three-year project that involved the employment of one full-time community care development coordinator in the community development organisation, Hull Developing Our Communities (Hull DOC). The project worked within an inter-agency framework, with a multidisciplinary Steering Group overseeing its development. In addition, the Joseph Rowntree Foundation funded a three-year evaluation of the pilot project, undertaken by the Centre for Housing Policy, University of York.

'Community care development' as an approach has few precedents. As with the only other study (Barr et al, 2000), the project was directly informed by the process of 'community development'. The Community Development Foundation defines this as:

A range of practices dedicated to increasing the strength
of community life, improving local conditions, especially
for people in disadvantaged situations, and enabling people
to participate in public decision-making, and to achieve
greater long term control over their circumstances. (www.
cdf.org.uk)

The Hull model of community development included a focus on the
following key elements:

- Local communities: the project was set up to work at a local,
  geographical level, working with local residents as well as agencies.
  The starting point was not specific client groups or communities
  of interest.
- Tackling disadvantage: as with much community development work,
  the project sought to address issues of social inclusion wherever
  relevant.
- Community-led focus: the project was designed to help communities
  to identify their own needs, rather than starting with predefined
  ideas of need. It had no brief at the outset to develop services or
  activities in particular ways, or to particular models.
- Participation: a crucial element of the project was the participation
  of community members, both generally and those with specific
  community care needs.
- Activity: the project was explicitly concerned with generating
  increased activity at a local level.
- Sustainability: the project was concerned with ensuring that any
  activities were not contingent on the long-term support of the
  project for their success.
- Empowerment: there was an overall concern with giving control
  to local communities and helping them to articulate their needs to
  more formal agencies.

The 'community care' component of the project was less well defined.
The project Steering Group members, as well as some local social and
health professionals, understood the project as being about the provision
of low-level support services. However, community representatives
interpreted the term in a much broader sense as representing a 'caring'
community and the process of trying to regenerate community spirit,
rather than referring to any formal statutory definition. In addition,
some local players involved in the project were quite unclear as to the
meaning of the term.

The project coordinator developed a staged approach to community care development at the local level, drawing on the above community development principles. It was possible to discern five key stages to this process:

(1) Selecting project areas

At the outset, the Steering Group chose two areas for the project to focus on. Two contrasting deprived neighbourhoods of Hull were selected: a primarily social housing area (New Bilton Grange) and an area of mainly private housing (Hessle Road). It is important to note that the communities were not consulted about the project working in their areas. While in one area the project was welcomed immediately, in the other this process took some time. In future work, it was agreed that local areas should be consulted about their potential involvement.

(2) Identifying unmet care and support needs

A process of identifying unmet care and support needs was ongoing throughout the project. However, the project commenced with a period of consultation with community groups and agencies and gathering of data on needs. Social services and health recorded unmet need for a period of two weeks. In one area, this stage of the project was greatly facilitated by a participatory appraisal research project being based locally and run by the same organisation that employed the project coordinator. Identifying need in the other area was much more difficult.

(3) Building up relationships and partnerships

The project established a local office base in each area, choosing to site itself in existing community facilities (church premises in both areas), rather than formal statutory or voluntary sector settings. However, identifying a base in one area proved difficult; this impacted adversely on the project, making it hard for the project to develop a community presence.

A process of meeting and building relationships with community members and agencies was an early task. Once the project had met groups and agencies separately, community lunches were held in both areas, providing an opportunity for introductions and cross-fertilisation of ideas in an informal setting. Partnerships with the community (individuals and groups) and, in some cases, agencies, emerged from this process.

> 'What I do, as the team manager, is go to the community lunches, the networking meetings that occur, and that is extremely valuable in as much as I go, you always meet different people, you get talking about what kind of things might be going on at the community centres, what things are going to be set up, how you can link in.' (Health representative)

(4) Working with existing and new community groups

A large role of the project involved capacity building with local groups and networks (ODPM, 2004). The project provided flexible support to help local people set up new community groups and activities, as well as helping existing groups to extend their role. Over the three-year period, the project worked very closely with a number of active community members[1] who were sometimes struggling to get initiatives off the ground; providing support with confidence raising, applying for funding, developing constitutions and so on. Once established, the project provided ongoing support to groups and activities on a needs-led basis. An important part of the project involved helping groups to identify relevant resources to ensure the long-term sustainability of activities (with £500,000 being generated for new initiatives in the area over the three years). One member commented:

> 'Well, to be honest, [the project] has got a lot of knowledge that we haven't got, where to get money from or who to approach if you need help. I mean, I'm totally new to community work.... [The project] has got a lot of contacts, without which we wouldn't, couldn't have got as far as we have.' (Active community member)

(5) Developing a community care development strategy

The final aspect of the process of community care development was working towards the adoption of a community care development strategy at the City of Hull level. This involved participation in city-wide forums and representations to statutory and voluntary sector organisations. Although most of this work was undertaken by the coordinator and Steering Group members, active community members also got involved in some presentations to promote the work of the project in their area to a wider audience. While the project did not succeed in developing a city-wide strategy as intended, it did have a direct input into the establishment of two new projects in Hull: a research project focusing on people with learning difficulties and the community, and a second Community Care Development Project, established in another area by social services and the local council.

> 'To get something fairly new on the agenda and to get it accepted, you know, so that it becomes part of the strategy for the city, takes longer than three years. It's as simple as that really, because you are talking about changing an awful lot of people's minds.' (Project worker)

'Community care' developments

The process of community care development gave rise to a number of new initiatives at the local level that would not have occurred without the input of the project. In most cases, these initiatives represented outcomes of the project, in so far as they were the consequences of the direct intervention of the project. However, due to the facilitative nature of the project, initiatives often represented an interim stage towards final outcomes (for example, the project led to the setting up of activities, which then produced outcomes for those involved). In some cases, outcomes or benefits were contested. The three key types of developments arising from the project are outlined below: community networks, facilities and activities. Within each category, two questions are considered:

- To what extent were these 'community care'-related developments?
- To what extent did the initiatives lead to community care outcomes in terms of meeting unmet support needs within the local communities?

New community networks

One of the main outcomes of the project was the establishment of new community 'networks', where local people and, to a lesser extent, representatives of organisations came together in formally constituted groups to address locally identified needs.

In one area, a 'Community Network' was set up by key community stakeholders to provide support to local residents in addressing issues of individual and community concern. This network was a successful grass-roots development with widespread community support that proved sustainable beyond the end of the project, its development assisted by initial funding from the Community Initiative Budget (£50,000) and a subsequent major grant from the European Regional Development Fund (£234,800) for the appointment of four workers. The network was not centrally concerned with community care issues, rather it responded to wider concerns of the community. However, following considerable worries over the anti-social behaviour of young people in the area, the network established a Youth Network to attempt to address these issues (see sections below). In addition, the network represented the area on other forums and bodies and organised community events more generally. It was recognised by formal statutory and voluntary sector bodies as a key contact point for the local community.

'I think the great value of the network is it provides structure and identity for the community to get into relationship with other bodies.' (Community member)

In the same area, a 'Community Care Forum' was set up specifically to address care and support issues. This was established by the project itself (no further funding) to bring community groups and local agencies together to discuss and respond to community care needs. Regular meetings were held over a period of a year, and while the forum was useful in bringing people together who had shared interests in addressing community care needs, the group dissolved when the pilot project ended. A number of reasons were given for this. First, joint working arrangements had constrained progress, including the lack of representation by health agencies, and group members having different overall objectives for the forum. Second, the group experienced difficulties in getting initiatives off the ground, largely due to a lack of funding and volunteers (see section below). However, the forum ultimately dissolved because ownership by the community and local agencies had not sufficiently been achieved.

These networks did not lead directly to any measurable outcomes for more vulnerable members of the community, but in the case of the Community Network indirectly had an impact through the establishment of activities (see below).

Establishing new/extending existing community facilities

Many agency representatives, and some community members, felt that an important benefit of the project was extending the range of community 'facilities' (that is, buildings/venues) available to local residents. In both the study areas, support to, and work with, the local church led to the opening up/extension of church premises for community purposes, when previously there were inadequate resources available to achieve this. In addition, in one area, a local community centre opened its doors to young people, where previously the centre had been predominately used by older residents. A purpose-equipped youth facility was also established in the local church. In the second area, the project was also instrumental in setting up consultative mechanisms to work towards the establishment of a community centre.

As with community networks, these new and extended facilities did not represent community care outcomes in themselves, but in some cases led to processes and activities that met the needs of more vulnerable members of the community (see below). In addition, local organisers recognised that they themselves benefited hugely from their involvement in running community facilities.

'Well, I repeat myself time and time again, for us, God loving, you've all got husbands, we haven't, to us [the community centre] is a lifeline.'

'It's surprising how many people who come in now are alone....' (Active community members)

New community activities

A range of community activities emerged with the support of the Community Care Development Project. A number of modest but popular activity-based groups were set up including a crafts group, a local history group and an indoor bowls club. A major development in one area was the establishment of a community-led, inter-agency youth network, with outreach and centre-based activities. At the request of the local community centre, a health garage was set up and run from the centre for the local community. A range of other one-off activities were arranged with the assistance of the project, including lunches for older residents and hosting summer activities for disabled children.

Activity-based groups

The activity groups (for crafts, history and indoor bowls) proved successful initiatives that ran during and after the pilot, usually on a weekly basis, attracting an average of 10-15 people each week. They were organised by local community members, and supported by the project. The groups had not conceived of themselves as having a particular role in supporting people who were defined as falling within a community care group. Rather, they encouraged local people to use the activities, irrespective of whether they had a disability, mental health problem and so on. While the groups supported few people who were in touch with formal services, a number of people with disabilities, particularly older people with mobility issues, were members of community groups. In this way, the groups may have offered a preventative, low-level support mechanism to people.

Further, some groups clearly had a general philosophy that incorporated a concern for caring for other community members, or addressing wider social issues that were of direct importance to the health and social welfare of communities. A couple of the groups explained that a guiding principle of the group was to be as welcoming as possible to more vulnerable members of their community who might have limited opportunities to socialise. A couple of interviewees who had worked with the Community Care Development Project felt that this philosophy had been directly influenced by the role of the project and its focus on community care issues.

> 'There are a lot of lonely people on estates that don't see anyone and I think that the idea behind this group was to have somewhere that people could come and, whether you're interested in crafts or not, it's a get-together and I mean, we do different things, and there's always something that someone can do, we try and find something don't we?'
>
> '... even if someone wants to come and have a talk.'
>
> 'If they just want to come and sit and have a cup of tea.'
>
> 'Just to get out of their house and meet somebody....' (Active community members)

Another active community member commented:

> 'It goes further than just groups because what it does is it brings people together, some of the people who come to these groups now didn't mix, didn't socialise, so its alleviating the social exclusion of people, they are becoming socially included ... I think there is an element of it in all groups,

but with these groups, because they were set up under that auspice, I think people have come together wanting to care more.'

Youth activities

Arguably, a definition of community care should include caring for marginalised young people within the community. The Community Network (see above) set up a Youth Network that ran centre-based activities two to three times a week with support from the youth service and sports development, and funding via the Neighbourhood Support Fund (£76,800) and the Single Regeneration Budget 6 (£131,000). Nearly 70 young people between the age of 10 and their early twenties were supported in the first year. This work led to some positive community-oriented benefits. First, the police, youth workers and some community members, although not able to measure the impact precisely, felt that the young people had reduced their anti-social behaviour and criminal activity that had been perceived as impacting on the decline of the area.

> 'This is a particularly bad area, in that the youth in the area were, over the last two years, have been absolutely running amok, its been really difficult to control them.... I mean our aim is to lock them up!... But that is only short-term hits really, in the longer term there has to be some way of stopping the kids doing it the first place, and I think that the Network and its associates have been working with the kids for quite some time now, they've been diverted from the streets into youth clubs ... and [the area] is improving.' (Police representative)

In addition, there were signs that the young people were caring more for themselves and the wider community. One of the aims of the Community Network was to address intergenerational conflict in the area and, in small ways, this was starting to be recognised. For example, some young people would join in with the local bowling group. However, most agency representatives recognised that there was a long way to go before this aspect of the Youth Network's aims would be met. These examples of increasing community caring were only witnessed by a minority of residents, many of whom were already predisposed in favour of attempting to include young people. For many residents, however, the issue of intergenerational problems remained.

Health garage

Responding to the expressed needs of community members, the Community Care Forum (see above) supported the development of a time-limited (six weeks) 'health garage' in one area. This involved health professionals running open sessions offering surgeries, health promotion and allied activities in the local community centre. This initiative involved partnership working between agencies and community players (with funding from the existing Community Health NHS Trust budget and the community providing the venue) that attempted to address both statutory and community aspirations. Agencies were willing to try new ways of working, in community settings, where previously they had little involvement with the local area or community. Community members felt that a number of health benefits had arisen from the work of the health garage, although some of these were contested by health professionals, with the two groups placing importance on different health gains. For example, community members stressed the benefit of being able to discuss and share their health issues with other local people, whereas professionals were concerned that those using the service were often already visiting their general practitioner and they were duplicating effort.

Community lunches for older people

A couple of community lunches for older people were organised by the local church via the Community Care Forum. Despite the church securing funding to continue this activity, the lack of volunteers meant that community lunches were unable to be set up as a regular event.

Summer activities for disabled children

The local community centre hosted a summer camp, run by a voluntary organisation, for children with learning difficulties. However, as with the health garage, outcomes appeared to be contested. The workers had found the experience of using the local community centre quite problematic. They felt that the venue had been unsuitable as it had not been possible to provide the level of protective environment that they had hoped for their young users with learning difficulties. While the centre's committee and volunteers had been very welcoming, they had found other users of the centre less happy. They also lost equipment following a break-in. It was not possible to comment on whether the young people with learning difficulties were troubled by any of these issues. However, another local disability organisation explained how the same local community centre had been always welcoming to their users, with a couple of people regularly attending local activities and enjoying the social benefits of taking part in activity-based groups.

Generally, there was a perception that it was more difficult for community groups to support people actively with more pronounced community care needs. Social and health agencies explained that this might not be appropriate in many cases as often skilled staff might be required, but there were not the resources available to provide this lower-level support.

> 'Really I suppose a lot of our client group may be too ill or their needs are too complex really for them to be accessing local community things such as that because their needs couldn't be met, you know there wouldn't necessarily be the skilled staff there to help.' (Social services representative)

A successful model?

The overall aim of the project was to encourage and facilitate communities in their support of their more vulnerable members. The experience of the Community Care Development Project was that there was already significant informal caring of families, friends and neighbours within the two communities. The aim of the project was to explore whether these considerable resources could be developed within community groups and other grass-roots activity.

The extent to which the project's main aim was achieved is largely dependent on how 'community care' is understood. Overall, the project was most successful in addressing broad community development issues. However, as indicated above, community representatives defined the project's 'community care' role very widely as promoting a healthy and caring community. Using this definition, much of the general community development work could be considered as contributing to a community's ability to care for itself and its members. Increased participation and local activities are likely to be signs of a healthy and functioning community.

Using a more specific definition of community care, concerned with the support of more vulnerable members of the community, the project was less successful in meeting its aims. Nonetheless, the project did succeed in a number of areas. The project promoted and encouraged the development of a caring and supportive approach within new community activities. Community networks and forums also examined community and health issues that they might not otherwise have done. In addition, the work with young people, although problematic and challenging, appeared to mark an important turning point in the communities' ability to care for their youngest members. In addition, it was clear that young people were explicitly viewed by other local residents as a 'problem' and barrier in developing a 'caring' community. For example, many older residents did not feel safe living in the area. Addressing youth and intergenerational issues was likely to be a prerequisite to the development of other community care initiatives of a more traditional nature. In addition, prevention in terms of community safety issues and social exclusion agendas was being addressed as well as the support needs of young people.

Little activity was developed that sought to include local people who had more traditional community care needs. This did not mean that some community groups did not include individuals with, for example, depression, mobility problems or mild learning disabilities, rather that communities did not necessarily find it easy to establish contact with specific scheme-based initiatives in the area, or people who were presently isolated in the community.

There was a range of barriers to community care development. First, the community did not feel as though it possessed the relevant skills and experience to provide some types of support. In consequence, while community groups were able to set up and sustain interest-based activities, more complex social or health interventions required the explicit support of local reliable and skilled volunteers. The lack of social capital in the two areas meant that few volunteers were available to offer their services. In both areas there appeared only to be a small number of volunteers who were willing to, and interested in, organising groups and activities, reflecting the national lower levels of volunteering in deprived areas (Home Office, 2002) and the need for ongoing support in this area (Civil Renewal Unit, 2003).

Second, for larger interventions, such as the youth work and health garage, formal support from statutory or voluntary agencies was paramount alongside community volunteers. However, different priorities, timescales and cultures within the statutory sector could sometimes delay or even undermine the work of community groups. In addition, frequent staff changes in the formal sectors sometimes made planning of initiatives more difficult. While the project assisted key active community members in successfully negotiating and working alongside more formal agencies, the problem of power imbalance between the two sectors remained.

Third, it was also important to be aware that 'needs' were often contested, often defined differently by different parties, making the overall impact difficult to assess. For example, meeting some of the needs of young people (for example, in opening up community facilities for them), meant that some other members of the community felt that their needs had been put at risk (for example, in not feeling comfortable in using the community facility). The statutory sector also measured need differently to the community, as seen in the case of the health garage. The project attempted to bridge the gap between the two sectors but it was clear that ongoing development work was required to enable community and statutory sectors to communicate more effectively and agree (and fund) joint priorities for local areas, hopefully an area that will receive greater attention following the *Choosing Health* White Paper (DH, 2004) and Communities for Health pilots.

Perhaps most importantly, the experience of the Community Care Development Project highlighted how communities tended to prioritise high-profile and impact issues at a local level over care and support needs. In one area, pressing issues of widespread poverty, crime, out-migration and house clearances made it particularly difficult for the community to address more specific community care issues. In this way, the local context directly shaped the nature of the project. A lack of other community workers meant that the project felt a responsibility to respond to these community development needs. This meant that unmet support and care needs were at risk of being marginalised in local discussions as they were more individualised and therefore less visible. The experience of the pilot project suggests that community initiatives need to be supported by the formal sector in order to achieve successful community care development. However, even more importantly, there remains a clear need for future projects of this nature to support the involvement of community care and Supporting People service users more explicitly in local planning processes.

Note

[1] The term 'active community member' was chosen by the Joseph Rowntree Foundation Advisory Group as the preferable term to describe local people who were actively involved in community activities (including those leading initiatives).

References

Audit Commission (1998) *Home Alone: The Role of Housing in Community Care*, London: Audit Commission.

Audit Commission (2005) *Supporting People*, London: Audit Commission.

Barr, A., Stenhouse, C. and Henderson, P. (2000) *Caring Communities: A Challenge for Social Inclusion*, York: York Publishing Services.

Bayley, M. J. (1973) *Mental Handicap and Community Care*, London: Routledge and Kegan Paul.

Brownhill, S. and Darke, J. (1998) *'Rich Mix': Inclusive Strategies for Urban Regeneration*, Bristol: The Policy Press.

Burrows, R. (1997) *Contemporary Patterns of Residential Mobility in Relation to Social Housing in England*, York: Centre for Housing Policy, University of York.

Civil Renewal Unit (2003) *Building Civil Renewal: Government Support for Community Capacity Building and Proposals for Change*, London: Home Office.

Craig, G. (1989) 'Community work and the state', *Community Development Journal*, vol 24, no 1, pp 3-18.

DH (Department of Health) (2004) *Choosing Health: Making Healthy Choices Easier*, White Paper, London: DH.

Edwards, C. (2001) 'Inclusion in regeneration: A place for disabled people?', *Urban Studies*, vol 38, no 2, pp 267-86.

Fletcher, P. (2000) 'From client to community: linking community care into the regeneration agenda', *Housing, Support and Care*, vol 3, no 3, pp 11-14.

Home Office (2002) *Active Communities: Initial Findings of the Home Office 2001 Citizenship Survey*, www.homeoffice.gov.uk/

Home Office (2004) *Firm Foundations*, London: Home Office.

ODPM (Office of the Deputy Prime Minister) (2003) *Sustainable Communities: Building for the Future*, London: ODPM.

ODPM (2005a) *Creating Sustainable Communities: Supporting Independence: Consultation on a Strategy for the Supporting People Programme*, London: ODPM.

ODPM (2005b) *Sustainable Communities: Homes for All*, London: ODPM.

ODPM (2005c) *Improving Delivery of Mainstream Services in Deprived Areas: The Role of Community Involvement*, London: ODPM.

Putman, R. D. (2000) *Bowling Alone: The Collapse and Revival of American Community*, New York: Simon and Schuster.

Quilgars, D. (2000) *Low Intensity Support Services: A Systematic Review of Effectiveness*, Bristol: The Policy Press.

SEU (Social Exclusion Unit) (1998) *Bringing Britain Together: A National Strategy for Neighbourhood Renewal*, Cm 4045, London: HMSO.

Taylor, P. (2006) *Who are the Capacity Builders? A Study of Provision for Strengthening the Role of Local Communities*, London: Community Development Foundation.

ELEVEN

Neighbourhood Care Scheme: the 'Coronation Street' model of community care

Marylynn Fyvie-Gauld and Sean de Podesta

Introduction

This chapter draws on an evaluation of a Neighbourhood Care Scheme in Brighton and Hove. It presents a unique example of community and community spirit and demonstrates how volunteering can flourish in such a way that everyone benefits. Since 1998 the scheme has grown from 23 users and seven volunteers to involve over 300 users and 126 volunteers, representing in 2005–06 a total of over 2,812 visits and 5,098 volunteer hours. This scheme fits well with the philosophy of the White Paper *Our Health, Our Care, Our Say: A New Direction for Community Services* (DH, 2006), which calls for a more prominent role for the community and voluntary sectors in the delivery of social care.

The chapter questions, however, the capacity of volunteers to deliver such care on a consistent and long-term basis.

Background

The government has long recognised the important contribution the voluntary sector makes towards citizenship as a form of responsibility for others. As Charles Clarke pointed out when he was Home Secretary, 'The voluntary and community sector is the invisible glue that holds society together, builds social capital and empowers individuals to make a difference in people's lives' (ChangeUp and ChangeAhead, 2006). It is the ability of the community and voluntary sector to harness social capital within a network that helps create social cohesion. As Putman (2000, p 19) argues, 'social capital' calls attention to the fact that civic virtue is most powerful when embedded in a sense network of reciprocal social relations'. Perhaps because of the local nature of the community and voluntary sector it is in a unique position to create networks of trust that bind communities together and create opportunities for cooperative action (Cohen and Prusak, 2001, p 4). The community and voluntary sector is able to act flexibly and it is this that creates its strength by responding directly to the diversity of the community (Bowers et al, 2006).

As this chapter shows, the Neighbourhood Care Scheme (NCS) is well placed to create the opportunities necessary for people to volunteer and to provide a service that supports people within the community and helps in the fight against social exclusion. Perhaps because of its community ownership the scheme has the flexibility and also the concern of a small organisation; as one volunteer respondent suggested, 'it is homely'.

Certainly, given its aims, the NCS might have a role to play in the overall provision of health and social care to individuals in their own homes. However, its relative success in recruiting and utilising volunteers to provide neighbourly support to vulnerable people raises questions about how society is organised so that these neighbourly impulses have to be formally directed because occasions to exercise them do not naturally arise. This is a question not simply about how health and social care is provided to individuals who need it, but of how fellow citizens/neighbours relate to each other within the existing social set-up.

Background to the NCS

Brighton & Hove NCS is a good-neighbour scheme supporting older people (aged 60+) and other age groups with physical/sensory disabilities living on their own by recruiting local volunteers to support them in a variety of ways from social visits, through assistance with shopping and going out, to simple DIY and gardening. It was started in the 1980s as a project geographically conforming to the social services 'patch' areas and local government wards. The scheme was based on a key volunteer in each neighbourhood coordinating other volunteers who would visit vulnerable individuals identified by social services. This structure functioned well until the key volunteers left, after which time it became hard to maintain an active organisational presence in the different neighbourhoods. In 1998 Brighton & Hove City Council provided a grant to fund a volunteer coordinator; at that point the scheme had seven active volunteers and 23 users on its books. The new coordinator had the task of reviving the scheme in its existing areas and starting it in two additional neighbourhoods.

The years 1999–2003 showed steady increases in the number of scheme users, the number of volunteers and the amount of work that volunteers carried out. However, by March 2003 the scheme had reached saturation point, reflected in declining volunteer numbers and a backlog of assessments of new referrals. The scheme would have ultimately failed – ironically, a victim of its own success – had it not been able to attract significant new funding from the National Lottery Community Fund (now the Big Lottery) and private trusts to employ additional staff in 2004–05. In that year the scheme was again very active, its volunteers making over 2,200 visits and delivering 4,900 hours of direct support, compared to 3,500 hours in the previous year (see Figure 11.1). It was also remarkably successful in recruiting volunteers – over 60 in the period. By March 2005 it had 135 registered volunteers and over 300 users, and was again approaching saturation point (de Podesta, 1999, 2001).

Figure 11.1: Comparison of figures, April 1999–March 2005

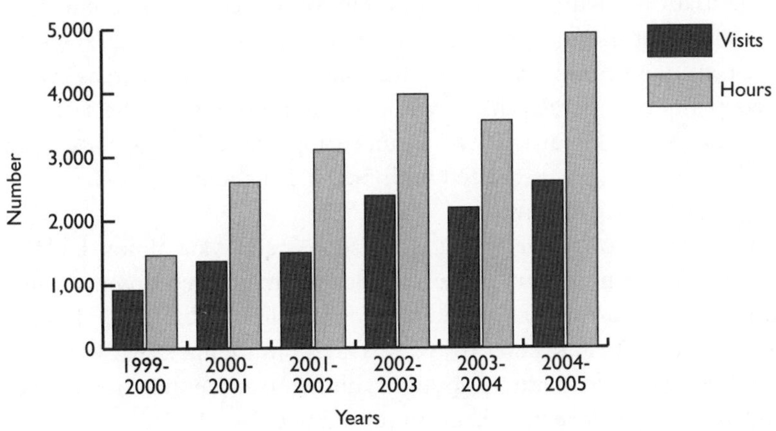

The evaluation

A three-year evaluation, on which this chapter is based, was commissioned by Brighton & Hove NCS and funded by the National Lottery Community Fund (now the Big Lottery). The aim of the evaluation was to assess the success of the NCS in terms of supporting people within the community and thereby eliminating social exclusion as well as providing a social service. In addition, the evaluation looked at why people volunteer and the reason behind the success of the NCS in attracting volunteers. Importantly, the evaluation determined whether the NCS is a unique scheme resting on the nature of a particular type of community or one that can be replicated, with or without modification, in other communities.

In order to make the evaluation as participatory as possible the volunteers were invited to design the questionnaires and conduct the interviews, with the University of Brighton acting as a managing agency. In 2004 and 2005 a total of 50 randomly selected volunteers were approached and 40 agreed to participate in telephone interviews. In 2006 it was decided to reduce the strain on the volunteers and, rather than interviewing them, mail out self-completing questionnaires, which resulted in a reduced total of 40 volunteers. Out of a total of 28 randomly selected users asked, 20 agreed to participate in face-to-face interviews in 2004 and 20 again in 2005.

Findings

More women than men volunteer, especially in social work and health organisations (Kuntz, 2001). Our random selection of volunteers revealed that 80% (n=32) were women compared with 20% (n=8) men, an uneven ratio reflecting the construction of women as carers, occupying the private, inside world while men occupy the political outside world (Saraga, 1998). Kuntz supports this, suggesting that male volunteers are associated with non-caring activities such as civil protection organisations.

Our evaluation suggests that while some people are almost lifelong volunteers, many others come to volunteering in retirement. While this may be as a way of continuing the discipline of the workplace, or as the complete antitheses to work (Davis Smith and Gay, 2006), the NCS appears able to attract younger volunteers more than many other organisations that seem reliant on retired people.

Volunteering

> 'I could not manage my life at present without my wonderful volunteer.' (Scheme user)

That voluntary and community groups can in some way rejuvenate or replace neighbourliness is a long-held belief, particularly by governments who have relied on the voluntary and community sector to plug the gaps left by the statutory services. Northmore et al (2006) argue that voluntary and community groups occupy a unique position spanning the statutory sector and the community and are able to provide ad hoc as well as more structured provision. They state: 'We believe the sector can develop and champion initiatives to stimulate and maintain neighbourly behaviour' (Northmore et al, 2006, p 61). Such community and voluntary activities depend on volunteers.

Our research asked how the volunteers rated volunteering, revealing that 97% (n=39) answered excellent or good. Respondents were also asked in what ways the NCS was of value to them personally. Clary et al (1998) identify five possible reasons for volunteering: shared values, self-development, social reasons, improvement to a career and a way of giving back to the community. Our evaluation replicated these reasons.

> 'Chance to help the community and meet nice people.' (Female, 35-44)

> 'It gives me contact with people outside my own home and meeting people.' (Male, 65-74)

> 'Gives me a reason for living, my son and husband have gone, it is nice to have someone who needs me.' (Female, 65-74)

> 'Doing something for someone else, you make a difference to someone's life; you show them that they have not been forgotten.' (Female, 35-44)

> 'The feeling of being appreciated by others.' (Female, 18-24)

> 'Greater sense of befriending skills – communication skills improved.' (Female, 45-54)

> 'More patient, greater understanding of the elderly.' (Female, 25-34)

> 'Patience, learning to speak clearly, understanding old age and lack of movement.' (Female, 45-54)

Values of volunteering

What creates value for volunteers? While altruism and self-interest have emerged as the dominant motives for volunteering, these should not be considered as two distinct and static forces; rather they should be seen in a combination of dynamic influences (Cnaan and

Goldberg-Glen, 1991). Our evaluation sought to find out how our volunteer respondents considered the NCS was of value to the people they assisted and to the community as a whole:

'Lonely people, pleased to see you.' (Female, 65-74)

'A huge difference, people are very grateful.' (Female, 45-54)

'The work I do for them benefits them.' (Male, 65-74)

The majority felt that volunteering had a positive impact on the community:

'Keeps the community together.' (Female, 35-44)

'It promotes a good and helpful atmosphere in the neighbourhood.' (Female, 35-44)

'For any one person to feel better is an improvement for the community.' (Female, 24-44)

'It improves any neighbourhood by creating a community spirit.' (Female, 25-34)

The evaluation wanted to know how the volunteers personally valued volunteering. The responses appeared to corroborate Hodgkinson and Weitzman's (1992) study, which revealed that volunteer involvement does appear to a large degree to be motivated by personal benefit:

'Selfishly I feel I brighten someone's day, for one afternoon a week it fills a lonely person's time.' (Female, 55-64)

'It is an opportunity to do something which is of help to others. I feel good about it. I enjoy being useful to others.' (Female, 65-74)

'Gives you an anchor, it's a commitment. It is nice to feel you can help someone who appreciates the company.' (Female, 65-74)

'Getting a sense of fulfilment.' (Female, 18-24)

'Feeling pleasure at being useful, gratified to be able to do something.' (Male, 65-74)

Volunteer motivation

What makes people volunteer, what motivates them and what sustains them in this role? There is a consensus that to a large extent volunteer motivation can be divided into two paradigms; altruism and egotism. According to Batson et al (1995) one cannot occur without the other and, as Atkinson and Birch (1978) argue, even if the motive behind the action may be constructed as selfish, the act itself is in all probability entirely benevolent.

According to Bussell and Forbes (2001), community activities attract half the population in the UK to volunteer at some point in their lives. However, while the number of calls on volunteers has intensified in order to address an ever-increasingly varied range of work, it would seem that the numbers of volunteers has peaked, which has inevitably led to organisations recruiting from a diminishing pool of volunteers (Gaskin, 1998).

With this in mind, and taken against the background that many organisations find recruiting let alone retaining volunteers problematic, we asked the volunteers what it was that helped them sustain their role as volunteers. Figure 11.2 shows that, as expected, the majority of volunteers said that they continued volunteering because it was rewarding. However, many also stated that being able to visit at times convenient to them was equally important. The issue of time is an important aspect in creating opportunities for people to volunteer. Nichols and King (1998) suggest that while people want to volunteer, the time it takes conflicts and competes with other aspects of their lives such as family and paid work. The strategy employed by the NCS is to give volunteers the opportunity to spend as much time as they feel able to commit, from half an hour per week or less to several hours. It

Figure 11.2: Factors that influence volunteering

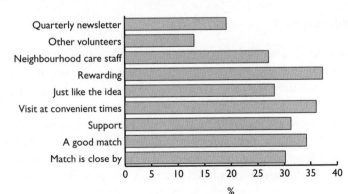

would appear that this is one of the most important aspects in volunteer retention; it also has the advantage of allowing busy professionals, inter alia, the opportunity to volunteer and thus create a large pool of volunteers and correspondingly increase the level of service.

The NCS operates in seven neighbourhoods of Brighton and Hove, encompassing well over 25,000 households and this local focus of the scheme also makes it possible to involve volunteers who might not otherwise be able to do voluntary work (for example, individuals with mobility problems, parents with young children).

Figure 11.2 also indicates that ensuring a good match between volunteer and user is essential. Again, it would appear that the localised nature of the scheme gives the organisation the benefit of being able to know both volunteers and users and in this way provide a suitable match.

An example of this was when XXX adopted Jack, a blind and lame retired working farm dog. He was a border collie. She did not want to leave him without proper attention when she was at work, so she contacted the NCS to see if an older person might enjoy his company. One of the NCS users suffered from chronic obstructive pulmonary disease, had a heart pacemaker and needed oxygen 16 hours a day. Her life had felt empty since she had had to give up her own border collie owing to her poor health. For the last three months of her life, however, until she went into hospital for the last time, Jack was dropped off at her flat each morning and picked up after work. The NCS user said her life was filled.

> 'Now I don't sit here feeling sorry for myself. I have a reason to get dressed in the morning, and take a short walk every day. I meet the neighbours and they're getting to know Jack.'

Volunteer support

Less attention has been paid in the literature to the contextual effects on volunteering and while evidence seems to be rather mixed, the impact of the community, regional characteristics and the organisation they volunteer with would appear to be important factors in the decision of volunteers to continue with their voluntary work (Kuntz, 2001). Some of the volunteers in our evaluation had been involved with the NCS for a long time and we wanted to ascertain if indeed, as Kuntz suggested, the organisation played an active role in their retention.

Figure 11.3 reveals that the most important form of support was the volunteer coordinator by telephone and in person. Our evaluation indicated that having an immediate response appeared to be important for the well-being of the volunteers. This illustrates that while organisations play an important part in sustaining volunteers, what underpins a successful structure is the nature of the personnel within the organisation. The role of the coordinator is clearly a key role in maintaining contact with the volunteers and helps both increase the volunteer numbers and assist with their retention.

Figure 11.3: Most important support

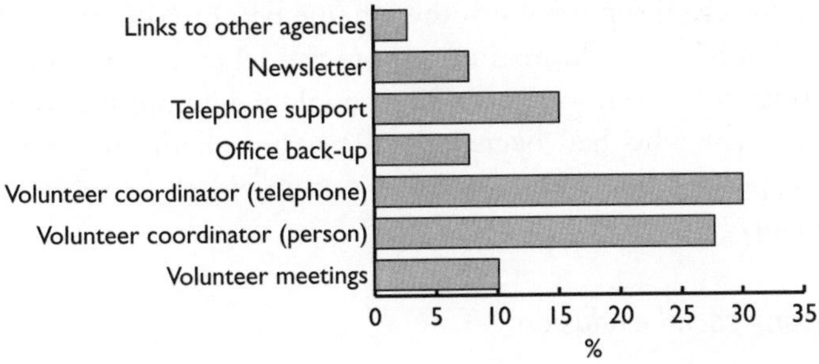

Supporting the users

Important aspects of the scheme are the psychological benefits of feeling supported or having the company of a reliable friend. Neighbours helping each other is a very basic, easily understood, human activity. One particular function of the NCS highlights the important difference in the complex relationship between the user and those people who are paid to care and those who volunteer. A great deal has been written on the gendered nature of care but rather less on the differences between paid care and unpaid voluntary care. Rose Galvin (2004) argues that people prefer to pay for services rather than rely on the goodwill of others, suggesting that paid care removes the obligation to feel and express gratitude for any help received. One the other hand, Deborah Stone (1999) maintains that once care becomes public it is redefined as a 'problem' contained by costs. In between this dichotomy of views, volunteering occupies a unique position where support is given on the basis of mutuality rather than patronage and is not merely a one-directional activity; it is the outcome of a relationship where the 'capabilities and autonomy of the recipient are foremost' (Side and Keefe, 2004, p 137).

A small example of the mutuality of volunteering took place at the end of December 2004 when a volunteer on her first visit to see a woman of 94 helped her to write a cheque out in aid of the victims of the Asian tsunami. When she got home the volunteer thought, 'I could do that', and also made a donation to the tsunami relief effort. Thus, a woman who could not leave her room in Brighton was able in a small way to help someone on the other side of the world and also influence her much younger volunteer – it is a two-way relationship.

In different areas and times of their lives, it is possible for an individual to be both a beneficiary and a volunteer. In 2004-05 four people who had received support from the scheme became volunteers. They included an 87-year-old man for whom the scheme had done some decorating and who now visits a 98-year-old neighbour for company, and a woman who had been helped by the scheme to overcome her agoraphobia and who now takes out an elderly woman in her wheelchair.

Combating social exclusion

Volunteering has a vital role to play within any community, not only because of the work carried out but also as a vehicle to help combat social inclusion. The transnational Volunteering into Participation (VIP) found that volunteers across five countries were able to offer help to people who otherwise would not have received any assistance, either through lack of social services funding, or because excluded groups are not adequately reached by official agencies (Kinds et al, 1999). The Social Exclusion Unit is currently running a number of projects looking at how mainstream services can meet the needs of excluded older people and initial findings have revealed the importance of involving local communities in the delivery of services (DH, 2005). Social exclusion was identified as the single largest issue in research undertaken by the Older People's Programme and commissioned by the Community Service Volunteers, Help the Aged and the British Red Cross (Easterbrook et al, 2006). The research found that the relationship between the volunteer and the person receiving the service was entirely different from that which exists between a service user and the statutory services, being more akin to friendship than duty, and that this difference is one that is valued.

For a woman in her fifties suffering from depression and chronic ME, a young local woman (a freelance journalist) provides regular social company, while several practical volunteers have done jobs (carpentry, decluttering) to make her new maisonette safer for her to live in.

Age and physical or sensory disability can effectively exclude people from the wider community and many of the people who use the NCS are largely housebound.

Figure 11.4 reveals that much of the volunteers' time is spent in low-intensity types of assistance of the kind that the government refers to in terms of reducing social exclusion. The government has identified this type of contact as having the advantage of early prevention, acting as a warning system and referral channel to other agencies as well as maintaining people in their own homes (DH, 2005, p 46).

> 'I know that if I do need my grass cutting, I just need to get in contact with XXX who rounds up the group to cut my grass.' (Male, 65–74)

> 'A great help with financial affairs and a lot of fun to talk to.' (Female, 65–74)

> 'I have wonderful care, out shopping.' (Female, 45–54)

Isolation, as previously mentioned, is one of the causes of depression and affects between 10% and 16% of those aged 65 and over. This is more than likely to be an underrepresentation of the reality as often depression in old age is treated as a normal part of ageing by older people and professionals alike. Rather than being a product of age, depression often occurs with the onset of illness among older people (NIMH, 2003).

Figure 11.4: Volunteer jobs

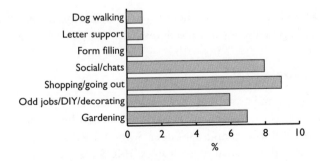

The Green Paper *Independence, Well-being and Choice* (DH, 2005, p 21) states that the proportion of older people living alone is likely to increase and that at present some 21% of people over 65 see their family or friends less than once a week and some not at all. A National Opinion Poll found that one in five people are alone for more than 12 hours per day (Age Concern, 2005). Such isolation has a negative impact on older people, especially those whose social life has diminished along with their physical abilities, and is a major cause of depression. Depression often goes unrecognised in old age because old age is often depicted as a depressing time of life (Manthorpe and Iliffe, 2005) and there is an expectation of depression among older people who will then not seek appropriate help, thinking that it is a normal adjunct to the ageing process.

With the expected increases in the numbers of older people, along with the government's commitment to a greater focus on preventative service or early intervention as set out in the White Paper *Our Health, Our Care, Our Say: A New Direction for Community Services* (DH, 2006), there would seem to be a very important place for groups such as the NCS, as described in this chapter, which attempt to help support people in their communities.

Perhaps as important are the relationships that develop between volunteers and the people they visit. The relationships may have boundaries, but importantly they are not professional relationships.

> 'The volunteer is a vital person, I am the only person who sees her socially.' (Female, 45–54)

> 'She looks forward to my visits; I am the only person to take her out.' (Female, 45–54)

> '[The visits] are of enormous value, my client is housebound and the visits prevent isolation and loneliness.' (Female, 25–34)

As shown in Chapter Twelve there is a key role for the voluntary sector in combating mental health problems (Manthorpe and Iliffe, 2005).

Conclusion

> 'The scheme provides a very valuable support. Help is given through the development of personal relationships, mutually beneficial to user and volunteer. Something that cannot be replicated in formal care services.' (NCS user)

Volunteers can provide an enormous human resource, contributing a number of different skills to assist those in need. For some they represent the only contact with people not being paid to help them. Essentially, volunteering provides that independent human interface that is so necessary and beneficial for people's well-being in the community, particularly for people confined because of incapacity and physical limitations (Gerain, 2002; Ostwald and Runge, 2004; Godfrey et al, 2005). It may also be argued that the connections between volunteers and beneficiaries of the scheme not only help to include people in the community but actually help to create the community. Putman (2000) contends that it is this element of social capital that not only helps the individual but also helps create a healthy and civil society.

Increasing pressures on statutory funding to cut the cost of caring and raise the levels of eligibility has inevitably resulted in a decline in low-level support. This has in turn exacerbated the demand for volunteer services. The challenge, then, for any voluntary or community group is to entice busy individuals to volunteer their time and then, importantly, to retain their services. While NCS policies and procedures are continually being developed it does not insist on an unduly rigid interpretation of these, which would stifle the vitality of the scheme. One of the major advantages of this flexible way of working is that the NCS is able to attract volunteers who may not normally volunteer. Within its criteria for selection of both beneficiaries and volunteers, it aims to include as wide a variety of people as possible. The variety of volunteers and their wide range of skills have enabled the scheme to carry out some large jobs and safely support individuals in very difficult situations. Equally, by having among its users individuals with needs that are relatively easy to address, the scheme can utilise the contribution of volunteers whose skills or confidence are limited. On many levels the NCS volunteers and users recreate and rejuvenate communities where neighbours help neighbours in a 'Coronation Street' model of community care.

The NCS is able to respond to individuals in a way that the statutory sector would find difficult. Not constrained within the target–setting culture of government, the NCS is able to operate as a fluid agency, sometimes providing unique and often innovative solutions to problems.

In the White Paper *Our Health, Our Care, Our Say: A New Direction for Community Services* (DH, 2006) the government lays great store on community involvement in health and social care services. As Barnes (2005, p 17) argues, quoting Curran (2002), care 'should be considered as a "public good"' in that if it is removed it is not only detrimental to those being cared for but also incurs a substitution caring cost to the state. It is therefore surprising that community groups such as the

NCS are increasingly experiencing difficulty in obtaining funding. The lack of statutory support for organisations like the NCS means they have to expend valuable time seeking financial support and are never certain of their future funding. In terms of costs, the NCS, as described in this chapter, provides volunteer hours equivalent to £73,500 per annum, taken at a cost of £15 per hour. However, this is a cumbersome calculation and does not take into account other costs in terms of loss of the effectively channelled, freely given competence and goodwill of hundreds of individuals involved in the NCS.

There are two enormous disadvantages that would result from the closure of any such community groups. First, there is the obvious loss of services to the community and to the users, who would not, in the present climate, have these services replaced by any statutory agency. Second, and perhaps more importantly, there is the loss of the symbiotic structure of volunteers, users and community built up over the years that would be almost impossible and extremely expensive to recreate. It is difficult to know what will happen to the NCS when the Lottery funding runs out.

References

Age Concern (2005) *NOP Generation Survey*, London: Age Concern.

Atkinson, J. W. and Birch, D. (1978) *Introduction to Motivation*, London: Macmillan.

Barnes, N. (2005) *Caring and Social Justice*, Basingstoke: Palgrave Macmillan.

Batson, C. D., Turk, C., Shaw, L. and Klein, T. (1995) 'Information function of empathic emotion: learning that we value the other welfare', *Journal of Personality and Social Psychology*, vol 68, no 2, pp 300-13.

Bowers, H., Macadam, A., Meena, P. and Smith, C. (2006) *Making a Difference through Volunteering*, London: CSV.

Bussell, H. and Forbes, D. (2001) 'Understanding the volunteer market: the what, where, who and why of volunteering', *International Journal of Nonprofit and Voluntary Sector Marketing*, vol 7, no 3, pp 244-57.

ChangeUp & ChangeAhead (2006) www.changeahead.org/html/intelligence.html

Clary, E. G., Snyder, M., Ridge, R. D., Copeland, J., Stukas, A. A., Haugen, J., et al (1998) 'Understanding and assessing the motivation of volunteers: a functional approach', *Journal of Personality and Social Psychology*, vol 74, no 6, pp 1516-30.

Cnaan, R. A. and Goldberg-Glen, R. S. (1991) 'Measuring motivation to volunteer in human services', *Journal of Applied Behavioural Sciences*, vol 27, no 3, pp 269-84.

Cohen, D. and Prusak, L. (2001) *In Good Company: How Social Capital makes Organizations Work*, Boston, MA: Harvard Business School Press.

Davis Smith, J. and Gay, P. (2006) *Active Ageing in Active Communities: Volunteering and the Transition to Retirement*, Bristol/York: The Policy Press/Joseph Rowntree Foundation.

De Podesta, S. (1999) *Just What the Doctor Ordered*, Brighton: Neighbourhood Care Scheme.

De Podesta, S. (2001) *Brighton & Hove Neighbourhood Care Scheme, Business Plan 2001–2005*, Brighton: Neighbourhood Care Scheme.

DH (2005) *Independence, Well-being and Choice: Our Vision for the Future of Social Care for England*, London: HMSO.

DH (2006) *Our Health, Our Care, Our Say: A New Direction for Community Services*, White Paper, London: HMSO.

Easterbrook, L., Bowers, H., Macadam, A., Patel, M. and Smith, C. (2006) *'Short Cut' to Making a Difference through Volunteering No. 1: Overview of the Research*, London: CSV.

Galvin, R. (2004) 'Challenging the need for gratitude: comparisons between paid and unpaid care for disabled people', *Journal of Sociology*, vol 40, no 2, pp 137-56.

Gaskin, K. (1998) 'Vanishing volunteers: are young people losing interest in volunteering?', *Voluntary Action*, no 1, pp 33-43.

Gerain, S. (2002) 'Corporate volunteering: an extension of corporate citizenship or a strategic escape from corporate giving', Paper presented at the Fifth International Conference 'Transforming Civil Society, Citizenship and Governance', Cape Town, South Africa, 7-10 July.

Godfrey, M., Townsend, J. and Denby, R. (2005) *Building a Good Life for Older People in Local Communities: The Experience of Ageing in Time and Place*, York: Joseph Rowntree Foundation.

Hodgkinson, V. A. and Weitzman, M. S. (1992) *Giving and Volunteering in the United States*, Washington, DC: Independent Sector.

Kinds, H., Munz, A. and Horn, L. (1999) *Volunteering into Participation: A Strategy for Social Inclusion*, Volunteering England Community Partnerships Consultants.

Kuntz, L. I. (2001) 'Self-interest or goodwill?', *Unesco Courier*, vol 54, no 6, p 26.

Manthorpe, J. and Iliffe, S. (2005) 'What should you expect at your age?', *Openmind*, no 132, pp 6-8.

Nichols, G. and King, L. (1998) 'Volunteers in the Guide Association: problems and solutions', *Voluntary Action*, vol 1, no 1, pp 21-32.

Northmore, S. M., Sampson, R. and Harland, S. (2006) 'Involving the voluntary and community sector', in T. Pilch (ed) *Neighbourliness*, London: Age Concern, The Smith Institute.

Ostwald, S. and Runge, A. (2004) 'Volunteers speak out: motivations for volunteering', *The Journal of Volunteer Administration*, vol 22, no 1, pp 5-11.

Putnam, R. (2000) *Bowling Alone: The Collapse and Revival of American Community*, New York: Simon and Schuster.

Saraga, E. (1998) 'Abnormal, unnatural and immoral? The social construction of sexualities', in E. Sarage (ed) *Embodying the Social: Constructions of Differences*, London: Routledge, pp 139-85.

Side, K. and Keefe, J. (2004) 'The role of unpaid work in maintaining individual and community health in Atlantic Canada: a case study', *Canadian Woman Studies*, vol 24, no 1, pp 129-38.

Stone, D. (1999) 'Care and trembling', *The American Prospect*, no 43, pp 61-2.

TWELVE

Challenging stigma and combating social exclusion through befriending

Bill McGowan and Claire Jowitt

Introduction

Mental health policy has made great strides in the last 20 to 25 years in attempting to shift the delivery of mental health services from the large outdated asylum system. The attempts at consolidating the closure of the asylums, while ensuring the build-up of alternative locally based community care services, have not been without their problems. Criticisms have been levelled at the fragmented and piecemeal build-up of alternative forms of community care throughout the 1980s and 1990s, where gaps in services have been highlighted and where concerns have centred around public safety in relation to homicides in the community and the increased prevalence of mental health problems among the homeless and in the prison population. The wider policy initiatives leading to the mixed economy of healthcare, the creation of the health/social care divide and the emphasis on greater involvement of communities and the voluntary sector in delivering services for vulnerable people have been a mixed blessing.

In the coastal town of Hastings in the southeast of England, a Befriending Scheme for people with mental health problems was established in 1989. The scheme was set up on a shoestring and survived for 15 years during a turbulent period of major national policy changes by attracting core funding from a succession of commissioning agencies beginning with health services, social services, the local health trust and latterly the local primary care group. It was a well-respected local service making a difference to the lives of vulnerable individuals with mental health problems and received the local civic pride award for its work in 1997. However, the service was voluntarily decommissioned in January 2006 as it had failed to attract adequate funding for service delivery and development (core funding had for a number of years been diminishing) and there were concerns regarding its ability to maintain the quality standards for which it was renowned. This chapter takes a critical look at the functions of the Befriending Scheme against a background of severe socioeconomic deprivation and explores what we have learned about its potential role in challenging stigma and combating social exclusion within communities.

Hastings: the socioeconomic context

The southeast of England is perceived as an affluent area on a broad range of socioeconomic indicators. Despite this, there are identifiable pockets of social and economic deprivation throughout the region. Hastings, a coastal town in the county of East Sussex, is a mixed urban/rural resort and retirement centre (Forest and Gordon, 1991; OPCS, 1991). It resides within the wider Hastings and Rother Area, which combines a significant rural area with the urban centres of Hastings, St Leonards and Bexhill. During the 1980s and 1990s these three urban areas displayed high levels of deprivation and poverty with particularly high levels of unemployment, unmet mental health needs, families under pressure and a large population of people of pensionable age and above (East Sussex Brighton & Hove Area Health Authority, 1998; East Sussex County Council, 1998). Hastings, with a population of 82,000, displayed high levels of overcrowding, low levels of home ownership and car ownership, low levels of property values and was dependent on a low average wage service sector (Hastings Borough Council, 1998). It had the highest level of teenage pregnancies in the county, a high level of standardised death rates for both men and women and very high suicide rates. This consistent picture of relative material and socioeconomic deprivation was reflected in the Jarman Indices, Breadline Britain Indices and the Department of the Environment Index of Local Condition scores for the area (East Sussex County Council, 1998).

A community under pressure

The health status of a community is closely associated with the wider social, economic and physical environment in which people live. What determines the socio-emotional resilience and health of an individual (or lack of it) is often where they live, the occupational group to which they belong, their socioeconomic status, quality of life, level of self-esteem and sense of identity as mediated through the 'lived social experience' of the neighbourhood and surrounding environment. Many behavioural aspects of the social environment also have an impact on the health experience of communities. Offending and anti-social behaviour in particular evokes a sense of fear, anxiety and insecurity. This influences the individual's perception and sense of ontological safety, impacting on the day-to-day experience of individuals and the community. In this respect, reported crime statistics for Hastings during the 1990s showed that it was highest in the county on a number of important public safety indicators. It had the highest rates of burglary, murder/manslaughter, criminal damage, drug-related offences and crime committed by under eights in the county (East Sussex Brighton and Hove Area Health Authority, 1998; East Sussex County Council, 1998).

The mental health experience of the community

There is strong evidence linking social inequalities and health inequalities (Acheson, 1998) and there is a close correlation between physical health and mental health (Bowie et al, 2000). According to the 1999–2002 local Community Care Plan, as much as one fifth of the population of East Sussex experienced mental health problems. This picture was not uniform as there were wide geographic variations in mental health need across the county and while most were supported within the primary care sector, a much smaller proportion experienced severe and enduring mental health problems. On the Mental Illness Needs Index (MINI) profile, Hastings borough had a level of mental health need greater than the national average and for the previous 11 years the suicide rates in East Sussex had been consistently higher than the national average although the overall trend was towards a decline. Over the same period, however, against this county-wide trend, the suicide rates in Hastings and Brighton had been increasing and two Hastings wards in particular had very high standardised suicide mortality rates (East Sussex, Brighton and Hove Area Health Authority, 1998; East Sussex County Council, 1998). Because of this well-documented and politically acknowledged high level of deprivation and unmet need, the area had assisted area status and a number of regeneration policies had been implemented to improve the situation (East Sussex, Brighton and Hove Area Health Authority, 1998; East Sussex County Council, 1998).

Hastings at the turn of the 21st century

Despite significant government and European Economic Community investment in neighbourhood renewal and the designation of the area as one of 10 Health Action Zones in the region in 1999, Hastings today still displays persistent areas of social deprivation as reflected across a broad range of contemporary socioeconomic and health indicators, which continue to have a major negative impact on the health experience of the community. In particular, it is the highest ranked town among the southeast area Health Action Zones on the Department of the Environment, Transport and the Regions index of deprivation and is above the national average on six out of the 13 health categories of the Compendium of Clinical and Health Indicators (SEPHO, 2001). Despite major developments in the provision of health and social care services, it ranks in the top quintile for hospital admission rates for mental illness by local authority in the southeast region and is in the highest quintile for multiple deprivation as measured by the Index of Multiple Deprivation (IMD), which, as an indirect index of mental health need, correlates closely with areas of deprivation (Nurse and Campion, 2006). On the recently developed Health Poverty Index (SEPHO, 2006), Hastings displays 11 out of the 26 indicators for worst health poverty in the region. This complex combination of contemporary and historical health issues, population factors and socioeconomic factors appears to contribute to the persistent maintenance of levels of relative deprivation and experience of poor health in the population. For a more detailed discussion of the relationship between poor quality of life and common mental disorders, see Singleton and Lewis (2001). It was at the end of the 1980s, against this historical backdrop of severe socioeconomic deprivation, poor health experience, and under-resourced and underdeveloped community mental health services, that a group of local Hastings residents set up a Befriending Scheme for people with mental health problems and during the middle of the first decade of the 21st century that service was decommissioned.

On the nature of befriending

Befriending services create some of the conditions of friendship but not all. Friendship typically is a private, mutual and voluntary activity between two or more people. Friends provide companionship, stimulation, social comparison, intimacy and affection (Flynn, 1992). Befriending relationships, however, are not private – the support organisation continues to play a role. The relationship is not completely mutual, while the voluntary service recipient and the volunteer may both gain from the relationship. They are not in a relationship of equal power. The relationship is not entirely based on spontaneous choice although each may be given the opportunity to reject the other at the start and at any point throughout the prescribed life of the service arrangement (Dean and Goodlad, 1998).

In defining befriending, the Scottish Befriending Development Forum (1997) argues that befriending is different from a professional intervention in that befriending seeks to prevent an isolated lonely existence for vulnerable individuals in favour of a life that derives meaning from the sense of belonging and 'being cared about' rather than 'being cared for' as is often the case with professional involvement. In a nationwide review, Dean and Goodlad (1998) took as their starting point a definition derived from the Scottish Befriending Development Forum, which defined befriending as:

> a relationship between two or more individuals which is initiated, supported and monitored by an agency that has defined one or more parties as likely to benefit. Ideally, the relationship is non-judgmental, mutual, purposeful and there is a commitment over time. (Cited in Dean and Goodlad, 1998, p 5)

The forum also states that 'whilst friendship is a private, mutual relationship, befriending is a service' (cited in Dean and Goodlad, 1998, p 4).

Russell et al (1992, p 6) defined befriending as:

> the provision of ongoing quality support to distressed individuals for an indeterminate period of time. The activity should enable appropriate, realistic and healthy coping skills to be developed within a warm and trusting relationship. Befriending is intended to lessen the person's sense of social or personal isolation.

While it is accepted that befriending is not the same as friendship, for many lonely, isolated individuals it may be, at worst, the preferable form of social relationship, which is tolerable and acceptable to the individual concerned. At best, a befriending relationship may be the beginning of a route back to gaining the increased confidence and self-esteem necessary to enable the individual to recreate and develop their own unique social network. (For a discussion on the artificiality of the befriending relationship, see Parish, 1998.)

What befrienders do

A replication study using a modified version of an evaluation tool developed by Hardcastle and Cooke (1993) was conducted by Jowitt in

February 1997 as part of an internal audit of the Hastings Befriending Scheme. The results from this audit indicate that the four most frequent activities engaged in by the befrienders (in ordinal rank) were talking with their friend, going out with their friend, providing practical help and going shopping. Bradshaw and Haddock (1998) in a small-scale study of a Befriending Scheme in Wigan identified a wide range of activities undertaken by the befrienders but the four most commonly reported activities were having a conversation, going out to a café, going for a meal and going shopping. Other less prominent activities reported included going out for a walk, collecting welfare benefits together, cooking, learning to use a computer, reading the Bible, ten-pin bowling, playing video games, going to the cinema and going for a drink. Both Parish's and Dean and Goodlad's research concurs with the above and confirms that 'what befrienders do' within the befriending relationship falls into four broad categories; in short, the relationship is about 'being available', 'spending time with', 'doing things' together and 'going to other places' together.

The value of befriending

In exploring issues around what is important about befriending, Buchan (1994) identified a number of themes that users of befriending services valued. These are the resources brought by the befrienders, such as cars for outings, the befriending relationship itself and the personal qualities of the person befriending such as supportiveness, perseverance and regularity. In the Dean and Goodlad (1998) study of what users valued, a number of themes emerged. These were the centrality of the personal relationship with their befriender, the value of going on outings and pursuing leisure activities and the importance of the relationship they had with the organisation. In the same study the accounts of what the befriending volunteers valued fell into four categories. These were the enjoyment they derived from the personal relationship with their befriendee, the sense of worth they get from volunteering, enjoyment of the befriending activities especially the outings and leisure activities and awareness of the user's enjoyment and recognition that they valued the befriending relationship.

A comparison of the entry expectations expressed by volunteers on the Association for the Pastoral Care of the Mentally Ill (APCMI) training programme with the values expressed as outcomes for befrienders in the Dean and Goodlad (1998) study points to a close correlation between the aspirational expectations on entry and actual achievements at the exit point referred to in the latter study.

The social policy context

A growing awareness of befriending as an important intervention in mental health is reflected in its inclusion in a number of policy initiatives; its inclusion as a good practice service model (Dunstable Befrienders) in the recent National Service Framework for Mental Health (DH, 1999) is an important milestone. The framework sets seven national standards for mental health services, with standard one addressing the promotion of mental health and the reduction of discrimination and social exclusion associated with mental health problems. As Berry (2001) points out, the inclusion of standard one in the National Service Framework puts mental health promotion centre-stage for the first time in the history of mental health service policy development.

The framework states that:

> Mental health promotion is most effective when the intervention builds on social networks and intervenes at crucial points in people's lives and uses a combination of methods to strengthen the individual to enhance their psychological well-being and communities in tackling local factors which undermine mental health. (DH, 1999, p 15)

In *The Report of the Committee of Inquiry into the Care and Treatment of Christopher Clunis* (Ritchie et al, 1994), two recommendations were made for the involvement of community volunteers with people who have mental health problems. One relates to the need for befrienders or advocates in relation to social services statutory aftercare duties under the 1983 Mental Health Act. It recommends that statutory authorities and voluntary agencies working in the field of mental health should recruit, train and support members of the public who wish to be Section 117 befrienders. This is perceived as a means of mobilising volunteers from the community in creating local support networks for vulnerable individuals, thereby bridging the transition from hospital to community. Overall, its inclusion within the National Service Framework identifies befriending as an important element in service provision and supports the proposition that befriending may help to prevent or reduce discrimination through its role in promoting an awareness of mental health issues and as a mechanism for mobilising community resources and encouraging community participation.

The emerging evidence base for the promotion of positive mental health through befriending

While befriending is slowly gaining national public recognition as an important community resource, it has only recently received the serious attention it deserves by policy makers and researchers as an intervention, having previously been a much applauded but under-resourced and under-researched intervention in the field of health and social care. There have been a number of important descriptive accounts of befriending services spanning a wide range of client groups in the literature: Gay and Pitkeathley (1982), Moffat (1986), Bowyer (1987), Jackson (1992), Ward-Panter (1992), Collis (1993), Cox (1993), Francis (1995), Petrioni (1997), King (1998) and Lepski (2002). It is only recently that a sustained attempt has been made to ascertain a clearer picture of the nature and benefits of befriending and to generate a debate about its status and value as a voluntary sector activity. A number of reports have sought to ascertain both the scope and the nature of befriending services (Russell et al, 1992; Dean and Goodlad, 1998; Parish, 1998) and a number of interesting qualitative papers have emerged, which attempt to describe in more detail and evaluate with greater clarity the nature, value, cost-effectiveness and impact of befriending as an intervention (Kingdom et al, 1989; Pound, 1990; Hardcastle and Cooke, 1994; Bradshaw and Haddock, 1998). More recently, two randomised controlled trials have been reported (Harris et al, 1999a; Sensky et al, 2000). In the case of the former, befriending was positively evaluated alongside a control intervention in relation to women with chronic depression, and in the latter, a modified form of cognitive behavioural therapy for individuals with a diagnosis of schizophrenia (resistant to medication) was evaluated, in which befriending as the control was evaluated positively during the first stage of the trial but less so during the six months follow-up.

Overall, this emerging research evidence suggests that befriending as a supportive intervention can increase a client's self-esteem and by definition their social and psychological well-being; enhance confidence and competence in relating to significant others; increase access to, and involvement with, existing social networks and community resources; reduce social isolation/exclusion and combat loneliness. In particular, in relation to individuals with schizophrenia, a befriending intervention can bring about substantial symptom relief and, in the case of women with chronic depression, promote the remission of depressive features.

The Hastings APCMI Befriending Scheme

Background and beginnings

The Association for the Pastoral Care of the Mentally Ill (APCMI), now the Association for Pastoral Care in Mental Health (APCMH), is a national charitable organisation founded in 1986 by a family who wished to educate the general public and combat prejudice towards people with mental illness. The organisation now has many branches throughout the UK. Although it started life as a pressure group, its work has expanded to include a diverse range of service responses, with each branch providing a voluntary service intervention that addresses the particular needs of the local community. The Hastings branch was set up in October 1989, when the national development officer of the National APCMI, prompted by a story in the national press about the lack of community facilities for people with mental health problems in Hastings at the time, contacted a local vicar with a reputation as a welfare entrepreneur, who set up a meeting with a group of parishioners from a local church. A series of events was set in motion, which culminated in the establishment of the Hastings APCMI Befriending Scheme for the Mentally Ill (for a fuller discussion of the origins, see McGowan and Jowitt, 2003).

The Hastings APCMI Befriending Scheme was registered under the 1985 Companies Act and had as its objectives:

- to seek to improve the quality of life for people with mental health problems in the Hastings area, through social contact and befriending;
- to contribute to the preventative work carried out by other agencies;
- to enhance and strengthen the community integration of people with mental health problems by increasing their social networks beyond the mental health circles;
- to raise public awareness of some of the difficulties faced by people suffering from mental illness;
- to enable volunteers to participate in the community care initiative, thus involving the community itself in the delivery of services.

The organisation implemented the above objectives through the Befriending Scheme, the purpose of which was to recruit, train, match and provide ongoing support and training for members of the local community who were prepared to befriend people who were lonely and isolated as a result of mental health problems.

Recruitment of volunteers

Volunteers were drawn from the local community. Six weeks before the training course started, a weekly advertising campaign was conducted through the local papers, local radio, Ceefax, on posters and hand bills. Volunteers also heard about the training programme by word of mouth through the grapevine. As a broad rule of thumb, the office received about 30 expressions of interest, of whom 10 to 15 (50%) would turn up on the night, 8 to 10 (30%) would complete the course and 5 to 6 (15%) would go on to befriend. The befriender volunteers remained active within the scheme for an average of two years and three months, 50% remained for one year or less, 25% for two to three years and 25% for four to six years.

Background of volunteers

Individuals in the local community who came forward to befriend were from a variety of backgrounds, expressed a variety of motives and held differing expectations as to what was on offer and what they might contribute to the scheme. They also had different levels of motivation, which reflected variation in their willingness and ability to make an emotional, personal and social contribution to the Befriending Scheme.

Entry expectations of volunteers

On the first night of each training programme an audit of participants' entry expectations was conducted. Overwhelmingly and in ordinal rank, the top three themes that emerged were to 'enhance their awareness of mental health issues', to 'gain a better understanding of the Befriending Scheme' and the expression of a 'wish to give something of themselves' (altruism). Other recurring expectations, although less prominent than the first three, were to 'test out suitability for the befriending role', to 'acquire new skills', to 'meet new people' and to 'learn more about local mental health services'. This motivational profile mirrors similar work on motivation for volunteering drawn from the work of both Parish (1998) and the National Centre for Volunteering (1997) survey, in which similar themes emerge, reflecting a combination of self-interest and altruism.

Preparation for befriending

Volunteers were prepared for a befriending role through a carefully designed training programme. The training programme ran one evening a week for two hours over a seven-week period and included a one full-day workshop. Participation in the programme enabled the training team over the course of the programme to appraise and evaluate the participants' potential and suitability for the befriending role. Conversely, exposure to the course processes and responses to the course content enabled the participants to 'test themselves out' as to their suitability. There was no compulsion to befriend during the training stage but at the end of the training programme participants who wished to go forward to befriend were interviewed and, if successful, a commitment to befriend for one year was agreed. This was formalised through a contract between the participant and the organisation. Befrienders undertook to visit their befriendee once a week for two hours over a period of a year. Matching of befrienders to befriendees followed on from the selection stage. This was undertaken with great care and befrienders were only allocated a friend if the match had an 80% chance of success. During the befriending stage continuous support was provided through a combination of regular monthly group meetings and three-monthly individual supervision with the coordinator. For a more detailed discussion of the modus operandi of the Befriending Scheme, the assessment and support structures for befrienders and management of the befriending processes (see McGowan and Jowitt, 2003).

Befriending and stigma

The last two stated objectives of the Hastings Befriending Scheme (page 201) were 'to raise public awareness of some of the difficulties faced by people suffering from mental illness' and 'to enable volunteers to participate in the community care initiative, thus involving the community itself in the delivery of services'. The organisation sought to achieve these objectives through the training programme, which, although primarily designed as a foundation programme for the preparation of potential befrienders, also provided a stand-alone 'mental health awareness' educational programme. This suited participants who wished to explore issues relating to mental health but had no wish to befriend.

Promoting mental health awareness

Within the training programme a good balance was struck between the provision of information and the provision of 'safe experiential space', which enabled participants to draw on their personal experiences and explore their own values, beliefs and attitudes towards people with mental health problems. After the first two sessions the programme became progressively more 'experiential' and over the ensuing five sessions the participants took increasing responsibility for generating material for discussion. 'Progressive immersion' in this learning process promoted personal reflection and enabled the participants to appreciate and empathise with the experience of mental distress. This had the positive effect of enhancing the individual's level of self-awareness, promoted their self-confidence and enhanced their interpersonal sensitivity, all of which were prerequisites for undertaking a befriending commitment. This 'experiential' approach was central to the transformation of the participants' negative fears, prejudices and insecurities surrounding mental health issues. By the end of the programme these early preconceptions were replaced with a more positive attitude coupled with a realistic appraisal of the complexity, challenges, dilemmas and risks associated with individuals with mental health problems.

Over the past 15 years, while 225 volunteers completed the APCMI training programme, only 106 (49%) went on to befriend. The 119 participants (51%) who chose not to befriend nevertheless represent an important long-term investment in the fight against prejudice and stigma. By taking their new insights and learning back into the community, the course completers may well have proved to be useful ambassadors for mental health by influencing positively the attitudes of their friends, neighbours and family members towards individuals with mental health problems.

Befriending and social exclusion

The thrust of government policy over the past two decades has been to encourage voluntary participation, in the belief that volunteering can enhance or create a greater sense of belonging, community identity and greater social capital within communities. More so, with the development of the pluralist welfare market, the voluntary sector now assumes a greater policy prominence and community care is charged with enabling those previously excluded to participate within the community and to make a contribution to community life. This communitarian view is concerned with social rights, social responsibilities and the recreation of community where volunteering is regarded as the civic responsibility of all citizens. There is an underlying assumption that volunteering as a civic duty provides a 'social dividend' and, by enabling people from different backgrounds to work together, helps build 'community' and foster mutual respect, social cohesion and tolerance.

The present government's intention to ensure the active involvement of the community in combating social exclusion has resulted in the creation of the Social Exclusion Unit, which in the summary report of its action plan (SEU, 2004) published 26 action points subsumed within six broad categories. While it is clear that befriending has a central role in contributing to three of the Social Exclusion Unit's six categories (action on stigma and discrimination, tackling social exclusion and supporting families and community participation), it might also be argued that it has a secondary role to play in relation to a fourth category (employment). Although not its primary focus, befriending may be an important intervention for individuals who, having successfully accessed employment following treatment for mental health problems, require consistent interpersonal support in order to sustain them in employment.

Dean and Goodlad (1998) explore the issue of befriending as an activity related to community care, social exclusion and volunteering. Although social exclusion is a very recent term and is still a matter of debate, they point out that it is often defined by reference to an economic model that defines exclusion as 'exclusion from the labour market' and assumes that community interventions are those which provide access for users and volunteers to such social networks as might operate as a bridge to employment. Dean and Goodlad argue, however, that, for some, 'labour market participation' is not an option and settle for a broader 'social' definition that defines inclusion as 'being accepted and being able to participate as fully as possible as part of a family, a social circle, a neighbourhood, and as a visible participant in the wider society' (Dean and Goodlad, 1998). For them, befriending is viewed as a 'bridge' to community participation and has the potential to extend social and interpersonal contact beyond the residential home, the family home and paid carers. They have developed six models as criteria against which to evaluate the effectiveness of befriending services in promoting participation and countering social exclusion. The theme title of each model suggests an underlying central function and related outcome: integration into community services and facilities; creation of new social links; integration into existing social networks; integration into affinity and identity groups; integration into mutual support groups; and full citizenship. They conclude that Befriending Schemes meet the criteria relating to the first three models of participation and social inclusion and that befriending seeks to tackle forms of social exclusion and supports 'community participation'. They argue that befriending, by involving members of the community in volunteering, complements the existing health and community care services and represents an important form of 'social capital' – care by the community, in the community, for the benefit of the community. For a fuller discussion of the relationship between befriending, social networks, social support and social capital, see McGowan and Jowitt (2003).

The demise of the Befriending Scheme

The Befriending Scheme was a 'single issue' organisation with an office, a part-time administrator and a full-time coordinator. The coordinator managed the service on a day-to-day basis and coordinated public relations, referrals, recruitment, training, matching, supervision, support and reviews. Strategic management was overseen by a management committee. Over time, the coordinator's primary work in providing support and supervision for befrienders became displaced by the increasing need to fundraise as the proportion of core funding became progressively eroded. Increased demands in relation to Criminal Records Bureau checks, health and safety assessments and 'grey areas' regarding insurance cover took their toll on a slim, overstretched team as service fatigue set in and the possibility of increasing capacity remained a forlorn hope while the organisation lurched from one relentless fundraising cycle to another without any break and very little additional financial benefit.

Alongside this, cutbacks in local service provision led to the insidious but noticeable withdrawal of community mental health and other support services to befriendees ostensibly on the grounds that they had a befriender visiting regularly. This led to disproportionate extra responsibilities being placed on the Befriending Scheme, leaving it managing unacceptably higher levels of risk as it was working increasingly with individuals with more challenging and complex needs. After much soul-searching, the ultimate conclusion was drawn that a 'good-enough' service could not be maintained under the prevailing circumstances and the service was decommissioned in January 2006.

Conclusion

Despite a compelling body of evidence emerging in support of befriending as an important 'midstream' public health and social care intervention, there remains a general lack of sustained financial investment for service provision, research and development. Indeed, despite the existence over nearly three decades of a London-based international organisation 'Befrienders International' (www.befrienders.org) dedicated to supporting befriending across the globe (361 centres in 41 countries), the distribution and development of befriending services around the UK remain disappointingly haphazard and fragmentary.

It remains to be seen if the launch of the Mentoring and Befriending Foundation (www.mandbf.org.uk) in 2005, a Home Office-funded national strategic body for offering support to practitioners and organisations throughout the UK, will rectify this dismal situation.

In addition to its contribution to the promotion of positive mental health, befriending has enormous potential for raising public awareness of mental health issues and for the mobilisation of latent community resources. Through its training programme it can educate the general public and through its Befriending Scheme, as a volunteer networking strategy (Froland et al, 1981), it can promote 'community participation'. By so doing, it has the potential to create and strengthen social networks, combat social exclusion, enhance the health experience of vulnerable individuals in the community and make a valuable contribution to community development on the ground.

It would be utopian to suggest that Befriending Schemes in and of themselves will have any substantial impact on the structural causes of discrimination, inequality and social exclusion, since, as in the case of the Befriending Scheme showcased in this chapter, they share (in terms of funding priorities) the marginalised status of many of the client groups which they serve. They remain part of a significant group of highly valued voluntary sector initiatives that struggle to survive from one inadequate short-term contract to the next. It is clear that befriending interventions have the capability but not yet the capacity to tackle discrimination and exclusion on a large scale but no doubt will continue to do so in small but highly significant ways and make a difference to the quality of everyday life for vulnerable individuals in need.

References

Acheson, D. (1998) *Inequalities in Health*, London: The Stationery Office.

Berry, R. (2001) 'Developing a national strategy for mental health promotion', *International Journal of Mental Health Promotion*, vol 3, no 4, pp 29-34.

Bowie, C., Jackson, L. and Brown, P. (2000) *Inequalities in Health in the South East*, Royston: South East Public Health Observatory (SEPHO).

Bowyer, C. (1987) 'Setting up a Befriending Scheme for Greenwich MIND', *SPRING Newsletter*, no 7, pp 21-30.

Bradshaw, T. and Haddock, G. (1998) 'Is befriending by trained volunteers of value to people suffering from long-term mental illness', *Journal of Advanced Nursing*, vol 27, no 4, pp 713-20.

Buchan, R. (1994) *The Experience of Being Befriended: A Study Based on Interviews with Members of a Mental Health Befriending Scheme*, Aberdeen: Voluntary Services Aberdeen.

Collis, J. (1993) 'Befriending in Robin Hood country (volunteer befriending for people with mental health problems in rural areas)', *New Directions*, vol 4.

Cox, A. D. (1993) 'Befriending young mothers', *British Journal of Psychiatry*, no 163, pp 6-18.

Dean, J. and Goodlad, R. (1998) *Supporting Community Participation: The Role and Impact of Befriending*, Brighton: Pavilion/Joseph Rowntree Foundation.

DH (Department of Health) (1999) *The National Service Framework for Mental Health: Modern Standards and Service Models*, London: DH, p 24.

East Sussex, Brighton and Hove Area Health Authority (1999) *East Sussex Community Care Plan 1999-2002*.

East Sussex County Council (1998) *Poverty Profile of East Sussex*, Lewes: East Sussex County Council.

Flynn, P. T. (1992) 'Friendly visiting: considerations and resources', *Educational Gerontology*, vol 18, pp 305-16.

Forrest, R. and Gordon, D. (1991) *People and Places: A 1991 Census Atlas of England*, Bristol: School for Advanced Urban Studies/Bristol Statistical Monitoring Group.

Francis, J. (1995) 'Alcohol: less talk, more do. CATCH, a volunteer Befriending Scheme in Chichester which offers more than counselling for people with alcohol problems', *Community Care*, 4 May, p 10.

Froland, C., Pancoast, D. L., Chapman, N. and Kimboko, P. J. (1981) *Helping Networks and Human Services,* Beverly Hills, CA: Sage Publications.

Gay, P. and Pitkeathley, J. (1982) *Just Like a Friend: Befriending Discharged Psychiatric Patients,* King's Fund Project Paper No 32, London: King's Fund.

Hardcastle, B. and Cooke, A. (1993) *An Evaluation of the Hastings APCMI Befriending Scheme,* Hastings: Hastings Health Authority.

Harris, T., Brown, G. and Robinson, R. (1999a) 'Befriending as an intervention for chronic depression among women in an inner city 1: randomised controlled trial', *British Journal of Psychiatry,* no 174, pp 225-32.

Hastings Borough Council (1998) *Facts and Figures: Useful Information about Hastings and St Leonards,* Hastings: Hastings Borough Council.

Jackson, C. (1992) 'Community mothers: trick or treat?', *Health Visitor,* vol 65, no 6, pp 199-201.

Jowitt, C. (1997) *The APCMI Befriending Scheme Co-ordinators Report 1994-1997,* Hastings: Hastings APCMI.

King, M. (1998) 'DOSTI – Befriending Scheme for Asians with mental health problems in Hillingdon', *Open Mind,* no 76, p 18.

Kingdom, D.G., Collis, J. and Judd, M. (1989) 'Befriending: cost effective community care', *Psychiatric Bulletin,* no 13, pp 350-1.

Lepski, J. (2002) 'Befrienders', *Newsletter for the Medical Foundation for the Victims of Torture,* no 21, pp 4-5.

McGowan, B. and Jowitt, C. (2003) 'Promoting positive mental health through befriending', *International Journal of Mental Health Promotion,* vol 5, no 2, pp 12-24.

Moffat, C. (1986) 'Befriending in Belfast', *New Society,* no 76, p 21.

National Centre for Volunteering (1997) *Safe and Alert: Good Practice Advice on Volunteers Working with Vulnerable Clients,* London: National Centre for Volunteering.

Nurse, J. and Campion, J. (2006) *Mental Health and Well-Being in the Southeast,* London: Care Services Improvement Partnership (CSIP), Department of Health.

OPCS (Office of Population, Censuses and Surveys) (1991) *Census of Population,* Cm 430, London: HMSO.

Parish, A. (1998) *Volunteers and Mental Health Befriending,* London: National Centre for Volunteering.

Petrioni, P. (1997) 'The impact of a volunteer community care project in a primary health care setting', in P. Petrioni and C. Petrioni (eds) *Innovation in Community Care and Primary Health,* London: Churchill Livingstone, pp 53-9.

Pound, A. (1990) 'The development of attachment in adult life: the Newpin experiment', *British Journal of Psychotherapy*, vol 7, no 1, pp 77-85.

Ritchie, J., Dick, D. and Lingham, R. (1994) *The Report of the Committee of Inquiry into the Care and Treatment of Christopher Clunis*, London: HMSO.

Russell, J., Dexter, G. and Bond, T. (1992) 'Differentiation between advice, guidance, befriending, counselling skills and counselling', Summary report, The Advice, Guidance and Counselling Lead Body.

Scottish Befriending Development Forum (1997) *Let's Befriend: A Befriending Resource Pack*, Falkirk: Scottish Befriending Development Forum.

Sensky, T., Turkington, D., Kingdom, D., Scott, J. L., Scott, J., Sidde, R., O'Caroll, M. and Barnes, R. E. (2000) 'A random controlled trial of cognitive-behavioural therapy for persistent symptoms in schizophrenia resistant to medication', *Archives of General Psychiatry*, vol 57, pp 165-72.

SEPHO (South East Public Health Observatory) (2001) *A Profile of the Health of Local Populations in the South East Region using the Compendium of Clinical and Health Indicators 2000*, SEPHO, www.sepho.org.uk

SEPHO (2006) *Health Poverty Index: An Atlas of Indicators for the South East*, SEPHO, www.sepho.org.uk

SEU (Social Exclusion Unit) (2004) *Mental Health and Social Exclusion: Social Exclusion Unit Report Summary*, London: Office of the Deputy Prime Minister.

Singleton, N. and Lewis, G. (2001) *Better or Worse: A Longitudinal Study of the Mental Health of Adults Living in Private Households in Great Britain*, London: Office for National Statistics.

Ward-Panter, J. (1992) *A Door Opens on the Special Hospitals*, Open MIND No 56, April/May, pp 16-17.

THIRTEEN

Paid care workers in the community: an Australian study

Jane Mears

This chapter looks at issues of concern to those working in domiciliary care in Australia. As the Australian population continues to age, older people and their carers will need more formal support and care in their own homes. At present this work is done primarily by home care workers. This sector of the workforce, already growing rapidly, will continue to grow. Recent reports have expressed concern about the low wages paid to these workers, the lack of career structure, the lack of entry qualifications and the paucity of training opportunities and the effect this could have on the recruitment of workers and the quality of care provided in the future. The social and political context is similar to Britain, where the delivery of social care is becoming more and more fragmented and privatised. As this care takes place in the privacy of people's homes, hidden from the public gaze, we do not generally observe care workers going about their daily work. This chapter focuses on these paid care workers and provides some insight into how they provide community care that aims to maintain and enhance community and social connectedness for the older people they are caring for.

Introduction

Historically, in Australia there has been a very heavy reliance on family care for frail older people and those with disabilities, with residential care seen as a last resort. From the 1970s, after much lobbying from groups representing older people and carers, a number of government inquiries were held. The reports from these inquiries recommended radical changes to this system. The most influential was the aptly named report *In a Home or at Home* (McLeay, 1982). This report recommended a range of policies to minimise 'inappropriate' admission to residential care, and to support family carers and older people to live in the community for as long as possible.

In 1985, under the Hawke Labor government, the beginnings of a serious attempt to set up a community care infrastructure came about with the introduction and implementation of the Home and Community Care (HACC) Programme. The main aim of the programme was to keep frail older people living in the community, building up community services to support them and, significantly, their carers in the community.

The period from 1985 saw the virtual restructuring of residential care in Australia and the emergence of a viable array of home and community care services (Gibson, 1998, p 33). The HACC programme encapsulated a dramatic change in moving from a reliance on residential care to community care as the favoured policy option. Its introduction was hailed as the 'first rational, cooperative system of older person care, enabling older people to remain in their own communities until they reached the final stage of their life' (Jamrozic, 2001, p 70). It targeted funding to government and non-governmental organisations to provide community care to older people and their carers. As part of this programme to foster community care and support carers, income support for carers was introduced.

With the election of the Howard coalition government in 1996, we have seen the implementation of policies based on principles of economic liberalism and the New Public Management fundamentally changing and reforming public administration to develop new relationships between the market, state (or public sector) and the non-government welfare sector, shifting responsibility from the state to the family wherever possible.

The assumptions underlying this government's policy were stated clearly in an Audit Commission report:

> There is now greater appreciation that governments can produce better results if they operate more like referees than supervisors, specifying the rules and the results required. Delivery of desired outcomes is usually better if opened up to competition.... Service delivery should be as competitive as possible. Service suppliers whether public or private should be required to tender or otherwise compete for the right to deliver government services ... this helps ensure service efficiency. (Officer, 1996, p viii)

This report was commissioned immediately after the government was elected and its findings released in the first year of the first term of the government.

In 1997 the National Strategy for an Ageing Australia was released. This strategy placed independence and self-provision as goals to be attained and emphasised the need for cost containment and efficiency, in addition to improving service quality and responsiveness. This strategy heralded a move towards a user pays policy for services to older people, with increased daily fees for hostels and nursing homes (now known as residential care facilities) and the widespread introduction of user charges in HACC services (Fine and Chalmers, 1998, p 7).

> This was aimed not so much at reducing the utilisation of nursing home service (although it may well have had this effect) as increasing funding by users, developing a more market based approach to their utilisation and shifting responsibility away from government. (Fine and Chalmers, 1998, p 18)

Funding for community care comes from the federal government, mostly through Aged Care Assistance Packages (ACAPs). Organisations tender for these packages. The organisations that 'win' the tender, then employ care workers to work in the homes of older people and those with disabilities, meeting their care needs. Budget constraints place major limitations on the type and amount of care that is provided. There is constant pressure on service providers to provide more care for less money. There are long waiting lists of those needing care, and a concern expressed by some service providers that those with less urgent need may be missing out altogether.

Concern has also been expressed in regard to the need for skilled workers to provide care for older people. Care work is a rapidly growing sector of the workforce. A recent Senate Inquiry reported that:

> With Australia's population ageing, demand for aged care services will increase. This will require not only adequate facilities but a skilled and committed workforce. The aged care workforce is facing significant challenges ... expansion of the community care sector has led to increasing demands for skilled workers; and poor pay for personal carers make it difficult to employ staff. (Senate Community Affairs References Committee, 2005, p xi)

The same inquiry also found that some organisations were experiencing great difficulty recruiting and retaining workers and made salutary comments on pay rates: 'Care workers receive relatively low wages. The hourly rate is less than that of checkout operators in supermarkets' (Senate Community Affairs References Committee, 2005, p 8). It is not just the poor pay rates, but also the lack of career structure, the lack of entry qualifications and the paucity of training opportunities.

Insights from paid care workers

How have care workers in Australia fared in the political climate described above? The focus of this chapter is on paid care workers, employed by the Benevolent Society of NSW, a non-profit independent provider of community care. The Benevolent Society is funded to provide community care and maintain older people in their homes for as long as possible. Budget constraints limit the care that it can provide, both the amount and the type of service. However, this organisation has a strong commitment to a social model of care, and aims to maintain and enhance social and community connectedness for those receiving care. The purpose of this chapter is to examine how, despite budgetary constraints and poor pay, the paid care workers employed by the Benevolent Society manage to fulfil the goal of providing good-quality care that meets the needs of the clients and fulfils the organisation's commitment to maintaining and enhancing social and community connectedness.

The data utilised in writing this chapter are taken from interviews for a study that was carried out in 2004-05 in partnership with the Benevolent Society (Mears, 2007, in press). The aim of the project was to examine the 'private' world of care work. Twenty-three care workers and 10 care coordinators and managers were interviewed. Interviewees were mostly women, aged 30–60, with the average age being in the mid-fifties. About a quarter of the participants were sole breadwinners. They had worked for the Benevolent Society for periods ranging from three months to 10 years; most had worked as care workers for at least five years. The majority were employed as permanent part-time workers, working up to 20 hours per week, and a few were employed as casuals, called to 'fill in' when the permanent part-time care workers were sick, or unable to work. All the care coordinators and managers were employed full time. For most of those interviewed care work was a job they had come to later in life. A significant proportion of the care workers were 'older workers' (aged over 45) when first appointed. This was not a 'first job' for any of the people interviewed for the project. They came with a wide range of previous work experience, both paid and unpaid.

The care provided to the older person is set down in a care plan, and is negotiated by the care coordinator in consultation with the older person and the family. There are three aspects to this plan, focusing on the needs of the older person and the ways to achieve good-quality care in regard to their health, personal and most importantly, social well-being. Despite the pressure to cut costs, the 'social' aspects of the care plan continue to be maintained and emphasised.

> 'We also provide them with social support, just to talk if they want to talk, or an outing, or for coffee down to the local shops, into the plaza for banking needs, anything they want to do, within reason, we're allowed to do, to make their life a little bit easier.'

A central theme that emerged during the interviews with the care workers for this study was the commitment they had to 'working with people'. It became clear that also of prime importance were the relationships forged between the care workers and the older people, and ensuring that older people maintained social and community connectedness.

Those interviewed had become care workers because they wanted to work with people, particularly older people, and they had been employed by the organisation often because of their experience as family carers and they were judged to be 'caring' people. Establishing trusting personal relationships enabled the care workers to perform a range of caring activities they would be unable to do without an intimate knowledge of the older person. These activities included less tangible and quantifiable goals of the caring enterprise, such as improving and maintaining the emotional and psychological well-being of the older people, and maintaining the independence of and empowering the older person. These relationships take time and skill to build up. The relationship formed between the care worker and the older person is of crucial importance, and clients and care workers inevitably become very close. In some instances, the care worker is the only visitor the older person sees from one week to the next. A lot is invested in this relationship.

The care workers saw the development of good relationships as essential, if they were to provide good-quality care. They spoke of the importance of investing time and energy into 'getting to know' the older person in order to build a 'working relationship'. Care work is firmly embedded in relationships. Knowing someone well, forming trusting relationships, ensuring the older person felt comfortable with the care worker, and indeed trusted the care worker, enabled the care workers to do the job properly and enable the older person to maintain social connectedness. This requires time and great skill; 'a caring person', with the ability to feel empathy and respect for older people, and requiring investment of time and energy that is not easily measured or quantified. They described their work as meaningful and rewarding because of these relationships; they liked working with older people and felt they were making a difference.

Becoming a care worker

Care workers were very committed to their work and had taken on the work because they wanted to care for older people. They derived much pleasure from their day-to-day interactions with the older people.

> 'They've got a life of experience, a world of experience, and they're interesting. They're all go, with a great sense of humour and they are all different characters.'

> 'I love the job because it is varied. I love the variety. I like people and I like meeting them. And I like helping them. I like getting paid for it too ... I just love my little job. I really do. I love the people. They are all different and you just respect the differences and enjoy it.'

Some had become disillusioned with prior work and entered care work as it offered the opportunity to do meaningful work that was personally satisfying. Some had worked in nursing homes or as human resource managers and managers in the finance industry. They spoke graphically of the effects of economic rationalism on the organisations they had been working for. They felt 'economic imperatives' and cost-cutting had led to the loss of personal contact and personal fulfilment in these jobs. Care work enabled them to connect with people in a meaningful way. They spoke of wanting to work in a 'caring environment', doing a job where one could derive intrinsic satisfaction from work that was useful and constructive.

> 'I worked for a bank for a long time and I got sick of being told to sell fries with that, to sell more and more services, when people came in for their withdrawals. I just got tired of that. I wasn't interested anymore.'

One participant described doing care work as a chance 'to give something back' to society, after one of her adult children was badly injured in a car accident. She felt that the job enabled her to make a meaningful social contribution.

'I ended up being manager of a building society. Then my daughter was nearly killed in a car accident. Very touch and go. And it changed my life. It just did, it changed. Up until then my job was the most important thing to me, but then after the accident I reassessed everything and I thought, "I don't want to do this anymore. I want to do a job where I'm appreciated, where I can help other people more." I know it probably sounds stupid, but it was like giving thanks for us getting her life back. I don't know, part of it's guilt maybe, or part of it's you want to give something back.... So that's how I started out.'

A number of the care workers had previously given up paid work to care full time for older and frail parents, friends and adult children with disabilities. When this caring ceased they found themselves wanting, and needing, to re-enter the workforce. Paid care work was seen as an ideal job by these women. Most lacked confidence in their ability to take on paid work. They were re-entering the workforce as middle-aged women, with no current work experience. Care work provided employment opportunities for these older workers and provided a comfortable transition back into paid work, doing work they were familiar with, enjoyed, and were confident they could do well.

'I just needed something different, but wasn't looking for anything in particular. I was looking in the local paper and there was a care worker's job, helping with personal care, something that I thought I would never be able to do. But after doing it for my mum I thought, "I can do this".'

'I cared for my mother-in-law when she was dying, seven or eight years ago. And when she passed away, I thought, "That is a job I think I might like to do".'

Care work, with the possibility of working flexible hours, was also attractive as it enabled women to combine work and family responsibilities: 'Now that my kids are older I just wanted to come back and do some part-time casual work during school hours and this just fits it perfectly.'

Some of the care workers had themselves been clients of the service. When their caring responsibilities ceased it was suggested to them that they may like to apply for a job as a care worker. For many it was this informal, unpaid caring experience that led them to realise they were 'good' at this work.

What makes a good care worker?

This question provoked a great deal of discussion. The care workers had very firm ideas about what made one a good care worker. They outlined in detail particular personal qualities and skills that were necessary and made the key point that a good care worker was a person who was able to relate well to people.

What they placed at the top of the list were personal qualities such as patience, maturity, the ability to empathise with older people, to be sensitive to and recognise people's needs, to be flexible and take initiative and, in addition, having a good sense of humour.

> 'It is not so much skills, you've got to have patience. If you don't have patience, well, don't work here.'

> 'Patience, a lot of patience is involved. Most of the people that I talk to [other care workers] have had similar things in their lives. They've either cared for a mother or father or someone. They've had a lot of caring in their lives. So I think it is something that you learn.'

Along with patience went maturity. Several of the participants spoke of the importance of having had life experience, of being mature and therefore possessing the qualities that come through maturity that enable the workers to deal sensitively and respectfully with older people. Some felt that with maturity, for some people, also came the understanding and the ability to appreciate and value older people.

> 'Maturity is important. I really believe that they [the younger workers] look at things in a different way.'

> 'Because I'm that bit older I have a little more patience than I would have had as a younger women. And you identify more.'

They spoke about being sensitive to people's needs and also being flexible. They had to be flexible, change their approach for each person and to try and organise their work to ensure that needs were met, while recognising and respecting difference and diversity.

> 'There is great job satisfaction in what we are doing. And as you get older, I think you get a little more understanding of older people. You've got that experience behind you, so you are a little more sensitive to their needs and you

want to give them as much independence, self-respect and dignity as possible.'

'I guess it all comes back to personality. You have to have the ability to actually meet them there instead of trying to do things your way, to go along with them as much as possible. Not to be exercising your own will.'

And a sense of humour is vitally important.

'You need to be able to laugh at some situations. You need a sense of humour.'

Particular skills that were singled out were communication, problem-solving and negotiation skills. In order to build a relationship, you need highly developed 'people skills', to be able to empathise and 'connect', to talk, to listen and to respond appropriately. It is a two-way relationship.

'People skills. You've got to know how to talk, how to relate.'

'I think you need good listening skills and you need to empathise with people. And be able to look at things from their point of view. I like to look at it as if it was my mum or dad that I was dealing with.'

'I think the most important thing is communication. You have got to be able to communicate with elderly people. If you're a bit young you just can't relate.... You've got to be able to ask them questions about their family, get them talking. That's the most important thing.'

To be a good care worker, one needs to be able to put into practice these principles, to maintain and enhance the independence, dignity and quality of life of the older people. This is not easy. It takes a great deal of thought, skill and experience to be able to respect someone's wishes, empower them and yet ensure that, at the same time, they are safe and well cared for.

'Independence. It's not a matter of us saying, "Give me your bank book, and give me your money." No, we always take them with us and keep explaining to them what has to be done.'

'I let them do as much as I can. If I'm doing a meal I ask if they want to help, even if it is only, "Where do you keep your potatoes?" I mean you know where they are, but you say, "Can you get me a couple of potatoes, or can you get me something out of the fridge, or where are your garbage bags?"'

The theme of this chapter is the ways in which the care workers enhanced social connectedness. The care workers felt that it was important to provide social support, if that was needed. They saw the nurturing of emotional well-being as an important priority, far more important than some of the more easily measured tasks set out in the care plan.

'Their emotional well-being is important. Most of the time I think that's more important than getting the house clean. Sometimes they just want you to sit and have a cup of tea with them.'

'Don't go in there saying, "I can't talk today because I've got to do this and that and that and it's written on my care plan." I'll leave a note in the book saying, "Sorry girls, didn't get a chance to do it today".'

It was through getting to know the older person and building up a relationship that enabled them to do their job and to continually monitor health and well-being.

'But you do watch. You do notice when they're a bit shaky, or they're not sitting the way that they normally sit, or they've arranged their table in a different way to what they do normally. Or, they get very repetitious with things and all of a sudden you'll see a change and you think, "Hang on a minute. That's not like them." You are always watching their health.'

A particularly striking example of a positive outcome based on astute and careful observation is a case in which a care worker picked up on the fact that her client had thrush, an extremely uncomfortable, but not life-threatening, vaginal infection that is very easily treated. It would have made a huge difference to the quality of this woman's life to have had the condition diagnosed and treated previously.

'In the end you can talk to them personally about different things and they'll start telling you what their problems are, like that lady that had the thrush. Now she'd had that for about five years, and nobody had picked up on it. I noticed by the way she was walking there was something wrong.'

Rewarding and meaningful work

As can be seen from some of the quotes above, the care workers interviewed really enjoyed their work and they spoke at length about the intrinsic rewards. However, they did not earn much money.

'Well, I feel that I'm working a lot. I'm only rostered to do 15 hours. My minimum hours are 15. Generally 20. But I feel like I'm nearly working a full-time job sometimes. And I get my pay and it is like $260 a week. And I'm thinking, What am I doing?'

'I know the bank work I was doing wasn't great. I wasn't very high on the scale. I wasn't a very high grade. But six years ago I was earning something like $17 an hour in that job and I'm still only earning $14 here, and this is a harder job.'

The care workers were very clear that they did not do the job for the money: 'So you are never going to get a million dollars out of this job…. If you want to be a millionaire this is not the right job.' And, as they pointed out, many good care workers leave because the pay is so low.

'You find a lot of the good workers that I've worked with leave because of the pay…. They are so good and they would stay I'm sure and it suits them with their families. Most of them are young mothers. It is just so hard. They will go out and get any sort of job that pays more, whereas they are very suitable to this.'

The attraction was that the work was personally fulfilling. Every day the work was different and varied; new pleasures and new challenges arose.

'To me this is just the most rewarding job that anyone can have…. I just love my job … I am so lucky because I have got beautiful, beautiful clients. I thank God for this opportunity to be able to do this kind of work. I really believe that this is what I was put on this earth for. And I do a good job. And I just get so much pleasure out of it. There is not a day where I wake up and go, "Oh no, I've got to go to work today." I get up and I'm ready to go. I just love it. I absolutely love it.'

One of the reasons they enjoyed care work was that they could see they were making a tangible difference to the lives of the older people they were caring for.

'The most valuable thing, the best thing I can say about my job is that when someone passes away, you know that you've made a difference to their life. You know that you've made their life happier and that you've actually done something for them. And the families are so grateful, and they say to you, "Mum or dad couldn't have managed without you." If someone does pass away it helps you to deal with it, that you've actually made a difference to their life.'

'I like the idea that I'm making a difference to somebody else's life. Well, more so to an elderly person's life. That's what I like about the job.'

They also liked the freedom and control they had over their work. Most of the time they worked without any direct supervision. They spoke of this as one of the attractive features of the work. Care workers need to be able to work alone, unsupervised.

'There's a lot of trust put in us, and a lot is left up to our own discretion. We have to know our guidelines and we have to know what we can do, but most things, within reason, we can do.'

'You've got a sense of freedom. When I was in the building society, you've got your manager breathing over your shoulder, telling you you are not meeting quotas and not selling our credit cards and insurance and all that sort of stuff. I took that for so many years. But here you've got the freedom of being out on the road. You've got no boss breathing over your shoulder and it's lovely, just being outside working.'

Those interviewed enjoyed the work and thought that they would stay working where they were in the foreseeable future.

> 'I hope to stay here. And I would like to do more work especially with the dementia clients because I really enjoy that. I find that it is very challenging. But I really enjoy it.'

> 'I would like to stay in that role, yes. I just find it fulfilling. I have been in the office, but I prefer caring for people.'

> 'I love this type of work. At this stage I haven't got any plans to do anything different.'

> 'I've got no plans to go anywhere. I'm very happy with what I'm doing.'

Conclusion

> 'Some people might have the image that maybe it is a nice little job you have that you go and make little old ladies cups of tea. It is far from that.'

What emerged from the stories the care workers told was that care work is indeed, 'far from that'. Care work is highly skilled and requires very delicate negotiations between personal and work relationships. Indeed, as the care workers cogently argued, to care properly for someone, you need to know them, to form a relationship. In an environment where budgets are tight and resources are scarce, these care workers are managing to continue working with older people as active participants in the care relationship. They are attempting to work in ways that improve quality of life, are socially inclusive and respectful, while making a genuine attempt to empower older people and enhance their independence.

> 'They should be seen as professionals. They shouldn't be seen as house cleaners. You see these people who are just doing just hard work, emotionally hard work. Physically hard work and having all these amazing skills and they are just not recognised.'

The managers are very well aware of the context they are working in. Using the 'language of the market', one of the managers described what they were doing: 'That is how we sell ourselves, as a relationship-based service.'

This research shows that these care workers are indeed providing a 'relationship-based service'. Care is based on relationships and, as Barnes emphasises in Chapter Four, is a basis for social life.

> At different points of our lives we all need care. This arises from our physical and biological vulnerability and our incapacity to support ourselves at crucial points in our life course. Care may, therefore, be regarded as a fundamental condition of human existence. Because it is not something we can do always for ourselves, but must rely on others, care is, itself, an inherently social activity.... Care may be considered as providing a basis for social solidarity, or, as we more commonly refer to it, for social life. (Fine, 2004, p 218)

The findings reported here would indicate that the community care infrastructure and the provision of good-quality care through this infrastructure, is largely sustained by the goodwill, good nature and general commitment to the sector of a group of committed workers.

It is important to tell the stories of the care workers in this study who, despite all the pressures to the contrary, managed to provide care based on building relationships with the older people they were caring for. They saw maintaining social and community connectedness as central to their work. If we wish to retain these care workers in the long term we need to recognise the importance of providing 'social care' in the broadest sense and that maintaining and enhancing social and community contact is at the core of care work. This is the reason these care workers are doing the work. It is important this story be told, not only to the older people being cared for, but also for the care workers and indeed for us all.

References

Fine, M. (2004) 'Renewing the social vision of care', *Australian Journal of Social Issues*, vol 39, no 3, pp 217-32.

Fine, M. and Chalmers, J. (1998) *Who Pays? The Impact of User Pays and Economic Policy on Older People*, Sydney: NSW Committee on Ageing.

Gibson, D. (1998) *Aged Care: Old Policies, New Problems*, Cambridge: Cambridge University Press.

Jamrozic, A. (2001) *Social Policy in the Post Welfare State: Australians on the Threshold of the 21st Century*, Frenchs Forest, NSW: Pearson Education.

McLeay, L. (1982) *In a Home or at Home: Accommodation and Home Care for the Aged: Report of the House of Representatives Standing Committee on Expenditure*, Canberra: Parliament of the Commonwealth of Australia, Australian Government Publishing Service.

Mears, J. (2007: in press) *The World of Care Work: Report on Research Project 'Talking to Care Workers'*, for The Benevolent Society of NSW.

Officer, R. (1996) *Report to the Commonwealth Government, National Commission of Audit*, Canberra: Australian Government Publishing Service.

Senate Community Affairs References Committee (2005) *Quality and Equity in Aged Care*, Canberra: Australian Government Publishing Service.

Part Four
Comparative perspectives

FOURTEEN

The care of older people in Sweden

Christina Hjorth Aronsson

Introduction

In Selma Lagerlöf's (1891/1997) *Gösta Berling's Saga* the powerful major's wife, Mrs Celsing, is cast out into the cold winter, both literally and socially, because of her bad behaviour.[1] Out there, in the cold, there is no responsibility on the part of the public to help or support her. Instead, this formerly powerful lady has to rely on the kindness of others for something to eat and somewhere to sleep. Lagerlöf's fictional world, as with pre-urban communities, is rooted in an environment where farmers and crofters lived in a feudal system, and the survival of such an individual was a matter of benevolence on the part of the church, villages or generous individuals. This literary parallel sometimes helps Swedish students to understand the historical dimensions of social constructions and that state interventions in relation to citizens are, to a large extent, variable across time and space. When the major's wife was excluded, care of the individual was a spontaneous moral reaction within families and between people. It was not a subject for debate, either within the education system or in pre-urban society.

The aim of this chapter is to explain how a care discourse was elaborated within the Swedish welfare state with universal rights for the care of citizens. The author's focus will be on the care of older people, a matter of social and political importance because of the ageing population and the complex difficulties within welfare of balancing services and expenditure. We should remember, however, that the care of older people is but one element in the welfare state, which, due to the macro-economic crisis at the beginning of the 1990s and throughout that decade, became the subject of major changes. These changes included an increase in decentralisation to the municipalities and an increase in user financing as well as higher fees and income-linking for services delivered to citizens. Another important change was an increase in the publicly financed services provided by private agencies (Lundberg and Palme, 2002). (See also Korpi and Palme, 2003, for a discussion about how new financial situations in the post-industrial welfare states influence, among others, old-age pension systems and an increase in pre-retirement pensions as a consequence of mass unemployment.) All these changes have significantly influenced the form and content of care for older people in the municipalities, for service users as well as for staff members. This is illustrated at the end of this chapter with some figures highlighting current problems in the care of older people.

Social care encompasses those public activities that include the help and support of people with different kinds of disabilities, or who, because of age-related diseases, are in need of help. Within the field of welfare policy, social work practice has been variously handled, but is, nevertheless, included in a single piece of legislation – the Social Services Act (SFS, 1980/2001:453). Growing demands for academic education and efforts to improve the evidence base now characterise social work and social care (see Abbott, 1988; Murphy, 1988; Perkin, 1996).

Citizenship and rights

The need to support those not part of the labour force because of their age, youth or poor health has always been recognised, in all kinds of communities. This is part of our condition as social beings, building social organisations and systems. Different approaches have been applied by each new generation, each contributing new ways of acting and behaving with regard to one another; rules that are in place generally look upon the labour force as in some way responsible for persons outside it. But these approaches are not only a matter of what kind of institutional solutions to the intergenerational problems or health problems a community has, they also contribute to the discourses that develop, thus reproducing action and organisation systems. Care is looked upon as a discourse, specific to time and space, for different kinds of communities.

Quoting Esping-Andersen (1990, p 21) with reference to T. H. Marshall, 'social citizenship constitutes the core idea of a welfare state'. The end of the 19th century was a turning point in Swedish society due to industrialisation and urbanisation. These changes resulted in a thorough restructuring of civil society, the family sector, urban space and working life as people were forced into towns in order to find paid work, which for most became the dominant source of income.

Housing conditions in towns and in the countryside were disastrous. Insurance against accidents, poverty and sickness did not exist and individual vulnerability was enormous. Parallel to these social and infrastructure changes was a political and ideological struggle concerning governmental power that ended in parliamentary victory for the Social Democrats in 1932, when the building of the Swedish model for a welfare society, characterised by universal rights and financed by high taxes, began. Policy areas important in the building of a welfare society have included social, labour market, finance and housing policy. A social housing policy greatly influenced by society was seen as necessary both for social reasons and as an important strategy for enforcing high employment levels and, therefore, income tax contributions (Hjorth Aronsson, 1999). Universal social rights were one of the cornerstones for building the welfare system. Social citizenship constructions were a prerequisite of the rights the individual had in case of accidents, illness and ageing as well as the right to schooling and education, and even to cultural events. This is what Esping-Andersen (1990) calls a decommodification policy of the Scandinavian model. There has been, and still is, legislation controlling state intervention in relation to municipalities. State subsidies and state policy instruments safeguard Swedish citizens by determining how they create locally based welfare policies. A state with a strong public sector should guarantee a community-based security net for all on an individual level.

The evolution of social care for older people will be the subject of this chapter. Of central importance is the fact that care, from the very early establishment of the welfare era, has been a matter for the public sector and a major part of social policy. This means that liberal-conservative charity and voluntary initiatives have been, for ideological reasons, repressed by public initiatives. Today more voluntary initiatives exist and, increasingly, private ones are seen in the welfare arena where the care of older people provides a number of examples. One conclusion seems to be that the voluntary sector has hardly any role to play in welfare and provides no real alternative for users (Dahlberg, 2004, 2005). Private management still plays a small part in the care of older people, but is receiving increasing attention from government (Proposition 2005/6:115; Socialstyrelsen, 2006).

To sum up, the care of older people and their social citizenship and rights have been seen as the responsibility of the public sector. Only now is there a slight tendency for the government to allow private alternatives in welfare provision for older people.

The need concept

In a dictionary of sociology, need is defined as something necessary for the survival of the individual or the organisation (Marshall, 1998). Needs are sometimes contrasted with wants or desires that should be fulfilled. The satisfaction of a person's needs has, in the late modern welfare debate, become a mantra both professionally and in the political struggle. Individual needs are defined by a complex relationship between the individual and the resources at hand, and the efforts of social workers to assess, value, decide and finally satisfy the needs in question, not forgetting the network of relatives an individual might have (Knight and Walker, 1985; Kaufman, 1994; Sand, 2005; Socialstyrelsen, 2005a). Financial compensation and needs assessment is another area where the concept of need is used to ensure that people can manage to live comfortably on their pensions (Bond et al, 1993). The complex concept of need can be understood in relation to help, personal support and care as a construction of what is available in terms of services and personal support, as defined by administrators and politicians. Holistic goals formulated within the legal framework to allow Swedish municipalities to work for quality of life, and supporting an independent life for older people, have been fragmented into a catalogue of individually assessed needs (SFS, 1980/2001:453; Socialstyrelsen 2005a). Satisfying the needs of older people in the municipal context has been left to politicians and administrators to a much greater extent than is the case with childcare, for which the state has largely retained overall responsibility (Trydegård and Thorslund, 2001; Rauch, 2005). Comparative studies between municipalities, looking at their policies and work on social care for older people, show that the differences have increased. The former, and originally universal, Scandinavian welfare model has become more fragmented (Rauch, 2005).

To sum up, the complex concept of need is socially constructed as well as being a political *mantra*. The complex needs of older people are to a growing extent met by support built on assessments of a catalogue of fragmented help interventions.

The care concept

Care, seen as help, support and attention to a person's individual predicament is a spontaneous and universal act of solidarity between human beings. It is the 'willingness to help your neighbour', to use a Christian term. Bauman (1993) argues for intuitive, spontaneous willingness to give care whenever necessary. He strongly rejects efforts to codify caring into ethical guidelines. From another perspective, as part of paid social care work, professional care ethics have developed with or without feminist approaches. The paid care work that we have been used to counting on in Swedish welfare is to a large extent a consequence of the entrance of women into the labour market. This began with home helpers in the 1940s but grew to a larger scale during the 1960s and 1970s. The transfer to a situation where both parents in the household leave home for paid work evoked demands for new ways to satisfy home-help requirements within nuclear families. It also created a female-dominated labour market of helpers (Eliasson and Szebehely, 1992). There was a move away from the responsibilities of the family to the community. Eventually this became a task for the public sector, and was legitimated by society through legislation, staff training and state directives to the municipalities (Szebehely, 1995). Simultaneously, however, alongside this ongoing translation from a private to a societal sphere, there remained a great responsibility within the family for the care of near relatives; something that could be defined as hidden, silent, time-consuming and never-ending work (Sand, 2005).

The empirical and theoretical research by the Norwegian sociologist Kari Waerness (1996) has been of profound importance to the evolution of a care discourse in Scandinavia. Influenced by an Anglo-Saxon tradition, and in order to identify different kinds of caring and cared-for individuals, Waerness developed various typologies in order to conceptualise differences between service and care, and symmetries in the relationships between giver and taker in these kinds of relationships. Her main concept – *rationality of caring* – was first introduced in a seminar in Stockholm in 1981 and developed in an article in 1984. Waerness argued that caring should be both (a) a relationship characterised by quality and understanding of the context at hand and consciousness of the existential conditions of the individual and (b) a planned and evolved practice characterised by rational action in paid, female-dominated work. Significantly, she strongly rejected the community care ideology that was evolving during the 1980s, principally with the argument that this kind of restructuring of people's everyday lives could no longer offer opportunities for community care as a realistic alternative within the care sector (1985). Her argument was that the emergence of women as major players in the labour market was a reality, and thus women were not an alternative in a supposed voluntary community care ideology. Looking back over the last 20 years we realise that women not only make up a large part of the labour force within the health and social care sector but simultaneously are responsible for a great deal of the private care within their nuclear families, as well as care for relatives. In retrospective studies Waerness (1999) has demonstrated the risks: over-rationalised and cost-effective care, leading to stressed social care staff who are unable to take an empathic approach to the care takers. Abstract care bureaucracies develop formal relationships with people whose real need is for personal service and care.

To sum up, Waerness has been of great importance to the research and practice of care in Scandinavia, and the definition of care. In her construction of the *rationality of caring* she includes both quality of care, and one-to-one relationships, typified by the special quality of the relationship between giver and taker. Her rejection of the community care ideology points to the difficulties of a welfare society that was too big, too expensive, and in search of alternative solutions to its contemporary problems; in this case all too unrealistic.

Ageing and care – the forming of a discourse

Citizenship and rights, needs and care can in a social historical perspective be looked upon as key concepts on which state, church and local community have been forced to and have tried to take positions. Looking to older people, the so-called client mixture (*klientelblandningen*) in the poor houses was, for hundreds of years, the kind of 'solution' that local communities developed to take care of the poor, old and chronically ill, physically as well as mentally. This responsibility for the old and the poor was defined as elementary survival (Odén, 1983a, 1983b; Gustafsson, 1987).

In 1940 a government commission noticed that homes for older people still had problems with their client mixture (SOU, 1942:56; Olofsson, 1993; Olsson, 1993; Edebalk, 1994). The state became aware of persistent, negative conditions affecting older people in these communities. A new policy for older people, including nursing and care, was introduced and one specific kind of housing for these people, the municipal elderly home (*ålderdomshemmet*), became the model for the whole country. Legislation concerning older people remained in the form of the Poor Law Act (Edebalk, 1990, 1991, p 41). During the next three decades the building of homes for older people proceeded, as did the building of medical care and nursing homes in response to an increasing number of older people with sustainable diseases.

Society began to question whether older people's homes were merely repositories and the basis of the ideology of normalisation was formulated as a critique of the system. It was felt that older people should be given the opportunity to remain at home for as long as possible, if necessary with home help. So in 1952 the National Board of Health and Welfare published the first directives for a home-help organisation for older persons in the municipalities. Alternatives to institutional care for older people were to be investigated (Szebehely, 1995). Supplementary home help became a favoured option for older people's care in the politics of the period, with residential care seen as a resource only for those with more severe care and nursing needs. Needs began to be met in the home by the municipalities (Szebehely, 1995).

What emerged in those years can be regarded as the foundation of contemporary home care for older people. The main actors in this development were women, simultaneously housewives with their own households. The paid home help proceeded with the help of their tacit knowledge.

The number of older people with severe nursing and care needs increased. This corresponded to increasing demands for home help and the establishment of institutional care for those older people whose needs were severe (SOU, 1977:99; Szebehely, 1995). At the beginning of the 1970s the *principle of normalisation* was crystallised. This principle became, and still is, the dominant ideology within Swedish care of older people (SOU, 1975:39, p 55; Proposition 2005/07:115).

To sum up, individualisation, personal integrity, home-help services and state subsidies contributed to normalisation. The expansion progressed at different rates in different municipalities. From a professional perspective it was enough to be a woman. A new kind of female profession was evolving – home helpers as the creators of public care. What was not considered were the demands put on frail relatives. The problems they currently face and the support they receive will be dealt with in the next section.

The current situation with regard to the welfare of older people

Normalisation began in an era when municipalities, in the name of a universal welfare tradition, were able to satisfy care needs. It eventually received legal support in the form of the Social Services Act and still influences actions taken concerning the care of older people (SFS, 1980/2001:453; Proposition 2005/06:115).

Contemporary analyses, however, indicate that a fall in the proportion of older people receiving home-help services is only partly explained by their reduced needs. (The number of people receiving home help fell over a 15-year period [between 1988/89 and 2002/03]: Socialstyrelsen,

2005a).A redefinition of the concept of need has occurred. Developments in recent decades indicate that society's total financial resources decide how many older people will be defined as needing help, rather than the health and capabilities of the people themselves (Gurner and Thorslund, 2003; Socialstyrelsen, 2005a). Special housing has, due to cost, been replaced by home-help services, which include domestic duties as well as personal care, meals-on-wheels, security alarms and daily activities. Nurses provide medical care in the home (Trydegård and Thorslund, 2001). The legal regulation of municipal responsibility, and the Reform Law on older people (the ÄDEL reform) in 1992 gave the municipalities 'the responsibility for the administration of nursing homes and home nursing care. The municipalities were also given the financial responsibility for ... "bed-blockers"' (Thorslund et al, 1997, p 199).

The contemporary situation is characterised by a growing insight that 'the pendulum' has swung too far in favour of home-help services. Special housing has been accepted too readily. Persons with severe dementia are those first to receive priority in institutional settings, and thereafter, those with greater care needs. Personal care of a wife/husband puts huge demands on spouses, who are often frail and of a great age themselves (Sand, 2005; Szebehely, 2005).

Demographically, Sweden has the oldest population in the world: the number of persons 80 years and older (sometimes described as the fourth age) making up slightly more than 5% of the total population (over nine million in 2004). According to official statistics this is expected to be the case up to 2050, although with big regional differences (Socialstyrelsen, 2005b, p 37). Women live longer than men; the ratio of women to men in Sweden, aged 80 plus, is 8:1. Most women live the last years of their lives alone, while the majority of men live their last years with a partner. In this same age group 78% of women live in single households, while the male proportion is 38% (Socialstyrelsen, 2005b).

> The average life expectancy increases for both men and women who are married or cohabiting and it is also expected that they will live together for more years than earlier generations. As in Great Britain, prognoses indicate that the number of older women in Sweden living with a partner will increase. (Socialstyrelsen, 2005b, p 38).

Figure 14.1 shows costs for primary medical care, hospital treatment including specialist treatment and municipal care for older people (including municipal medical care) by age group and sex in 2003 (Socialstyrelsen, 2005b, p 275). Costs for medical treatment for men

Figure 14.1: Medical/specialist treatment, primary healthcare and municipal social care (home help and special housing), cost (thousands of SEK) per person, by gender and age group, 2003

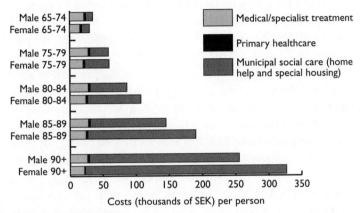

Source: Socialstyrelsen (2005b, p 275)

and women are comparatively constant through all age groups. The increasing costs are in the municipal care of older people for both sexes. Women of the highest ages dominate in special housing for older people (Socialstyrelsen, 2005b, p 275). Worthy of note is that municipality costs for special housing are about double those for home-help services in ordinary housing.

Estimated costs for social care of older people according to the Social Services Act and the Health and Medical Services Act are published by the National Board of Health and Welfare. Table 14.1 illustrates costs, in thousands of millions of SEK, for 2003 and 2004, at a national level.

Table 14.1 illustrates the municipal priorities of living in ordinary housing with home and medical help, where the increase was 6.2% between 2003 and 2004. There was a slight decrease in the costs for

Table 14.1: Total costs for care of the elderly (thousands of million SEK)

	2003	2004	Change 2003–04 (%)
Social care of older people, total	78,245	79,470	1.6
– Ordinary housing	23,998	25,495	6.2
– Special housing	52,786	52,523	–0.5
– Open activities	1,461	1,452	–0.6

Source: The National Board of Health and Welfare (2005c, p 7).

special housing as well as for open activities. Looking at the proportional costs in 2004, about 65% of the total referred to special housing, 33% referred to home-help services in ordinary housing and almost 2% to daily open activities (Socialstyrelsen, 2005c, p 8).

Statistics for municipal services given to persons 65 years and above during 2005, according to the Social Services Act (SFS, 2001:453) and the Health and Medical Services Act (SFS, 1982:763), are provided in Figures 14.2 to 14.5 (Socialstyrelsen, 2006).

Figure 14.2 illustrates the percentage of the population aged 65 and over, of different age classes, living permanently in special housing or receiving home-help services. Home-help service dominates for people up to 90 years of age. By age 95 special housing is the dominant form of help. In total, about 235,400 persons or 15% of the population aged 65 and over, received one of these forms of help in 2005. In comparison with the situation in 2000, the number of persons aged 65 and over living in special housing or with home-help services decreased by 3,800 persons. At the same time, as the number of people in special housing fell to 15% (n=17,800 persons), those with home-help service increased to 12% (n=14,100 persons).

The proportion of people with home help in 2005 was 9% of those aged 65 and over (n=135,000). The increase occurred in the age group 80 years and over, while for those people aged 65-79 there was a decrease (Socialstyrelsen, 2006). This might illustrate a more stringent assessment.

Figure 14.2: Percentage of persons aged 65 and over permanently living in special housing or with home-help service on 1 October 2005

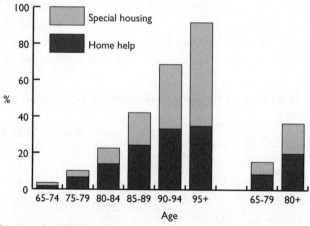

Source: Socialstyrelsen (2006, p 16)

Among those receiving home help on 1 October 2005 the percentage of women was higher than that of men. For people aged 95 and older, more men than women received home help (see Figure 14.3).

Figure 14.4 shows hours per month for which it has been decided a person should receive home-help in their ordinary homes. Only 38% received one to nine hours per month and about 23% received between 10 and 25 hours per month. Approximately 0.5% received 200 hours or more.

Figure 14.3: Percentage of the population aged 65 and over with home-help service living in ordinary housing on 1 October 2005

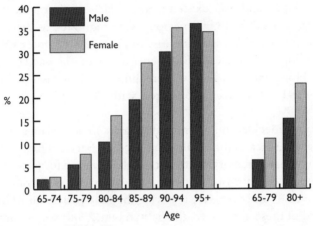

Source: Socialstyrelsen (2006, p 18)

Figure 14.4: Percentage of the population receiving home-help services plotted against allocated help hours/month on 1 October 2005

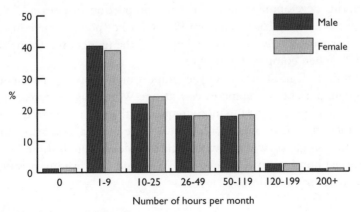

Source: Socialstyrelsen (2006, p 19)

Of those receiving home help about 10% received assistance from private agencies, that is, from a provider contracted by the municipality. Compared with 2000 this represents an increase of 3% (Socialstyrelsen, 2006).

Those helping a relative in their home are able to receive benefits from the municipality, paid on behalf of the person receiving care. On 1 October 2005 about 5,300 persons were permitted relative care benefits (*anhörigstöd*) by the municipalities. At the same time about 1,800 older people received help from a relative who was contracted by the municipality, most often a husband/wife (Socialstyrelsen, 2006).

Home medical care (*hemsjukvård*) delivered by the municipality to persons aged 65 and over existed in about 50% of the municipalities. On 1 October 2005, 48,000 persons were registered as receivers of home medical care. This is an increase of 7% on 2000 figures. Of those receiving home medical care, 70% were aged 80 or older and 65% were women. Home medical help was, in almost 70% of cases, combined with home-help services. Compared with 2000 this represents an increase of 9%.

Day care is decided on an individual basis, in accordance with the Social Services Act or the Health and Medical Services Act, and takes the form of shared activity, treatment or rehabilitation for persons with, for example, dementia or mental or physical disabilities. About 12,200 persons aged 65 and over were receiving this kind of help on 1 October 2005, and of these about 64% (Socialstyrelsen, 2006) were women.

Around 100,400 persons aged 65 and over lived in special types of housing on 1 October 2005, representing a decrease of 15% (n=17,800) since the year 2000. The number of people aged 65-79 has fallen by 1% (n=7,000) since 2000, and those aged 80 and over have decreased by 2% (n=10,800). In relation to the total population aged 65 and over, this development means that the proportion of persons living in special housing has fallen from 8% to 6%. For persons aged 80 and over permanently living in special housing, the reduction is from 20% to 17% when compared with 2000.

Figure 14.5 illustrates how the proportion of those permanently living in special housing increases with age. Women aged 75 years and over live in special housing more frequently than men, due to the fact that they often live longer with one or more medical conditions and are often single or widows with high care needs. Of all those living in special housing on 1 October 2005, around 13% lived in privately owned accommodation.

Figure 14.5: Percentage of the population aged 65 and over living permanently in special housing on 1 October 2005

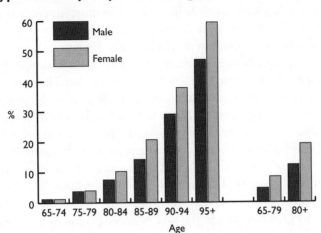

Source: Socialstyrelsen (2006, p 21)

Summary

The social care discourse of the Swedish model evolved in an era of universal welfare solutions distributed by the public sector, with the state as the conductor and the municipalities determining and distributing services as the providers. Legally, questions concerning older people came under the Poor Laws, a situation that persisted until the Social Services Act came into force in 1980. Since then, service is the overall terminology for the satisfaction of social and personal needs, services and care. Different housing solutions have been discussed and tried. Since the middle of the 1970s the principle of normalisation has been dominant, leading to a contemporary situation characterised by a lack of special housing for older people most in need of care; this also affects those with medical needs who are not in hospital. This situation has also been marked by a growing ageing population, lack of educated social care staff and rising costs. Changes in family structure and a high proportion of women in the labour market have also contributed to a situation whereby society can no longer count on women to take responsibility for the unpaid care of older relatives.

Statistics show that the costs are mainly matters for the municipalities, increasing with the age of individuals; costs for the county councils are comparatively constant for ages 65 and over. The increase in costs has been in services to those living in ordinary housing at the expense of those living in special housing. The number of persons permanently living in special housing in 2005 was 100,400, a decrease of 15% on

2000 figures. The management of special housing represents 65% of the total costs of care for older people. The proportions of people living in ordinary housing with home-help services and those in special housing also indicate the stricter needs assessments that are made before anyone is judged in need of a place in special housing. The home-help services provided to people living in their own home increase with age. Overall, a higher percentage of women receive help than men, illustrating their tendency to live alone as widows or as single people. Relative care benefits are a supplement to home help, whereby a relative receives money from the municipality for help to a person according to their assessed needs. Home medical care to persons aged 65 and over, mostly women, was delivered in about half of the municipalities, an increase between 2000 and 2005. Day care was provided for about 12,200 people of aged 65 and over, most of them women. Private initiatives still play a small, but growing, part in the care of older people in Sweden.

The social care of older people is currently characterised by a fragmentation of help, where needs are judged ever more stringently and without a holistic approach. There is a need for consolidation of resources, in terms of money, staff, knowledge and responsibility, given to the care of older people. To complete this chapter, reference should be made to the government Bill that was presented at the beginning of 2006 (Proposition 2005/06:115). The main propositions are listed below:

Government suggestions for policies on nursing and the care of older people (Proposition 2005/06:115)

Organisation:

- policy instruments on a national level to increase management of nursing and care;
- agreements between county councils and municipalities about participation of physicians in the municipal medical care of older people;
- development of medical treatment in private homes with the municipality as principal organiser;
- education and support for staff who care for older people; organisation development.

Medical care:

- increase in rehabilitation;
- attention to nutrition;
- attention to the pharmaceutical treatment of older people;
- physicians involved in the care of older people on a municipal level;
- increased quality in the treatment of people with dementia;
- staff continuity in medical treatment of older people.

Social care:

- legal suggestion: legal right to home service for persons of aged 67 years or over;
- special attention to ageing in a multiethnic society;
- strengthening of legal rights in the Social Services Act (SFS, 2001:453);
- attention to good and purposeful housing for older people;
- health promotion and preventative measures for older people.

The next few years will show to what degree the state, county councils and municipalities will be able to meet the challenges and consolidate their resources in order to develop care for older people that is effective, professional, well organised and ethically defensible. Key actors will be professionals and politicians, as well as researchers and teachers.

Note
[1] Selma Lagerlöf (1858-1940), storyteller, winner of the Nobel Prize for literature.

References

Abbott, A. (1988) *The System of Professions: An Essay on the Division of Expert Labour*, Chicago, IL/London: University of Chicago Press.

Bauman, Z. (1993) *Postmodern Ethics*, Oxford: Blackwell.

Bond, J., Coleman, P. and Peace, S. (eds) (1993) *Ageing in Society*, London: Sage Publications.

Dahlberg, L. (2004) 'Substitution in statutory and voluntary support for relatives of older people', *International Journal of Social Welfare*, vol 13, no 2, pp 181-8.

Care, community and citizenship

Dahlberg, L. (2005) 'Interaction between voluntary and statutory social service provision in Sweden: a matter of welfare pluralism, substitution or complementarity?', *Social Policy and Administration*, vol 39, no 7, pp 740-63.

Edebalk, P. G. (1990) *Hemmaboendeideologins genombrott: Åldringsvård och socialpolitik 1945-1965*, Lund: Meddelanden från Socialhögskolan.

Edebalk, P. G. (1991) *Drömmen om ålderdomshemmet: Åldringsvård och socialpolitik 1900-1952*, Lund: Meddelanden från Socialhögskolan.

Edebalk, P. G. (1994) 'Möllermodellen – svensk socialförsäkring 1944-1951', *Socialvetenskaplig tidskrift*, no 1, p 6.

Eliasson, R. and Szebehely, M. (1992) 'Äldreomsorgens särart och särbehandling', in R. Eliasson (ed) *Egenheter och allmänheter: En antologi om omsorg och omsorgens villkor*, Lund Studies in Social Welfare, Lund: Arkiv Förlag, No VII.

Esping-Andersen, G. (1990) *The Three Worlds of Welfare Capitalism*, Cambridge: Polity Press.

Gurner, U. and Thorslund, M. (2003) *Dirigent saknas i vård och omsorg om äldre*, Stockholm: Natur and Kultur.

Gustafsson, R. Å. (1987) *Traditionernas ok: Den svenska hälso- och sjukvårdens organisering i historie-sociologiskt perspektiv*, Stockholm: Esselte.

Hjorth Aronsson, C. (1999) 'Struktur, handling och rumslig morfologi: två fall av förnyelse och byggande i urban miljö', Doctoral dissertation, Department of Sociology, Uppsala University.

Kaufman, S. (1994) 'The social construction of frailty: an anthropological perspective', *Journal of Aging Studies*, vol 8, no 1, pp 45-58.

Knight, B. and Walker, D. L. (1985) 'Toward a definition of alternatives to institutionalization for the frail elderly', *Gerontologist*, vol 25, no 4, pp 358-63.

Korpi, W. and Palme, J. (2003) 'New politics and class politics in the context of austerity and globalization: welfare state regress in 18 countries, 1975-1995', *American Political Science Review*, vol 97, no 3, pp 425-46.

Lagerlöf, S. (1891/1997) *Gösta Berling Saga*, Iowa City: The Penfield Press.

Lundberg, O. and Palme, J. (2002) 'A balance sheet for welfare: Sweden in the 1990s', *Scandinavian Journal of Public Health*, vol 30, no 4, pp 241-3.

Marshall, G. (ed) (1998) *A Dictionary of Sociology*, Oxford: Oxford University Press.

Maslow, A. (1970) *Motivation and Personality*, New York: Harper Collins.

Murphy, A. (1988) *Social Closure: The Theory of Monopolization and Exclusion*, Oxford: Clarendon Press.

Odén, B. (1983a) 'Åldrandet och arbetslivet: en introduction', in L. Tornstam (ed) *Äldre i samhället – förr, nu och i framtiden, del 2: Probleminventeringar*, Stockholm: Liber förlag, pp 69-80.

Odén, B. (1983b) 'Åldrandet, familjen och de sociala relationerna: en introduktion', in L. Tornstam (ed) *Äldre i samhället – förr, nu och i framtiden, del 2: Probleminventeringar*, Stockholm: Liber förlag, pp 125-36.

Olofsson, G. (1993) *Det svenska pensionssystemet 1913-1993: Historia, struktur och konflikter*, Lund: Arkiv No, pp 58-9.

Olsson, S. E. (1993) *Social Policy and Welfare State in Sweden* (2nd edition), Lund: Arkiv.

Perkin, H. (1996) *The Third Revolution: Professional Elites in the Modern World*, London and New York: Routledge.

Proposition 2005/06:115 *Nationell utvecklingsplan för vård och omsorg om äldre*, Stockholm: Riksdagens Tryckeriexpedition.

Rauch, D. (2005) 'Institutional fragmentation and social service variations: a Scandinavian comparison', Doctoral thesis, Department of Sociology, Umeå University.

Sand, A.-B. (2005) 'Informell äldreomsorg samt stöd till informella vårdare – en nordisk forskningsöversikt', in M. Szebehely (ed) *Äldreomsorgsforskning i Norden: En kunskapsöversikt*, Köpenhamn: Nordiska Ministerrådet, pp 197-241.

Socialstyrelsen (2005a) *Hemtjänsten och de äldres behov – en jämförelse över tid* [*Home-help Services and the Needs of the Elderly – A Comparison Over Time*], Stockholm: The National Board of Health and Welfare.

Socialstyrelsen (2005b) *Folkhälsorapport 2005* [*Public Health Report 2005*], Stockholm: The National Board of Health and Welfare & Centre for Epidemiology.

Socialstyrelsen (2005c) *Jämförelsetal för socialtjänsten år 2004* [*Comparatives between Municipalities of Social Services in 2004*], Stockholm: National Board of Health and Welfare.

Socialstyrelsen (2006) *Äldre – vård och omsorg år 2005: Kommunala insatser enligt Socialtjänstlagen och Hälso- och sjukvårdslagen* [*Elderly – Nursing and Care 2005: Municipal Services According to the Social Services Act and the Health and Medical Services Act*], Stockholm: Socialstyrelsen.

SOU (Statens offentliga utredningar) (1942:56) *Utredning och förslag angående socialvårdens organisation m.m*, Stockholm: Socialvårdskommittén.

SOU (1975:39) *Statsbidrag till kommunerna*, Stockholm: Kommunalekonomiska utredningen.

SOU (1977:99) *Pensionär-75: En kartläggning med framtidsaspekter*, Stockholm: Pensionärsundersökningen.

SOU (2003:91) *Elderly Politics for the Future: 100 Steps to Safety and Development with an Ageing Population*, Stockholm: Allmänna förlaget.

SFS (Svensk författningssamling) (1980/2001:453) *Lag om Socialtjänst* [*Social Services Act*], Rikslex.

SFS (1982:763) *Hälso-och Sjukvårdslagen* [Health and Medical Services Act], Rikslex.

Szebehely, M. (1995) *Vardagens organisering: Om vårdbiträden och gamla i hemtjänsten*, Lund Studies in Social Welfare No IX, Lund: Arkiv Förlag

Thorslund, M., Bergmark, Å. and Parker, M. (1997) 'Difficult decisions on care and services for elderly people: the dilemma of setting priorities in the welfare state', *Scandinavian Journal of Social Welfare*, no 6, pp 197-206.

Trydegård, G.-B. and Thorslund, M. (2001) 'Inequality in the welfare state? Local variation in care of the elderly – the case of Sweden', *International Journal of Social Welfare*, no 10, pp 174-84.

Waerness, K. (1984) 'The rationality of caring', in M. Söder (ed) *Economic and Industrial Democracy*, London: Sage Publications, pp 185-211.

Waerness, K. (1985) 'Den nye 'community-ideologien' – en utfordring for sociologisk forskning', *Sociologisk forskning*, no 2-3, pp 21-36.

Waerness, K. (1996) 'Omsorgsrationalitet: reflexioner over ett begrepps karriär', in R. Eliasson (ed) *Omsorgens skiftningar: Begreppet, vardagen, politiken, forskningen*, Lund: Studentlitteratur, pp 203-20.

Waerness, K (1999) 'Kan travelhet skape grusomhet i den offentlige omsorgstjenesten?', in K. Thorsen and K. Waerness (eds) *Blir omsorgen borte? Eldreomsorgens hverdag i den senmoderne velferdsstaten*, Oslo: Ad Notam Gyldendal.

FIFTEEN

From old to new forms of civic engagement: communities and care in Germany

Frank Bönker

Germany is famous for the traditionally strong role of communities in the provision of personal social services. Until the 1990s, the bulk of these services, including social care, were provided by the so-called welfare associations (*Wohlfahrtsverbände*), non-profit organisations with deep roots in the local community. Strongly embedded in their respective socio-cultural milieu, the welfare associations were able to rely on a high degree of civic engagement. Moreover, the fact that they were organised along ideological lines guaranteed a strong cultural 'fit' between care givers and care receivers.

Since the 1980s, however, the role of the welfare associations in social care has undergone considerable change (Bönker and Wollmann, 1996, 2000; Heinze and Strünck, 2000). The welfare associations have not only lost market share, they have also become increasingly similar to commercial service providers. This double marketisation has been accompanied by changes in the level and form of civic engagement. On the one hand, the traditional forms of engagement, characterised by 'lifelong and humble volunteering' (Bode and Evers, 2005, p 113) within the confines of particular milieu and organisations, most notably the welfare associations, have suffered from erosion. On the other hand, new forms of civic engagement, with a more individualistic, project-type orientation, a greater demand for participation and a much less prominent role for the welfare associations, have gained importance and have increasingly attracted the interest of policy makers.

In this chapter, I analyse the changing forms of civic engagement in German social care, with a view to identifying major trends and policy issues. I start by sketching the old forms of civic engagement as they have defined the traditional social service regime. Next, I examine the factors that have contributed to the demise of this regime and to the erosion of the old forms of civic engagement. The third section then deals with the spread of new forms of civic engagement and discusses various attempts to encourage voluntary engagement in the field of social care. The chapter closes with a brief summary.

Civic engagement in the traditional social service regime

From a comparative perspective, the social service regime that prevailed in Germany until the 1990s stood out because of the dominant position of the welfare associations (Bönker and Wollmann, 2000; Heinze and Strünck, 2000; Bode and Evers, 2005, pp 107-9). The latter provided about two thirds of all personal social services and were also formally incorporated into policy making at the local and state level, thus playing a major role in the formulation and implementation of social policy.

Historically, the welfare associations have grown out of the numerous charities and self-help organisations that mushroomed at the local level in the late 19th century. Today, they are organised into six umbrella organisations. Three of these have been aligned with the churches – the *Deutscher Caritasverband* with the Catholic church, the *Diakonisches Werk* with the Protestant church and the *Zentralwohlfahrtsstelle der Juden in Deutschland* with the Jewish community. A fourth welfare association, the *Arbeiterwohlfahrt*, has been part of the Social-Democratic Labour movement. The two other associations – the Red Cross and the *Deutscher Paritätischer Wohlfahrtsverband* – have organised those that have stood outside the churches and the Labour movement.

The strong role of the welfare associations in both service provision and policy making dates back to the 1920s (Bönker and Wollmann, 2000, pp 329-31; Evers and Sachße, 2003, pp 61-71). It reflects the strength of corporatist traditions in Germany, as well as the strong influence of Catholic social thinking on German social policy. The power of Catholic social thinking has found its expression in the official endorsement of the famous principle of subsidiarity according to which social services ought to be provided by public authorities only if families and non-profit organisations cannot cope. In line with this principle, the 1961 Federal Social Assistance Act gave the welfare associations clear priority in service provision and obliged local authorities to support, and to cooperate with, the welfare associations.

The cooperation between the local authorities and the welfare associations manifested itself in the formal representation of the welfare associations in certain local committees. Moreover, the welfare associations enjoyed strong tax privileges and received substantial public subsidies, which added up to about a tenth of the welfare associations' revenues in the 1980s. Because of their powerful legal and political position, the welfare associations played a major role in the massive expansion of personal social services that took place in Germany in the 1970s and 1980s. In the course of this development, the welfare associations grew substantially. The number of regular employees almost tripled from 382,000 in 1970 to 1.12 million in 1996.

The strong role of the welfare associations in the provision of personal social services favoured a high degree of civic engagement. Since the welfare associations, most notably those affiliated with the churches and the Labour movement, were rooted strongly in their respective socio-cultural milieu and were part of a broader subculture of associations, they were able to rely on a high level of voluntary engagement. According to estimates, the number of volunteers stood at about 2.5 million in the 1980s, about half of whom were actually engaged in the delivery of social services. In addition, the welfare associations benefited from substantial donations. Despite the strong increases in revenues from service fees and public subsidies, such donations still accounted for about 5% of all revenues of the welfare associations in the 1980s.

Given the degree to which they are embedded in different ideological communities, civic engagement in the welfare associations was traditionally based on a strong sense of belonging to a particular community and the commitment to a particular ideological cause. It was seen as natural and/or as mutual social obligation rather than as a temporary individual project or a way of individual self-realisation. As a result, voluntary engagement was relatively stable and reliable and not limited to particular activities or life stages. Nor was it fraught with strong demands for participation.

The degree to which the welfare associations were embedded in different ideological communities also provided for a strong cultural 'fit' between care givers and care receivers. The coexistence of different associations made it possible for frail people to find a service provider representing, and catering for, their own community. In many cases, care receivers and care givers even knew each other from joint activities and/or joint membership of a particular subculture. Thus, the traditional German social service regime nicely illustrates Burton A. Weisbrod's famous argument that the involvement of non-profit organisations in service provision can help to meet the demands of citizens in diverse, multicultural communities (Weisbrod, 1988).

The demise of the traditional social service regime and the erosion of the old forms of civic engagement

Since the late 1980s, the provision of personal social services in the Federal Republic has undergone far-reaching changes. These changes can best be described as a 'double marketisation' (Bönker and Wollmann, 2000). For one thing, the welfare associations have lost substantial market shares to commercial providers. For another, the modes of service provision have changed and the welfare associations themselves have developed similarities with their commercial competitors. The demise of the traditional social service regime has been accompanied by an erosion of the old forms of civic engagement. These changes in both social service provision and civic engagement have been brought about by an interplay of changes in society, in policy and in the organisational strategies of the welfare associations themselves (Bode and Evers, 2005, pp 110-14).

To start with, the position of the welfare associations has suffered from socio-cultural mega trends such as individualisation, secularisation and the increase in female employment (Heinze and Strünck, 2001, pp 235-40). These trends have weakened the old milieu upon which the welfare associations have rested and have contributed to an erosion of the old forms of civic engagement. As the identification with the churches and the Labour movement has declined, voluntary engagement in, and for, the welfare associations has become less natural. Temporary interest in particular 'projects' has replaced unconditional lifelong faithful commitment. Citizens have paid more attention to the individual 'value-added' of civic engagement and have placed higher demands on their participation. As a result, the welfare associations have faced increasing problems in attracting volunteers and donations. This drying out of civic engagement has made the welfare associations closer in nature to other providers, most notably local governments and commercial providers.

Socio-cultural mega trends have also had some implications for the demand for services and the cultural 'fit' between care givers and care receivers. In the course of individualisation and secularisation, the demand for 'ideologically correct' services has fallen. Customers have paid less attention to the ideological background and affiliation of the service provider, but have become more interested in the quality of services in a more narrow sense. As a result, the welfare associations have lost one of their traditional comparative advantages. This change in demand patterns has further increased the pressure put on the welfare associations.

A second source of change has been changes in policy. In the 1990s, the regulation of German personal social services was put on a new footing (Bönker and Wollmann, 2006). These changes in regulation aimed at strengthening the position of self-help groups and commercial providers and at replacing the traditional forms of cooperation between local governments and welfare associations with market-type contracts. Reforms were motivated by concerns that the welfare associations had become too bureaucratic and that the quality and responsiveness of services and the efficiency of service delivery had suffered from the exclusive and cosy cooperation among the welfare associations and between the welfare associations and local authorities, which lacked transparency (Seibel, 1992; Meyer, 1997). These concerns were strongly inspired by the ideas of New Public Management, which were all the rage in the second half of the 1990s.

The introduction of a new long-term care insurance scheme in 1995/96 represented the single most important change in the regulation of personal social services (Evers, 1998; Ostner, 1998). The new legislation did away with the traditional privileges of the welfare associations in service provision and policy formation and accepted commercial providers as contract partners with 'equal rights'. The new rules paved the way for a substantial expansion of commercial service providers, particularly in the field of domiciliary care. In 2003, the proportion of licensed service providers who were commercial providers had increased to 55%, while that of service providers associated with the welfare associations had fallen to 43%, much less than before the mid-1990s (Statistisches Bundesamt, 2005, table 2.1).

The introduction of the long-term care insurance scheme not only weakened the position of the welfare associations, but also had a negative effect on civic engagement in care (Deutscher Bundestag, 2002, pp 251-2). First, the new legislation weakened those actors that had traditionally 'channelled' the bulk of civic engagement (the welfare associations), and strengthened those actors that normally do not draw on voluntary engagement, that is, commercial providers. Second, the very introduction of the new scheme has tended to discourage civic engagement. Even though the size of benefits has been limited right from the beginning, the new scheme has nourished the impression that civic engagement is no longer necessary, because the frail are now taken care of by a specialised, professional scheme. This impression has prevented citizens from becoming, or remaining, active and has led many local authorities and other actors to reduce their efforts to encourage civic engagement.[1] Finally, the introduction of the long-term care insurance scheme has given rise to a 'medicalisation' of services.

Based on a narrow, medical understanding of frailty, the new legislation has favoured an orientation towards the healthcare system in which civic engagement has traditionally played a much more limited role than in personal social services.[2]

A third reason for the erosion of the traditional social service regime and the old forms of civic engagement has been the reorientation of the welfare associations themselves. In the 1990s, the latter began to pay less attention to the encouragement of civic engagement and the integration of volunteers into service provision. For one thing, the growth and professionalisation of the welfare associations in the 1970s and 1980s favoured the rise of a new generation of professional managers. Partly 'socialised' outside the welfare associations and often keen on mimicking the structures of the apparently more successful and modern commercial providers, some members of this generation have tended to see civic engagement as a sideshow, if not as an outdated, pre-modern relic. This sceptical position towards volunteers has been echoed by some of the regular employees, who have feared that, in times of fiscal retrenchment, the encouragement of civic engagement might favour cuts in regular employment.

Not surprisingly, the 'self-commercialisation' of the welfare associations was most pronounced in East Germany where the socio-cultural milieu upon which the West German welfare associations rested were largely destroyed under communism. Thus, when the welfare associations were set up in the East, they could not build on the same foundations of citizen engagement that existed in the West. As a result, the new welfare associations in the East are more similar to commercial providers than their Western 'parents' (Angerhausen et al, 1998). The viability of such 'lean' welfare associations served as a model for the 'modernisers' in the welfare associations in the West.

Social care and the rise of new forms of civic engagement

The erosion of the traditional forms of civic engagement has gone hand in hand with the spread of new forms of activity. A number of empirical analyses suggest that, contrary to many fears, the readiness for, and the level of, civic engagement has not declined over time (Infratest, 2005). What we see, however, is a change in the forms of engagement. Civic engagement is increasingly motivated by individual interest in self-realisation and in a particular issue rather than by attachment to a specific group, socio-cultural milieu or community or by commitment to shared norms. It also comes with greater demands for qualification and participation. As a result, civic engagement has become more short term, more volatile and more project oriented. Moreover, the welfare associations have lost their role as the single most important framework for civic engagement.

The encouragement of new forms of civic engagement in personal social services has been an issue in both academic and political debates ever since the late 1970s. It has been discussed under different headings that reflect a shift in the Zeitgeist (Heinze and Olk, 2001; Olk, 2001). Initially, civic engagement was primarily seen as a means of counterbalancing the bureaucratisation of formal services. Later on, civic engagement was promoted as an alternative to formal employment, a way of closing gaps in the social net and a source of social cohesion and social capital. The broad interest in civic engagement is evidenced by the instigation of a parliamentary commission in 1998. This commission, which consisted of Members of Parliament, academics and other experts, not only came up with a voluminous report on the state of civic engagement (Deutscher Bundestag, 2002), but also stimulated the debate on civic engagement by commissioning research reports and by organising public hearings on the topic (Heinze and Olk, 2001).

In Germany, social care belongs to those fields that feature most prominently in the debates on fostering civic engagement (Landtag NRW, 2005, pp 518-21; Deutscher Bundestag, 2002, pp 250-4). One reason is the growing awareness that the ongoing demographic changes will produce a strong 'demand' for civic engagement in social care. Special attention has been paid to the increasing number of frail people suffering from dementia. Their needs are only partly addressed by the long-term care insurance scheme with its narrow understanding of frailty. Also, it is widely believed that looking after people with dementia is a type of care that can be undertaken relatively easily by volunteers.

A second reason for the interest in civic engagement in social care can be located on the supply side. There is some evidence that the existing potential for civic engagement in care is only partly exploited (Blanke and Schridde, 2001, pp 123-7; Deutscher Bundestag, 2002, p 92). According to one major survey, for instance, only about 5% of all Germans aged 14 and over are voluntarily engaged in social affairs (Infratest, 2005). At the same time, about 16% of those who would like to become involved would prefer to do so in the field of personal social services. Given such figures, many observers believe that it should be possible to increase the number of volunteers in social care. Among the different subgroups of potential volunteers, the 'young pensioners' – retired people who are still healthy and are looking for a new 'project' after decades of gainful employment – have become a major target group (Seiters, 2002). With their life experience and their awareness of the problems of ageing, they are seen as natural candidates for looking after frail older people.

Initiatives to foster civic engagement in social care have taken different forms. To start with, the welfare associations have rediscovered civic engagement (Deutscher Bundestag, 2002, pp 274-5). Compared to the early 1990s, they are now paying more attention to the recruitment and integration of volunteers and regard the latter as a major asset rather than as a relic. All welfare associations have made the involvement of volunteers a major part of their corporate identity. In order to become more attractive for interested citizens they have run advertising campaigns, have professionalised their human resources management and have tried to accommodate demands by potential volunteers for greater participation and a more project-oriented engagement (for examples, see Landtag NRW, 2005, pp 265-8).

The welfare associations have also been a driving force behind the mushrooming of volunteer bureaux (*Freiwilligenagenturen*) that has taken place since the mid-1990s (Heinze and Strünck, 2001, pp 245-7; Jakob and Janning, 2001; Deutscher Bundestag, 2002, pp 147-9). Set up by individual welfare associations, local authorities or alliances of local actors, these agencies have tried to recruit, to train and to place volunteers and to consult organisations interested in integrating volunteers in their work. Drawing on British, Dutch and US models, the main idea has been to bundle information and to create a single contact point for all those interested in civic engagement. The volunteer bureaux, of which there are an estimated 150, have promoted civic engagement in all kinds of fields, not only in social services (*Bundesarbeitsgemeinschaft der Freiwilligenagenturen*).

The activities of the welfare associations and the local authorities have been complemented by several initiatives at the federal level. The federal government has made a number of attempts to promote the role of volunteers in social care, especially the care of people with dementia. For example, it has co-financed a number of model projects testing new ways of integrating volunteers into social care. It has also introduced a supplementary long-term care insurance benefit for people with dementia.

The recruitment, qualification and integration of voluntary helpers were among the key issues in the federal government's programme 'Modern Services for the Elderly' (*Altenhilfestrukturen der Zukunft*), which ran from 1999 to 2003 (BMFSFJ, 2004). Within the framework of this programme, the government supported 20 innovative local projects.

The focus of these projects differed. Some concentrated on a better integration of different services; others aimed at exploring new forms of living or at improving services for those with dementia. In one way or another, however, a substantial number of projects tried to strengthen civic engagement and to provide a greater role for volunteers.

The support for model projects was extended and made on a regular basis in 2002, when the Red–Green government amended the law on long-term care insurance with a view to improving the situation for people suffering from dementia (Bundesregierung, 2004, pp 17–18). The new law obliges the long-term care insurance funds (*Pflegekassen*) to provide €10 million annually for supporting measures improving care for these citizens. The measures eligible for this support can take different forms, including courses for family members and volunteers, agencies for relief carers, and new forms of care for groups of sufferers by qualified volunteers. Due to German federalism, the eventual distribution of the money rests with the states. The care insurance funds do not cover all the costs. States and/or local governments are expected to bear half of the expenditure.

In 2002, the federal government also introduced a supplementary cash benefit of up to €460 per year for people with dementia. This benefit, which is only paid on top of the standard long-term care insurance benefits, can be spent on a number of specified services (§ 45b, SGB XI), most notably short-term and relief care not covered by the standard benefits and new forms of care for people with dementia. Again, special emphasis is put on care by volunteers. The government hoped that the new benefit, along with the financial support for model projects, would help to substantially expand the service infrastructure. Promoting care by volunteers has been seen as a way of improving the quality of support and of reducing the burden on the family without expanding costly formal intervention by professionals.

However, the expansion of services has progressed slowly (Bundesregierung, 2004, pp 29–34). By late 2004, the numbers both of model projects and of new kinds of services for people with dementia were much lower than originally expected and deemed necessary and desirable by the government. First, it took some time before the states adopted the complementary legislation required for the implementation of the new provisions. Second, the recruitment and qualification of volunteers was more difficult than expected. Third, the demand for services has remained lower than expected. In 2003, less than 10% of the 400,000 who were eligible actually claimed the new benefit for people with dementia. This reluctant take-up can partly be explained by a lack of information about the new benefit, and the limited availability of services. However, it also suggests that a substantial number of the frail, and their family members, still remain sceptical about care by 'strangers', be they professionals or volunteers.

The slow expansion of new kinds of care services for people with dementia shows that there are obstacles to strengthening civic engagement in personal social services. It shows how difficult it is to find volunteers, especially for more demanding and less attractive services, to integrate these volunteers into service provision, and to overcome reservations on the part of the 'clients' themselves. There are no simple solutions to these problems. Of course, there are calls for a better coordination of activities, a better 'social recognition' of civic engagement, more financial support for innovative projects and improved fiscal incentives for volunteering (see, for instance, Landtag NRW, 2005, pp 518-21). In an age of 'permanent austerity' (Pierson, 1998), however, all costly measures have met strong resistance.

Summary

This chapter has analysed the changing forms of civic engagement in German social care. It has shown that the traditional forms of civic engagement have suffered from erosion, but have been partly replaced with new forms of engagement. These changes in civic engagement have been a major factor in the transformation of the German social service regime. This is because the erosion of the traditional forms of civic engagement has contributed to the weakening and transformation of the welfare associations, which had dominated the provision of social services up until the 1990s.

As the chapter has shown, the encouragement of civic engagement in care has been ever present in German academic and political debates. A number of major reform initiatives are identifiable, especially since the mid-1990s. These initiatives have gained ground more recently with the federal government's attempts at promoting new forms of care services for those with dementia, which rely heavily on volunteers. However, these reforms have so far produced limited results. The slow expansion of the new services is evidence of the obstacles that exist to strengthening civic engagement and the role of the community in social care.

Notes

[1] In a way, this message is also conveyed by the federal government's regular reports on long-term care (Bundesregierung 1997, 2001, 2004). The first two reports, at least, do not raise the issue of civic engagement.

[2] However, it should be noted that some features of the long-term care insurance scheme have aimed at strengthening civic engagement. One of the main goals of the new scheme was to stabilise informal care and to promote 'a new culture of help and human devotion' (*eine neue Kultur des Helfens und der mitmenschlichen Zuwendung*) (§ 8(2), SGB XI). The measures adopted include courses and pension credits for informal carers as well as a special cash benefit (*Pflegegeld*) for frail people to be used for 'acknowledging' informal care, rather than for buying formal care. These measures have aimed at strengthening all kinds of informal care, including care by volunteers. In practice, however, they have mainly favoured care by family members, relatives and neighbours.

References

Angerhausen, S., Backhaus-Maul, H., Offe, C., Olk, T. and Schiebel, M. (1998) *Überholen ohne einzuholen: Freie Wohlfahrtspflege in Ostdeutschland*, Opladen: Westdeutscher Verlag.

Blanke, B. and Schridde, H. (2001) 'Bürgerengagement und aktivierender Staat', in R. G. Heinze, and T. Olk (eds) *Bürgerengagement in Deutschland: Bestandsaufnahme und Perspectiven*, Opladen: Leske and Budrich, pp 93-140.

BMFSFJ (Bundesministerium für Familie, Senioren, Frauen und Jugend) (ed) (2004) *Altenhilfestrukturen der Zukunft: Abschlussbericht der wissenschaftlichen Begleitforschung zum Bundesmodellprojekt*, Berlin: BMFSFJ.

Bode, I. and Evers, A. (2005) 'From institutional fixation to entrepreneurial mobility? The German third sector and its contemporary challenges', in A. Evers and J. Laville (eds) *The Third Sector in Europe*, Cheltenham, UK/Northampton, US: Elgar, pp 101-21.

Bönker, F. and Wollmann, H. (1996) 'Incrementalism and reform waves: the case of social service reform in the Federal Republic of Germany', *Journal of European Public Policy*, vol 3, no 3, pp 441-60.

Bönker, F. and Wollmann, H. (2000) 'The rise and fall of a social service regime: marketisation of German social services in historical perspective', in H. Wollmann and E. Schröter (eds) *Comparing Public Sector Reform in Britain and Germany: Key Traditions and Trends of Modernisation*, Aldershot, Burlington, Singapore and Sydney: Ashgate, pp 327-50.

Bönker, F. and Wollmann, H. (2006) 'Public sector reforms and local governments in Germany: the case of local social policy', in V. Hoffmann-Martinot and H. Wollmann (eds) *State and Local Government Reforms in France and Germany: Divergence and Convergence*, Wiesbaden:VS, pp 189-206.

Bundesregierung (1997) *Erster Bericht über die Entwicklung der Pflegeversicherung*, Deutscher Bundestag, BT-Drs, 13/9528, Bonn: Bundesregierung.

Bundesregierung (2001) *Zweiter Bericht über die Entwicklung der Pflegeversicherung*, Deutscher Bundestag, BT-Drs, 14/5590, Berlin: Bundesregierung.

Bundesregierung (2004) *Dritter Bericht über die Entwicklung der Pflegeversicherung*, Deutscher Bundestag, BT-Drs, 15/4125, Berlin: Bundesregierung.

Deutscher Bundestag (2002) *Bürgerschaftliches Engagement: auf dem Weg in eine zukunftsfähige Bürgergesellschaft: Bericht der Enquete-Kommission 'Zukunft des bürgerschaftlichen Engagements'*, Deutscher Bundestag, BT-Drs, 14/8900, Berlin: Deutscher Bundestag.

Evers, A. (1998) 'The new long-term care insurance program in Germany', *Journal of Aging and Social Policy*, vol 10, no 1, pp 77-97.

Evers, A. and Sachße, C. (2003) 'Social care services for children and older people in Germany: distinct and separate histories', in A. Anttonen, J. Baldock and J. Sipilä (eds) *The Young, the Old and the State: Social Care Systems in Five Industrial Nations*, Cheltenham, UK/ Northampton, US: Elgar, pp 55-79.

Heinze, R. G. and Olk, T. (2001) 'Bürgerengagement in Deutschland: Zum Stand der wissenschaftlichen und politischen Diskussion', in R. G. Heinze and T. Olk (eds) *Bürgerengagement in Deutschland: Bestandsaufnahme und Perspektiven*, Opladen: Leske and Budrich, pp 11-26.

Heinze, R. G. and Strünck, C. (2000) 'Social service delivery by private and voluntary organisations in Germany', in H. Wollmann and E. Schröter (eds) *Comparing Public Sector Reform in Britain and Germany: Key Traditions and Trends of Modernisation*, Aldershot, Burlington, Singapore and Sydney: Ashgate, pp 284-303.

Heinze, R. G. and Strünck, C. (2001) 'Freiwilliges soziales Engagement: Potentiale und Fördermöglichkeiten', in R. G. Heinze and T. Olk (eds) *Bürgerengagement in Deutschland: Bestandsaufnahme und Perspektiven*, Opladen: Leske and Budrich, pp 233-53.

Infratest (2005) *Freiwilliges Engagement in Deutschland, 1999-2004: Ergebnisse der repräsentativen Trenderhebung zu Ehrenamt, Freiwilligenarbeit und bürgerschaftlichem Engagement*, Berlin: Bundesministerium für Familie, Senioren, Frauen und Jugend.

Jakob, G. and Janning, H. (2001) 'Freiwilligenagenturen als Teil einer lokalen Infrastruktur für Bürgerengagement', in R. G. Heinze and T. Olk (eds) *Bürgerengagement in Deutschland: Bestandsaufnahme und Perspektiven*, Opladen: Leske and Budrich, pp 483-507.

Landtag NRW (2005) *Bericht der Enquete-Kommission 'Situation und Zukunft der Pflege in NRW'*, Düsseldorf: Landtag NRW.

Meyer, D. (1997) 'The provisions of the German charitable welfare system and the challenge of the free market', *German Studies Review*, vol 20, pp 371-98.

Olk, T. (2001) 'Sozialstaat und Bürgergesellschaft', in R. G. Heinze and T. Olk (eds) *Bürgerengagement in Deutschland: Bestandsaufnahme und Perspektiven*, Opladen: Leske and Budrich, pp 29-68.

Ostner, I. (1998) 'The politics of care policies in Germany', in J. Lewis (ed) *Gender, Social Care and Welfare State Restructuring in Europe*, Aldershot, Burlington, Singapore and Sydney: Ashgate, pp 111-37.

Pierson, P. (1998) 'Irresistible forces, immovable objects: post–industrial welfare states confront permanent austerity', *Journal of European Public Policy*, vol 5, no 4, pp 539-60.

Seibel, W. (1992) *Funktionaler Dilettantismus: Erfolgreich scheiternde Organisationen im 'Dritten Sektor' zwischen Markt und Staat*, Baden-Baden: Nomos.

Seiters, R. (2002) *Bürgerschaftliches Engagement und die Zukunft der Wohlfahrtsverbände*, Discussion paper: Bürgergesellschaft 20, Bonn: Friedrich-Ebert-Stiftung.

Statistisches Bundesamt (2005) *Pflegestatistik 2003: Deutschlandergebnisse*, Bonn: Statistisches Bundesamt.

Weisbrod, B. A. (1988) *The Nonprofit Economy*, Cambridge, MA: Harvard University Press.

SIXTEEN

The social care system for older people in Japan and the role of informal care: Long-term Care Insurance five years on

Michihiko Tokoro

Introduction

Japanese society is ageing rapidly. Currently over 20% of the people in Japan are over 65 years old, and this proportion will grow to 27.8% in 2020. How to cope with this ageing population has been on the agenda as an urgent policy issue since the 1980s, and continuous welfare reforms were made in the 1990s. The most important policy development in this field was the introduction of public Long-term Care Insurance (LTCI) in 2000. This aimed to reduce the heavy burden on the informal care system (the family) and to socialise the care of older people by expanding community-based social care services. Five years on, a review of LTCI is in progress. This chapter will explore current issues concerning Japanese social care policy and informal care.

An outline of the social care system for older people in Japan

The Japanese welfare system has been characterised by its residual aspects, in which care for older people was traditionally given mainly by the family, and more precisely by women. However, this arrangement should not be seen as explained by tradition or culture. At one point, Japan tried to develop the western style of welfare state, and the social service programme was expanding until the first oil crisis interrupted Japanese economic development. Then, in the late 1970s and 1980s, a popular argument arose, in favour of a Japanese-style welfare society in which the family and the informal sector would play a greater role in social care (Hiraoka, 2006). This was typical of the political ideologies of the period of low economic growth, which attempted to stem the expansion of social expenditure. It was argued that the Japanese welfare system should find its own development path, based on Japanese culture and tradition, rather than adopt a western-style welfare state.

Even though the 'Japanese-style welfare society' is a mere political slogan, the Japanese residual welfare system remained until at least the 1990s. Public social care for older people was provided on the basis of assessment of needs and financed by taxation and income-related charges. Eligibility was judged by local authorities, which had broad discretion. With limited resources they of course took into account the living arrangements of older people. The rationing of service resources usually meant that a higher priority in service allocation – often a place in a residential and nursing home – was given to single older people with low incomes, rather than to older people living with potential informal carers, or those with higher incomes. Those older people who were excluded by the old style of service provision were particularly unhappy with that system.

Local government administered the old system in which non-profit sectors also operated as service providers on behalf of public sectors under contract to local government. The quantity of service provision was limited, so many older people and their families faced difficulties in accessing public services. While there were not enough social care provisions, in particular community-based care services, many older people stayed in hospital for non-medical reasons, waiting for a place in a nursing home to become available (Hiraoka, 2006).

As concerns over the ageing population grew, Japan introduced LTCI in April 2000. The Japanese LTCI is unique in the way it integrates the social insurance system and 'mixed' social service provision for older people, with a 'care management system' in which care services are provided under a care plan made by social care professionals. During the process of implementing the LTCI, three policy goals were often stressed:

- establishing a social care system for all older people, supported by the whole population;
- improving the quality and efficiency of long-term care services, and separating social care from medical provision;
- reducing heavy dependency on long-term hospitalisation and the cost of medical insurance.

Japanese social policy preferred a social insurance rather than a tax-based system as the way to finance social services, although the LTCI is not purely 'insurance', as half of the finance for the scheme comes from general taxation. However, the self-image of insurance was considered important, in terms of presenting a clear link between *paying* for care and service *provision*. It was a practical option for the government, which needed to persuade the public to finance the new public care system.

The insured are those aged 40 years and over. They are divided into two categories: those aged 65 years and over (type 1) and those aged 40-65 (type 2). The insurance contribution varies as it is determined by local government, but the average premium for those aged 65 was approximately 3,000 yen per month when the new system was introduced. The individual service user is also required to meet 10% of the service cost, subject to an upper limit. There are several measures in place to reduce the contributions and service charges for those with a low income.

Today, LTCI covers most personal care services for older people, including home help, home-visit nursing, day care, rehabilitation, short-term (overnight) stays and equipment rental. For-profit organisations have joined the public sector and non-profit voluntary sectors in providing these community-based services. Service users choose the types of service, facilities and service providers for themselves, and it was expected that the providers – public, non-profit and for-profit – would compete with each other to obtain more customers in the social care market condition created by the new LTCI.

Welfare of older people under LTCI

Older people

Stereotypically, older Japanese people live in traditional extended families, but continuous social movement in families since the 1950s has changed this. It is estimated that the proportion of households with older people will increase from 23.8% in 2000 to 37.1% in 2025. In 1980, 50.2% of the households that had older members (aged 65 years or more) were three-generation households. The proportion of three-generation households declined to 23.7% in 2002, while houses with a single older occupant, and those with an older couple, increased from 10.7% to 20.2% and from 16.2% to 28.6% respectively during the same periods. In other words, half of the households containing older people have no younger members. If we look at the picture over the whole population, 8% of older males and 17.9% of older females live on their own, compared to 4.3% of older males and 11.2% of older females in 1980 (Social Security Board, MHLW, 2004). It is important to recognise that the current demographic and household patterns do not resemble the old arrangements for care by the family typical of the 1970s or 1980s.

While the numbers of older people living apart from their children are increasing, some do still live close to their children. The government's survey on older people living apart from their children shows that 10.3% have children living within five minutes' walk, and 45.9% live within one hour's journey (MLIT, 2003). Taking these statistics together with the data on three-generation households, it can be said that many older Japanese people still live close to potential informal care, as far as physical distance is concerned. However, a different government survey shows that the contact between older parents and their children living away from home, including conversations over the telephone, is relatively low. Over half of older people have contact less than once a week (Cabinet Office, 2006).

The circumstances of older people who are actually in need of support could be different from those set out above. The Comprehensive Survey of Living Conditions of the People on Health and Welfare for 2004 (CSLCPHW)[1] is the latest of a series of three-yearly surveys on eligible LTCI service users. According to this survey, household types are classified in accordance with their level of care need. In the case of level 4 or 5, where people are often admitted to nursing homes, the

Figure 16.1: Type of household and level of care needs

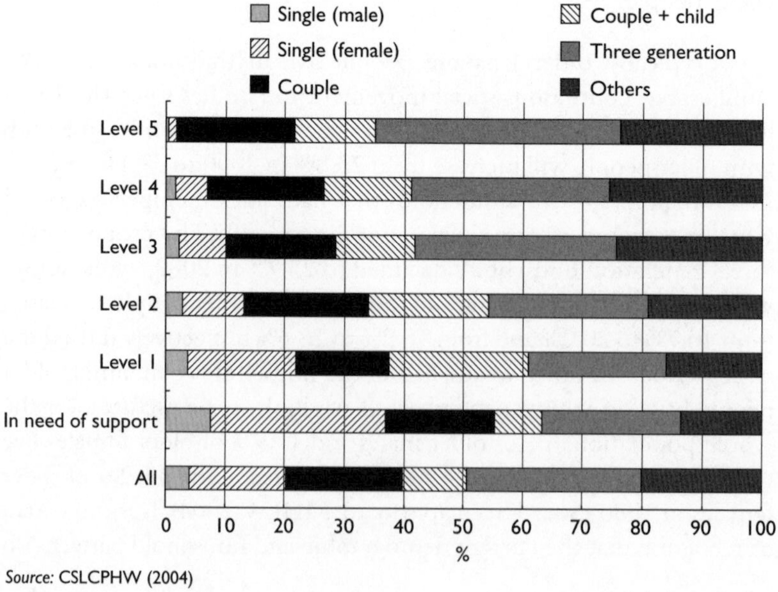

Source: CSLCPHW (2004)

proportion of single households is less than 10%, while households that include offspring are still in the majority (Figure 16.1).

Care services under LTCI

LTCI covers a wide range of care services, including community-based, institutional and some healthcare services. To access these, older people must have their care need formally assessed by the local authority. If they are considered to be in need, they are rated as 'in need of support' or 'in 'need of care' which has a further five categories (level 1-5) according to the level of care need in the original LTCI schemes (these categories were reorganised in the 2005 reform, which is explained later in this chapter). Between need level 1 and need level 5 they can then apply for care services, up to a limit that is set based on that level. For example, an older person who is 'in need of support' can utilise care services up to 6,150 units (approximately 61,500 yen or 300 GBP) and those who are 'in need of care level 5' can use services up to 35,830 units (approximately 358,300 yen or 1,800 GBP) per month. Then LTCI covers 90% of these care costs, and the user pays the remaining 10% as a 'user charge'. Simply put, users choose their own services with the support of a 'care manager', and they are then allocated a package of

Figure 16.2: Choice of community-based service by level of care needs

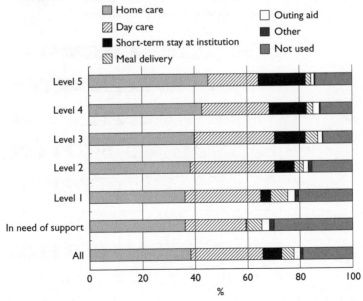

Source: CSLCPHW (2004)

care services that come from various providers. The aim of LTCI is to increase the number of care service providers and stimulate competition among them in the social care market.

Various community-based personal services are available under LTCI, but the choice of services tends to be diverse, depending on the care need or circumstances (Figure 16.2). People in lower need categories do not always take up the services to which they are entitled, or use the meal delivery services, while short-term stay services are those predominantly taken up by those in medium need categories. In practice, to use institutional care services, a person must fall into a higher need category.

It is interesting to note that there are still people who are not using the community-based care services for which they are eligible. There may be several reasons for this. Older people may dislike being supported (they are self-reliant), or may have sufficient family support (Figure 16.3). It is often suggested that the service charge (10% of service costs) may be too expensive for older people with low incomes.

Figure 16.3: Reason for not using services

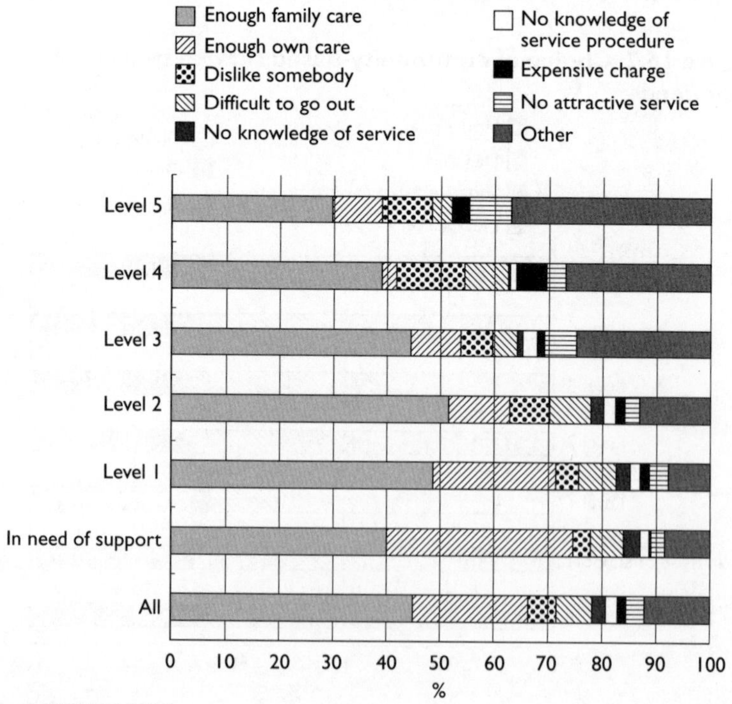

Source: CSLCPHW (2004)

Figure 16.4: Reason for not using services, older people and carers compared (level 1)

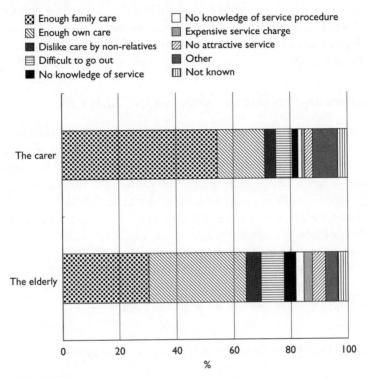

Source: CSLCPHW (2004)

The picture is seen to be more complicated if we compare the reasons given by older people and by their carers (Figure 16.4).

On the other hand, it has been pointed out that, as a consequence of having an insurance system, 'unnecessary' services are often arranged for older people. As mentioned above, the main aim of LTCI was to support older people living on their own in the community. LTCI offers a wide range of choice, from physical care services to home aids, and it was expected that older people would be able to choose the services that they really needed from this range. It appears, however, that services are often utilised unnecessarily. There is confusion here between 'what people need' and 'what they want'. The increase in the number of single males among older people may necessitate a particular type of support if we consider the traditional male breadwinner model of families, in which the man was very unlikely to engage in housework such as cleaning or cooking.

It was originally expected that care managers would make a 'care plan' for an individual older claimant according to their needs, but in many cases, care managers are employed by the care service providers, and work as a service manager for the providers, rather than as an independent social worker acting in the interests of older people (Hiraoka, 2006).

Carers and trends towards institutional care

In Japan, a third of main carers are spouses in the same household, followed by daughters or (some) sons–in–law (27%) and children (25%). It is notable that the carers are also ageing, over half being 50 or more years of age. Many of them have a job outside the household (40%). The employment of carers also affects the time they are able to give to older people. Comparing the 2001 and 2004 surveys, the average length of time a carer, employed or unemployed, is able to give has fallen (Figures 16.5, 16.6 and 16.7).

It is worth noting that the amount of time devoted to care by informal carers has decreased since 2001, but there is no clear improvement in the carer's own assessment of their health (Figure 16.8).

Figure 16.5: Main carer's relation to the older person

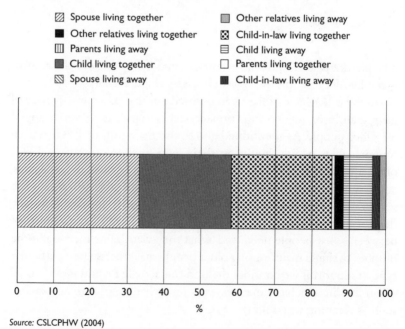

Source: CSLCPHW (2004)

Figure 16.6: Carer's age

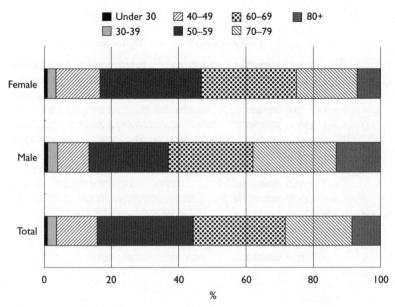

Source: CSLCPHW (2001, 2004)

Figure 16.7: Average time of care by carer's work status, 2001/04

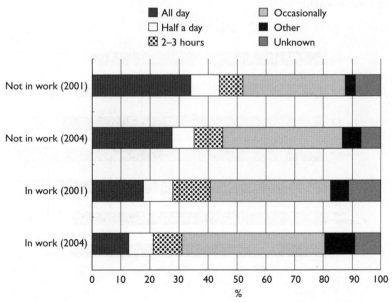

Source: CSLCPHW (2004)

Figure 16.8: Carer's health by the care need, 2001/04

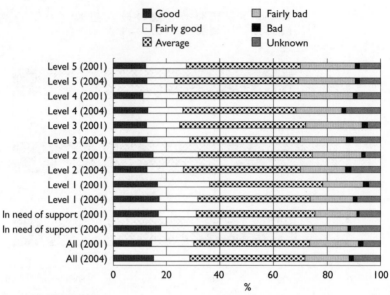

Source: CSLCPHW (2004)

Figure 16.9: Intention of using institutional care answered by the main carer

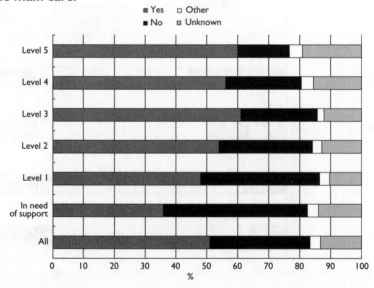

Source: CSLCPHW (2004)

It is also important to note that a general preference towards institutional care, for instance in nursing homes, still exists among older people and their carers. This preference is enhanced by increasing care needs, a view particularly expressed by carers (Figure 16.9). There may be some disagreement between older people and their carers about the desirability of institutional care. For example, in the case of level 2, half of the carers express a preference for institutional care, but this proportion is considerably higher than that for older people themselves (Figure 16.10).

Despite the differences, there still seems to be a strong demand for institutional care among service users and there are still long waiting lists for care of this kind. It is reported that 340,000 older people were on the waiting lists in 2005, and this is often seen as evidence of the shortage of care services (Ikegami, 2005; Ito, 2005; MHLW, 2005). One of the reasons for this is that payments for institutional care, particularly hotel costs, are seen as relatively generous, compared to care in the community.

There are still many older people staying in hospitals for social reasons, with 380,000 beds available in hospitals nationwide for those who need long-term medical treatment. LTCI covers the care service provision for older people in these hospitals under some conditions. A third (130,000), of hospital beds above were covered by LTCI in 2005, but this system has been criticised as it supports the social hospitalisation of older people as a convenient substitution for nursing homes, which

Figure 16.10: Intention of using institutional care by care needs

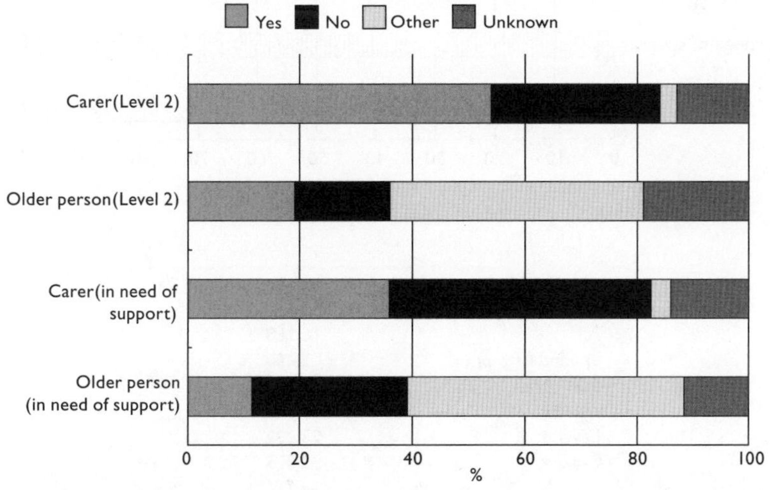

Source: CSLCPHW (2004)

usually have long waiting lists. The MHLW has estimated that in 2005 at least half of the 'patients' needed no medical treatment and were unnecessarily staying in hospital. These costs impose a heavy burden on both LTCI and the public medical insurance (Social Security Board, MHLW, 2005).

It is possible to argue that the trend towards institutional care shows the reality of informal care in Japan. Although the government regards this as a result of the relatively low cost of institutional care, the real problem is still rooted in the burden on family carers. From the start, LTCI was designed to more or less encourage family or community support, yet the demand for institutional care remains high.

Figure 16.11: Monthly spending on services by level of care need (yen)

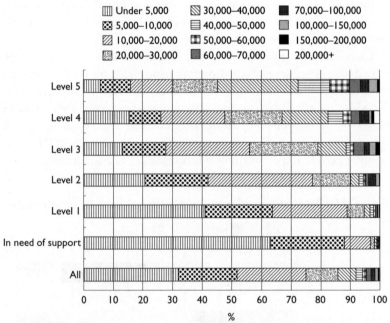

Source: CSLCPHW (2004)

	Average payments (yen)
All	16,188
In need of support	5,450
Level 1	10,102
Level 2	15,715
Level 3	23,232
Level 4	32,323
Level 5	33,771

Cost of care services under LTCI

The cost of care tends to increase, not surprisingly, according to the level of care needed (Figure 16.11). The average amount for all users who have to pay for themselves under the LTCI scheme is 16,188 yen (80 GBP) but this can be up to 33,771 yen for those at level 5. These care costs need to be examined in the context of household expenditure. The Family Expenditure Survey (2004) shows that in the case of an older couple, their average monthly disposable income is 204,134 yen and real expenditure is 235,065 yen. This means that the average household is already in deficit, and would find it difficult to meet the costs of additional services unless they have savings.

It has often been pointed out that the LTCI scheme imposes a financial burden on older people living on low incomes. The contribution for the insurance and 10% charge for service use have been a matter for debate since its introduction.

The average contribution for older people (aged 65+) was 2,911 yen in the period 2000-02. This went up to 3,293 yen in 2003-05, and would reach 4,300 yen in 2006-08 (Social Security Board, MHLW, 2005). The LTCI scheme has several provisions to help those on low incomes. Contributions are based on an income-related scale, which has five (or six depending on the local authority) bands. The reduced rate (50%) of standards contribution is applied to the lowest income group such as those living on public assistance (G1) and the higher rate (150%) is applied to the higher income group (G5). The local government can require additional contribution from the highest groups (G6).

There are more serious concerns over the effects of service charges (10% of service cost), which could prevent those in need from claiming assistance. If we look at the spending on care services by income group, spending tends to increase with income (Figure 16.12). However, according to the data in Figure 16.11, it is not certain whether older people, in particular those with low income, utilise all the services they need because the average spending is below what the LCTI would cover. It is also important to note that the user has to pay all the costs that are not covered when care services are needed beyond the limit set by their LTCI. This can be very expensive for older people. It can be shown that informal carers still contribute significantly to fill the need that is not covered by LTCI (to 2005).

Figure 16.12: Spending on care services by income level (the band of LTCI contribution, yen)

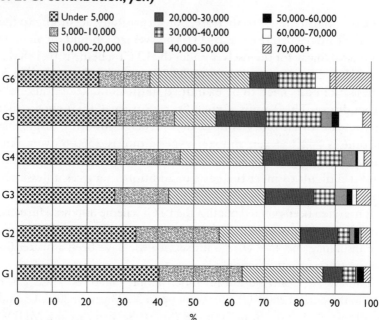

In addition to several measures to reduce the contribution and service charges, the public assistance system covers both contributions and service charges if the service users are living on benefits. The number of households that receive care service support from the public assistance system increased from 64,551 in 2000 to 141,009 in 2004. This is evidence that the financial circumstances of older people are deteriorating.

LTCI: the first five years

General picture

The Social Security Board, Ministry of Health, Labour and Welfare argues that LTCI is a success, on the basis of the following points. First, the social care services under LTCI have expanded dramatically. The number of older people who were assessed as eligible for care insurance services rose from 2.18 million in 2000 to 4.11 million in 2005, and the actual number of service users increased from 1.49 million to 3.23 million during the same period. This rapid increase can be seen as a success for 'socialisation of care'. The number of service providers has also increased. This is partly because new providers, including for-profit organisations, have joined the social care market. There were serious concerns about the shortage of care service provision and that people would be 'paying contributions for non-existent services' when LTCI came into force, but this situation did not arise.

Second, the 'needs assessment system' is seen as 'fair'. There were worries that need assessment could be biased, could fail to assess particular needs, or might function as a gatekeeper controlling service provision. There were particular concerns about need assessment in the case of dementia, where the extent of need can be very difficult to judge. But after minor amendments to the assessment system, it seems that there have been no real problems to date.

Third, there were no serious confusions over the administration of care provision at the local government level when LTCI was introduced. The insurer of LTCI is the municipality, which is responsible for management at local level. No serious administrative failure has been reported so far. An opinion poll shows that the vast majority of people believe that the burden of family care has reduced under LTCI (Social Security Board, MHLW, 2004, 2005).

However, several problems have already appeared in the LTCI system. Its expenditure rose from 3,600 billion yen in 2000 to 6,800 billion yen in 2005 (Uemura, 2005a). As examined above, there are still preferences for institutional care. It is also problematic that some users tend to consume services regardless of their need, and that service providers encourage their service users to utilise more services for business reasons. The creation of the social care market attracted a number of private social care providers. The availability of care services was a main concern when LTCI was introduced, but today, the quality of the services has become an important issue. Fraud cases, such as false claims to the insurer by the providers, and theft or abuse by care workers, are sometimes reported.

Also, LTCI is not always accessible to those on low incomes. The service charge works as a deterrent for them, meaning that this income disparity could lead to an unequal service utilisation among the older population. The availability and quality of services is still very dependent on the local environment. There are still shortages of service providers and provision in some rural areas, while a higher insurance contribution (premium) is required for the insured living in those areas that have a high proportion of older people. The areas where many nursing homes operate tend to require higher levels of insurance contribution, because they have attracted more frail older people. In addition, there is an increase in the numbers of single older households, which means that many such people in urban local authorities will face financial problems.

The recent social trend, described as a *U-turn to the city from the suburbs*, offers a more convenient lifestyle and less dependency on the car. It is reported that the level of contributions in some municipalities is 2.5 times higher than others.

The reform of LTCI in 2005

Expanding public expenditure has led to a review of the policy of social care, and in 2005, the first major reform of LTCI was carried out since its introduction. The government set the policy goal as creating a 'sustainable social care system'.

The main aspect of the reform is the introduction of what is called a 'prevention programme' for older people with lower needs which is managed by a newly established local support centre. The categories of 'in need of support' and 'in need of care level 1' will be reorganised into three categories, and those who are in these new categories will be provided with new 'prevention programmes'. The prevention programmes include exercise, dental healthcare and other community-based life support programmes (Uemura, 2005b). The prevention programmes were introduced to promote health, reduce care service provisions and to improve LTCI's finance. However, it is unclear whether these programmes actually improve the health of older people and reduce the expenditure from LTCI on them (Ikegami, 2005). Although the prevention programmes include nutrition improvement, it is not certain whether older males, who had never cooked in a traditional family, would ever pick up a pan (Sodei, 2005).

The reform has also tried to create strong incentives among users and carers for them to move away from institutional and towards community-based care. In the previous system, institutional care was regarded by family carers as a cost-effective option, as 'hotel costs' were covered by LTCI. So the reform made changes to this coverage, and 'hotel costs' (such as nursing homes) as an element of institutional care are now excluded from LTCI coverage.

These new initiatives were implemented in 2006, but several parts of the reform proposal were left out, notably the extension of LTCI coverage. LTCI basically covers the needs of the older population, based on insurance contributions from those aged 40 or over, and taxation. There have been arguments for the extension of coverage towards the younger population so that care services can be provided to people with disabilities. The financial basis of LTCI could be made more solid if contributions were required from the under-40s. This idea faced strong opposition from disabled people who worried about increases in charges. Currently the care service provision is based on an income-related selective system financed by taxation, and businesses feared extra financial imposts to support the employees' contribution. However, this issue will be given attention again in the next major reform in several years' time.

Prospects: LTCI and impacts on family policy

It is still too early to conclude that LTCI is a success or a failure, as there is a need to take many factors into account. The original aim of LTCI was to support older people living in the community and to reduce the burden of family care by providing various community care services in a context of welfare pluralism. Some data suggest that this goal has been more or less achieved, but there are several issues still needing attention.

It is important to remember that LTCI was not intended to replace all informal care with public care, even including community-based care services. Family care is always expected to underpin the policy emphasis when shifting from an institutional-based system, such as nursing home care, to community care. LTCI was a useful tool to keep the family involved in the care of older people. It is, of course, true that most older people prefer living in their own home, not in a care institution. The fact is that the current provision level under LTCI alone is not always enough to fulfil all the need, so some families are still seeking institutional care, which is probably considered as a clear replacement for informal care. This may be the case for older people with dementia.

The recent reform of LTCI was initiated in response to financial concerns. While the control of costs was highlighted, reducing the burden of informal care was no longer the main issue. It is symbolic that a 'sustainable care system' is what was stressed, instead of the 'socialisation of informal care'. This was a remarkable change from the early periods of LTCI in 2000.

However, the shift from institutional to community care could be problematic unless the environment of informal care is improved. Social care for those with dementia will be the next serious issue for the Japanese care system. It is not certain that the current system can support older people and their informal carers in the community. It is also important to consider the care costs for older people and their carers under LTCI. The current level of insurance contribution and the user charge (10% with a maximum limitation of charge on a service user set at approximately 38,000 yen) is often seen as a reasonable level, but their financial situation will inevitably bring a higher bill for many users. It is estimated that the insurance contribution may have to increase to 6,000 yen in 2012, over two times higher than at its introduction. In addition, outside the LTCI system, several social security reforms have already made the situation worse. In the public health insurance scheme, the charge for patients has increased, in particular, for older people. The pension reform in 2004 has introduced a capping system for pension payment, which aims to reduce the cost of pensions as demographic change occurs. With lower pensions and higher insurance contributions and user charges, informal care will have to play a vital role in the care of older people, just as before.

LTCI was introduced in order to reduce the burden of family care, and has been broadly accepted *and welcomed*, but it has begun to face financial realities. Unless the public shows strong support for the original aim and is prepared to put more financial resource into the system, it is very difficult to imagine a bright picture for older people and their carers in 2020.

Note

[1] The Comprehensive Survey of Living Conditions of the People on Health and Welfare for 2004 (large-scale survey) has collected data on older people who were assessed as being eligible for the care service covered by LTCI. The survey covered 10,000 households and 100,000 older people.

References

Cabinet Office (2006) *Survey on the Living Arrangements and Opinions of Older People: International Comparison.*

Hiraoka, K. (2006) 'Long-term care insurance in Japan', in H. S. Yoon and J. Hendricks (eds) *Handbook of Asian Aging,* Amityville, NY: Baywood Publishing.

Ikegami, N. (2005) 'Kaigo hoken no Kaikakuan to konngono tenbo', *Shakaihoken Junpo*, no 2240, pp 16–22.

Ito, S. (2005) 'Kaigohoken Kaikaku to Kaigo Hosho', *Wage and Social Security No 1396,* Junposha, pp 4–39.

Social Security Board, MHLW (Ministry of Health, Labour and Welfare) (2004) 'Kaigo Hoken no minaoshi ni kannsuru iken', ['For a reform of the Long-term Care Insurance'] *Kaigo Hoken Joho*, vol 5, no 6, *Shakaihoken Kenkyusho*, pp 2–35.

Social Security Board, MHLW (2005) 'Shakaihoshou shingikai/kaigofukyuuhibunnkakai shiryou', *Gekkann Kaigo Hoken*, no 111, pp 36–50.

Sodei, T. (2005) 'Kaigo Hoken no Souteigai', *Shukan Shakaihosho*, no 2357, pp 24-5.

Uemura, N. (2005a) 'Kaigo hoken no gonenkan no ayumi', *Gekkann Kaigo Hoken*, no 110, pp 64-5.

Uemura, N. (2005b) 'Kaigo hoken ha do kawaru?', *Gekkann Kaigo Hoken*, no 113, pp 64-5.

Conclusion

Susan Balloch and Michael Hill

In one sense there can be no conclusion to this book. The chapters represent powerful contributions to an international debate about how to meet both the costs and complex demands of care and the rights of citizens in advanced economies and ageing societies. This debate is very likely to continue into the foreseeable future with no immediately obvious solutions. Several issues, however, are clarified in this volume and some encouraging evidence provided on potential improvements in policy and practice.

One central concern repeated in several chapters and made particularly strongly by Barnes in Chapter Four is that 'care' is usually absent from discourses of citizenship, participation and civil renewal. The 'ethic of care', as a set of principles and practices, challenges the distinction between public and private virtues and enables connections to be made between care, citizenship and social justice. It encourages policy makers to look beyond conventional boundaries imposed on 'social care' and 'community' policies and think holistically about the best ways to improve people's lives. This includes not just older people and the conventional candidates included in a narrow interpretation of 'community care' but also young people (Stephen and Squires, Chapter Seven; Quilgars, Chapter Ten) and women who, as victims of domestic violence, are often isolated from any type of support (Wilcox, Chapter Eight).

In this context it is important that we do not overlook inequalities of care and the much more acute problems faced in meeting the care needs of those discriminated against on grounds of ethnicity or poverty. As Butt (Chapter Nine) reveals, black and minority ethnic communities' experiences of care are very variable and only rarely promote choice and control. This is less the result of inadequate legislation than the perpetuation of racial stereotypes and the imposition of a white, ethnocentric perception of care, which often fails to identify the needs of those living in diverse communities. The suggestion that a community development approach may be best for meeting the needs of black and minority ethnic communities, and indeed any groups experiencing discrimination and disadvantage, needs to be taken seriously in the social care world. It is endorsed in Germany by Bönker (Chapter Fifteen), who quotes how the traditional provision of social services through local welfare associations was very effective in meeting the demands of citizens in diverse, multicultural communities.

These considerations raise important questions about what 'community' means in these contexts. As has been emphasised in distinctions between 'care in' and 'care by' the community, citizenship is not enhanced if what occurs is abdication of the overall responsibilities of society and government to communities without the capacity to develop effective care strategies. There is moreover a need to consider whether these so-called communities have firm identities outside official stereotypes of little-understood ethnic groups.

The potential effectiveness of a community care development strategy is the particular focus of Chapter Ten by Quilgars, which is based on research in two deprived neighbourhoods in Hull. This had the objective of encouraging and facilitating communities in their support of their more vulnerable members. Developments encompassed new networks, a community care forum and new community facilities and activities. The project showed that while it was definitely possible to encourage a more caring and supportive approach within new community activities it was still difficult to make contact with people who had more traditional community care needs and/or were isolated in the community. The latter problem was exacerbated by the prominence of high-profile issues such as crime and community safety, which tended to overshadow care and support needs.

There is substantial evidence of the viability of looking beyond family care to neighbourhood support and to the social capital and resources that can be built up through voluntary and community sector activities (Fyvie-Gauld and de Podesta, Chapter Eleven; McGowan and Jowitt, Chapter Twelve). While positive evidence for the effectiveness of schemes within local communities such as befriending and mentoring is very strong, financial support for them from local authorities, health agencies and neighbourhood renewal funds is hard to obtain. Along with Quilgars, these chapters show both the potential of communities and voluntary organisations to enhance care and, at the same time, their vulnerability.

Returning to the primary source of care – still in all countries seen as 'the family' and, in particular, women – it is clear that individuals take the responsibilities of care with extreme seriousness and responsibility but are often pushed to their limits by the failure of services to understand the biographies of those they are trying to support or failing to appreciate the nature of relationships within which effective care is received. This is particularly the case for families providing care for members with increasing dementia (Brannelly, Chapter Six).

Recognising an ethic of care relevant to the whole of society asks us to move away from a narrow focus on care in the family setting to an acceptance of a public responsibility for care based on adequate funding, effective organisation and a properly trained and remunerated social care workforce.

This book has not sought to address in any detail the complex interface between health and social care. The importance of this is well illustrated by the needs of individuals with dementia and their families, with dementia often dismissed as a condition not needing medical or nursing care. Divisions and conflicts between health and social care agencies must, however, be confronted if a fairer care system is to be established. This involves understanding and resolving the different perceptions of rights and needs raised in the debate about the medical and social models of disability. It is also integral to any discussion of the costs of care and who should bear them.

In the UK the funding of social care has changed little since the 1940s. It is still based on means-tested care offered to a relatively small number of individuals through local authorities or privately purchased, in contrast to healthcare, which is still largely free through the National Health Service. Only in Scotland (Petch, Chapter Three) are personal care costs, in addition to health costs, covered by the state. The most radical recent proposals are centred around the expansion of direct payments and individual budgets, but the funding of these is not ring-fenced and progress on their development is very slow. The Commission for Social Care Inspection (CSCI, 2006) report on the state of social care in England berates the lack of information for people trying to purchase their own services, minimal support for carers and lack of choice over services used.

Sweden's system shares some of the characteristics of the UK systems, albeit in a context of much more effectively measured care. Both Germany and Japan, in contrast, have undertaken major reviews of their social care funding and attempted to establish more level playing fields in which basic care costs are covered by public funding, although at a fairly low level (Chapters Fifteen and Sixteen). They have gone from this down the route of creating long-term care insurance, offering the potential of more universal services (at least without rationing by means tests). Yet in both these countries there have been mounting concerns at escalating costs and inadequate services, hence rationing by strict tests of need remains of great importance. In Germany the scheme is criticised for being based on a limited, medical model of frailty and for contributing to the commercialisation of care and a fall in civic engagement through the voluntary sector. In Japan there has been concern that cheaper costs have encouraged long waiting lists for residential care. Additionally, a cap on pensions and increased insurance contributions and user charges mean that the emphasis on family and informal care has, if anything, increased. The evidence from both these countries suggests that while a national scheme is potentially fairer and easier for people to understand, in practice care still needs to be based within and around communities to be acceptable.

An interesting difference between German and Japanese care insurance is the way in which, in the former system, benefits come in cash that may be spent in any way (including the reimbursement of relatives) while in the latter it is services that are provided. The development of direct payments in the UK offers the potential for provisions comparable to those in Germany, should the current very limited acceptance of payments to relatives be extended. However, the fact remains that for all help of any substance (also disregarding here the limited grants of Attendance Allowance) there is also the application of a means test (often taking assets into account as well as income). The extent to which the use of means testing implies incomplete citizenship is, of course, a matter for debate.

One of the successes of the UK system of care has been the continued reduction in residential care and greater support for people living in their own homes. The privatisation of care has been a major feature of this, as indeed it has been in Germany and Japan, and even in Sweden the private market in care is now expanding. In essence there is no reason why properly regulated, commercially marketed care should be any less effective and acceptable than publicly provided care, which has certainly not escaped scandals related to failure and abuse. Yet we return to the issues highlighted earlier – that services provided by an impersonal organisation, with staff who are not part of their local community, will have more difficulty in providing what people want and need.

Mayo et al note in Chapter Five, quoting Le Grand (2003), that internationally there is evidence that public sector employees report a greater commitment for serving the community and helping others than those in the private sector. Logically there is no reason why this should be the case if terms and conditions of work, training opportunities and rates of staff retention are similar across public and independent sectors. Current evidence suggests, however, that this is often not the case, particularly where the public sector, as a major purchaser, forces down the price of services and hence staff salaries.

The quality of the social care workforce is integral to the effective working of any care system. Mayo et al (Chapter Five) and Mears

(Chapter Thirteen) highlight the strength of the commitment of the workforce and the centrality of their values but balance these against the difficulties faced. Mayo et al's study of front-line professionals in neighbourhood regeneration identifies the types of difficulties that have emerged, partly related to the inherent complexities of working with very diverse individuals and communities but also related to the New Public Management and partnership working, which sometimes leaves professionals little scope for making personal choices in a context of increasing bureaucratisation and central control. Lack of management support in difficult situations was also widespread. Such pressures 'distance' professionals from those they are trying to support demoralise them and are a likely contributor to high rates of turnover.

Workforce difficulties can also be compounded by low rates of pay, poor training and a lack of career structure. As Mears (Chapter Thirteen) shows, this is an issue with international dimensions and a problem for the home care workforce in Australia. While care workers recognised that their work was highly skilled, required delicate negotiations between personal and work relationships and the building of trust over time, they resented their low levels of pay and recognised that their commitment to their work and the satisfaction they obtained from it was being exploited. They also feared that cost-cutting would distance them from those they supported.

We do not wish to be naive about the resource problems that have to be faced in relation to the problems of care. Rationing decisions have to be made, and questions about how to share care responsibilities between the state, communities, families and individuals have to be confronted. What is unfortunate in this context is the way in which rhetoric about ageing societies and the so-called 'demographic time bomb' involves an exaggeration of these problems and a disregard of the continued importance of the mixed economy of care. Worse still, such rhetoric, in identifying those who need care as a problem group for society, implicitly denies the citizenship of these individuals. All citizens – to greater or lesser degrees – need care at times. A good society is one in which it is regarded as normal and natural that we both give and receive care in a social, economic and political structure that supports this activity.

References

CSCI (Commission for Social Care Inspection) (2006) *The State of Social Care in England 2005-06*, London: CSCI.

Le Grand, J. (2003) *Motivation, Agency and Public Policy*, Oxford: Oxford University Press.

Index

A

Acceptable Behaviour Contracts
(ABCs) 108-10, 112, 116-17
active citizenship 64, 65-6, 67, 160-1
see also community engagement
'active community members' 165-6
activity-based community groups
168-9, 173
age
maturity of paid care workers 214,
218
see also older people; young people
Age Concern Aberdeen Informal
Support and Care Project 42
Aged Care Assistance Packages
(ACAPs)(Australia) 213
altruism
as motive for paid care work 216-17
as motive for volunteering 181, 183,
202
in public sector 76
Alzheimer's disease *see* people with
dementia
anti-oppressive social work practice 28,
110, 112-17
antisocial behaviour management
105-17
and community care development
approach 170
enforcement and support 106-7
and families 108-17
Anti-Social Behaviour Orders (ASBOs)
25, 107, 116-17
Appleton, C. 117
assessment *see* need assessment
association: use of term 6
Association of Directors of Social
Services (ADSS) 142
Association for the Pastoral Care in
Mental Health (APCMH) 201
Association for the Pastoral Care of the
Mentally Ill (APCMI) 198, 201-6
Atkinson, J.W. 183
attentiveness and ethic of care 63, 70, 71
and civil renewal 131
people with dementia 95-6
Audit Commission 24, 142
Audit Commission (Australia) 212
Australia
paid community care workers 211-24,
285
job satisfaction 221-3
motivations for becoming care
workers 2161-7
political and economic context
211-14
qualities for care work 218-21

B

Badenoch and Strathspey community
social work team 41-2
Balloch, S. 34
Banks, S. 76-7, 80, 83
Barclay Report 21, 29, 41
Barnes, Marian 128, 129-31, 189, 224
Barr, A. 43-4, 161-2
Barron, J. 123
Batson, C.D. 183
Bauman, Z. 75, 232-3
Befrienders International 207
befriending services 193-4, 196-207
definition and nature of befriending
196-7
Hastings Befriending Scheme 193-4,
196, 198, 201-7
research on 200
and social policy 199, 204-6
value to user 198, 200
volunteers 202-3
Benevolent Society of NSW 214
Beresford, P. 28
Berry, R. 199
Berthoud, R. 144-5
Bevan, Aneurin 10
Big Lottery 179
biography of people with dementia 90,
93, 96, 99, 282
Birch, D. 183
black and minority ethnic communities
9, 141-53, 281
community development in Scotland
44
domestic violence survivors 129
evidence of needs 143-4
inequality and lack of support 144-7,
152
legislation and policy 147-8
practice shortcomings 148-51, 152-3
regeneration workers and ethical
dilemmas 82, 83
role of voluntary organisations 141,
146, 151-2, 153
Blunkett, David 59, 63-6

'boundary drawing' in professional
  work 84–5
Bowes, A. 44
Box, L. 151
Bradford Social Services Department
  150–1
Bradshaw, T. 198
Braithwaite, J. 116
Brighton & Hove Neighbourhood Care
  Scheme 31, 177–90
Buchan, R. 198
Bulmer, Martin 7, 27
Burnett, R. 117
Bussell, H. 183
Butt, J. 142, 144, 150–1

C

Cahill, M. 26
Calouste Gulbenkian Foundation 26
capacity building *see* community
  capacity building
care
  as concept 232–4
  care discourse in Scandinavia 233–5,
    241
  as devalued concept 59, 60–1
  feminist perspective 61–2, 133
  definition of care 62
  moral principles 63
  see also carers; ethic of care
Care Development Group 47
Care Inquiry (Scotland) 48
care insurance 12
  see also long-term care insurance
care plans
  Australia 214–15
  Japan 262, 268
Care 21 47
Care Values and the Future of Welfare
  (CAVA) 72
carers
  in black and minority ethnic
    communities 146
  domestic violence survivors as care
    givers and receivers 122, 123, 131–3,
    134
  gendered nature of care 61, 62, 233–4,
    235, 241
  and individual budgets 30
  and institutional care in Japan 268–72,
    276
  interdependency of care relationship
    65, 67, 91, 95–7, 98–9, 133, 134
  low status of care work 61, 71, 211,
    213–14, 221, 223
  as paid care workers 217, 218
  payments in Germany 257*n*, 284

of people with dementia 90–1, 92–3
  consultation and support for 94–5, 96,
    99
  relatives as carers in Sweden 235, 236,
    240, 242
  and rights-based approach 60
  support for 33, 46, 47, 90, 94–5, 96, 99
    black and minority ethnic
      communities 146–7
    in Sweden 240, 242
  unpaid carers in Scotland 46–7
  see also informal care
Carers Legislation Working Group
  (Scotland) 46
Carers Scotland 46, 47
categorical imperative 76
Catholic social thinking in Germany
  248
Census data on and black and minority
  ethnic communities 143–4
Chalmers, J. 213
charging for care *see* user funding
Charity Organisation Society (COS) 26
Cheetham, J. 43
child protection and domestic violence
  125
Children Act (2004) 116
children's hearings in Scotland 43
children's services 21, 25
  separation from adult services 27–8
children's workforce strategy 31
Chinese community: health needs 143
choice 29
  for black and minority ethnic
    communities 141, 146, 152
  and people with dementia 94–5
  and user funding in Japan 263
  see also direct payments; user
    empowerment
Choosing Health (White Paper) 160, 174
citizenship
  active citizenship 64, 65–6, 67, 160–1
  and black and minority ethnic
    communities 143
  citizenship discourse in social care 29,
    281, 285
  contractual model 105, 106, 109
  New Labour civil renewal agenda 59,
    63–7
  and people with dementia 100
  and social work 28
  and welfare rights in Sweden 230–1,
    234
city-wide community care development
  approach 165–6
civic engagement *see* active citizenship;
  community engagement
civil renewal 59, 72

and ethic of care 63-7, 71, 131
Civil Renewal Unit 64, 161
Clarke, Charles 177
Clary, E.G. 181
class and community 9-10
Cobb, J. 81
Commission for Racial Equality (CRE) 142, 148
Commission for Social Care Inspection (CSCI) 24, 142, 150, 283
commitments and community engagement 67-70
commodification of care 17
communitarianism 75
  Blunkett's civil renewal agenda 64
  and government 12-13, 17
  and universalism 15-17
  and volunteering 204-5
'communities of interest' 7-8, 45
  activity-based community groups 168-9, 173
  and domestic violence survivors 129-31
Communities Plan 160
Communities that Care 53
community
  definitions and use of term 5-6, 6-7, 107, 127-8, 129, 282
  and diversity 8-10
  and families 10-11
  as geographical concept 6-8
  and government 11-14
community activities 166, 168-72
community capacity building
  Community Care Development Project 161, 165
  in Scotland 52-3
community capital in Scotland 42
community care
  background 21-3
  and community development see Community Care Development Project
  definition and use of term 5-6, 163, 172
  in Japan 277
  New Labour policy 23-5
  paid care workers in Australia 211-24, 285
  for people with dementia 89-100
  Scandinavian critique 233, 234
  Scottish approach 44-5
  Scottish Social Attitudes surveys 48-9
  and vulnerable people 159-60
  see also home care services
Community Care Development Project 159-74, 282
  key stages 164-6

resulting initiatives and outcomes 166-74
  and statutory sector 173-4
Community Care Forums
  in Hull 167, 171
  in Scotland 44-5, 51
Community Care and Health (Scotland) Act (2002) 46
community cohesion 59, 64, 71, 72
community development (neighbourhood renewal)
  black and minority ethnic voluntary groups 141, 146, 151-2, 153, 281
  capacity building in Scotland 52-3
  and community care see Community Care Development Project
  and domestic violence survivors 126
  front-line professionals and ethical dilemmas 78-87, 285
  New Labour policies 23-4
  in Scotland 42, 43-5
  and social care 26-8
Community Development Foundation 162-3
Community Development Project 26
community engagement
  and befriending services 205-6, 207
  civic engagement and social care in Germany 247-57
  motivations and commitments 67-70, 71
    domestic violence survivors 129-31
  see also active citizenship; social inclusion
community facilities 166, 167-8
community groups
  and community care development approach 165, 166-74
  lack of formation for domestic violence survivors 122, 127, 128
  motivations and commitments 67-70
    domestic violence survivors 129-31
  see also voluntary and community sector
Community Health Partnerships (CHPs) in Scotland 50-1
Community Initiative Programme/Budget 126, 167
community links in antisocial behaviour work 114, 116-17
Community Network in Hull 166-7, 170
community planning in Scotland 45, 50
community psychiatric nurses (CPNs) and ethic of care 91-5, 98, 99
Community Safety Partnerships 110, 116

community safety teams 109, 110, 112, 113, 115
  and domestic violence 125-6
  and young people 116-17
community social work
  demise of 21
  in Scotland 41-2, 52-3
'community values' 107
community work
  education and training 28
  ethical dilemmas 78-87
  and social care 31, 160
competence and ethic of care 63, 71, 97
complementary service provision 91
conflict in communities and ethical
  dilemmas 82
Confucian family model 11
consultation
  and Community Care Development
    Project 164
  domestic violence survivors 127
  and local government 14
  minority ethnic communities 147,
    148
  people with dementia 94-5
consumerist movements 13
contractual model of citizenship 105,
  106, 109
Cooke, A. 197-8
coping mechanisms for front-line
  professionals 78, 85-6
'Coronation Street' model *see*
  Neighbourhood Care Scheme
'cosmopolitan' occupational groups 8
Council for Voluntary Service 162
Crime and Disorder Act (1998) 105
Crime and Disorder Reduction
  Partnerships 107, 124
criminal justice system
  and domestic violence 125-6
  see also antisocial behaviour
    management
crisis management and domestic
  violence 123
Curtice, L. 49

D

day care in Sweden 240, 242
D/deaf people in black and minority
  ethnic communities 145-6
Dean, J. 197, 198, 205
decentralisation 77, 78
decommodification of care in Sweden
  231
deinstitutionalisation policy 21, 22, 23
deliberative practices and feminist ethic
  of care 70-1

dementia *see* people with dementia
Department for Communities and
  Local Government (DCLG) 160,
  161
Department of Health: assessment
  guidance 148
'dependency critique' 66
dependency relationship
  and domestic violence 133
  negative view of 17, 65-6, 67, 133,
    134
depression
  in older people 187-8
  value of befriending 200
deprivation and mental health in
  Hastings 194-6
developing countries: remittances 15-16
Dewar, B. 45
direct payments 12, 13, 29-30, 71
  in Germany 255-6, 284
disability movement 44, 60, 61, 128
disabled people
  and active citizenship 66, 67
  in black and minority ethnic
    communities 143-4, 145-6
  and community care development
    approach 169
  activities for disabled children 171-2
  and community engagement 69
  exclusion from Single Regeneration
    Budget initiatives 161
  and Neighbourhood Care Scheme
    187
discrimination *see* race equality; racism
diversity and community 8-10
domestic violence survivors 121-36,
  281
  community-based projects 121, 126-7,
    129-31
  lack of community-based work 122,
    124, 134
  dominant definitions of domestic
    violence 122, 123-4, 134
  funding issues 124
  gendered aspects 122, 123, 127-9
  women as carers and need for care
    131-3, 134
  state-sponsored policies 122, 124-7,
    134
domiciliary care *see* home care services
Donald, S. 42
'double marketisation' in Germany 247,
  250
Dutt, R. 149

E

education and training 28, 32, 87
  befriending volunteers 203, 204
  care workers in Australia 213-14
  in Sweden 230
egotism *see* self-interest
emotional distance in professional work
  84-5, 87, 96-7
emotional well-being and paid care
  work 220
employment
  and befriending services 205
  and domestic violence survivors 125
empowerment
  of communities
    community care development
      approach 163
    in Scotland 44
  see also user empowerment
enforcement agencies and antisocial
    behaviour work 106-7, 108-17
'equalities commission' proposal 147,
  148
equality
  and 'dependency critique' 66
  see also race equality
Esping-Andersen, G. 230, 231
ethic of care 59-72, 131, 233, 281, 283
  feminist perspective 61-72, 133
  four principles 63, 92, 95-7
  and people with dementia 91-7
ethical dilemmas of frontline
    regeneration workers 75-87, 285
ethnic groups *see* black and minority
    ethnic communities
ethnocentric value base 149-50, 281
Etzioni, A. 127
Evandrou, M. 144
Every Child Matters (Green Paper) 25,
  116
Expert Carers Programme 33, 47
extended family in Japan 263-4

F

faith-based community organisations
  14, 248
families
  and care work 16, 17, 282
  informal care in Japan 261-2, 263-4,
    268-72, 277
  older people in Australia 211
  relatives as carers in Sweden 235, 236,
    240, 242
  and community 10-11
    young people and antisocial
      behaviour management work 105,
      108-17

support for disabled people 145-6
Family Resources Survey 144
feminist ethic of care 61-72, 131, 133
Ferguslie League of Action Groups
  (FLAG) 42
Ferns, P. 149
Fine, M. 213, 224
Forbes, D. 183
formal care sector *see* paid care
*Framework for the Assessment of Children
  in Need and their Families* 25
free personal care in Scotland 47-50
front-line community professionals and
    ethical dilemmas 75-87, 285
  coping strategies and support systems
    85-6, 87
funding 34-5, 283-4
  befriending services 193-4, 207
  and community care development
    approach 167, 170
  sustainability 163, 165
  and free personal care in Scotland
    47-8
  and needs assessment in Sweden
    235-6
  Neighbourhood Care Scheme 178,
    179, 189-90
  rationing of care services 34, 36, 48
  residential and nursing home care
    21-2, 34-5
  user funding
  Australia 213
  Japan 262-3, 265-6, 273-4, 275-6,
    277-8
  Sweden 229
  welfare associations in Germany 249
  for work with survivors of domestic
    violence 124

G

Galvin, Rose 185
gender issues
  and domestic violence survivors 122,
    123, 127-9, 131-3
  gendered nature of care 61, 62, 233-4,
    235, 241
  domestic violence survivors 131-3
  and home care services in Japan 267
  Swedish ageing demographics 236
  volunteering 180
General Household Survey 144
General Social Care Council 24
Germany 14
  civic engagement and social care
    247-57, 281-2, 283, 284
  new forms of civic engagement
    247-8, 252-6

traditional social service regime 247, 248-52
Giddens, A. 75
Gillies, V. 112
Glendinning, C. 29
global incapacity 98
Goodlad, R. 197, 198, 205
Gordon, D. 42
Gough, I. 15-16
governance 15
government and community 11-14
Griffiths, Sir Roy 21, 29
Guilds of Help 26

H

Haddock, G. 198
Hague, G. 127, 133
Halsey, A.H. 5
Hardcastle, B. 197-8
Harwin, N. 123
Hastings
  Befriending Scheme 193-4, 196, 198, 201-7
  demise 193-4, 206
  socioeconomic context 194-6
Haynes, P. 48, 90
'health garage' in Hull 168, 171, 173, 174
Health Poverty Index 196
Health Survey of England 143
healthcare
  health needs of black and minority ethnic community 143-4
  and social care 32-4, 283
    Community Health Partnerships in Scotland 50-1
  see also mental health
Heenan, D. 23
Heron, B. 113, 115
Hill, Michael 5
Hillery, G.A. 5, 127
Hirsch, D. 35
Hodgkinson, V.A. 182
Holman, Bob 10
home care services (domiciliary care)
  black and minority ethnic communities
    ethnic matching 150
    voluntary organisations 151
  in Germany 251
  limitations 22-3
  paid community care workers in Australia 211-24, 285
  in Scotland 42, 47
  in Sweden 234-40, 241-2
  and relatives' needs 235, 236, 240, 242

special housing 236, 237-8, 240-1, 241-2
Home and Community Care (HACC) Programme (Australia) 212-13
home living *see* independent living
Home Office: Active Communities Directorate 160
Home Office five-year strategic plan 105
hospital care for older people in Japan 262, 271-2
household types in Japan 263-5
housing
  special housing in Sweden 236, 237-8, 240-1, 241-2
  for vulnerable people 160
housing association movement in Scotland 42
Hugman, R. 77
Hull Community Care Development Project 159, 162-74, 282
humanism 15

I

identity groups 9
immigrant care workers 16
inclusion *see* social inclusion
income inequalities and race 145
income maintenance packages 16
independence and civil renewal agenda 65, 67
Independence, Well-being and Choice (Green Paper) 29, 30, 187-8
independent living 24
  and individual budgets 29-30
  Neighbourhood Care Scheme in Brighton & Hove 177-90
  and people with dementia 92-3, 94-5, 95-6
  Supporting People programme 160
  in Sweden 234-40
  see also home care services
independent sector 31
  home care services 22-3
  residential care 22
  in Scotland 42
  see also private sector; voluntary and community sector
individual budgets 29-30
individual enforcement practitioners 108
Individual Support Orders 111-12
individualism
  and demise of welfare associations in Germany 250
  and ethical dilemmas 75-6, 87
  and ethnocentric value base 150

and government 12, 72
  social work in Scotland 51-2
informal care (lay care) 23, 36, 172
  and Long-term Care Insurance in
    Japan 261-78
  payments in Germany 257*n*, 284
  and people with dementia 89, 91-5
  unpaid carers in Scotland 46-7
  see also carers; voluntary and
    community sector
institutional racism 144
institutional respite care 90
integrated systems
  health and social care 32-3, 34
  in Scotland 53
  see also joint working
interdependency of care relationship 60,
  65, 67, 91, 95-7, 98-9, 133, 134
  mutuality of volunteering 185-6
intergenerational problems 170, 173
Irish community: health needs 143
isolation
  and befriending services 197
  and depression 187-8
Issacharoff, Ruth 5

J
Jack, G. 25
Jamrozic, A. 212
Japan
  ageing population 261
  Long-term Care Insurance and role of
    informal care 12, 261-78
  costs of care 273-4, 275, 277-8, 283-4
  extended family and informal care
    261-2, 263-5, 277
  review and reform of LTCI 274-8
  trends towards institutional care
    268-72, 275, 276
  social care workforce 32
job satisfaction of paid care work in
  Australia 221-3
Joint Future Group 53
joint working 23, 33
  and community care development
    approach 167
  and community safety teams 109
  in Scotland 53
  unpaid carers 47
  see also partnership working
Jordan, B. 28
Joseph Rowntree Foundation 43, 151,
  162
Jowitt, C. 197-8
Jowitt, T. 26

K
Kam Yu, W. 144
Kant, Immanuel 76
Kelly, L. 129
Kendall, I. 31
Kilbrandon Report 43
King, L. 183
Kingsmill, D. 125
Kintrea, K. 42
Kittay, Eva 66
Kuntz, L.I. 180, 184

L
Lagerlöf, Selma 229
Laming Report 25
law and order *see* criminal justice
lay care *see* informal care
Le Grand, Julian 76, 284
Leadbetter, C. 52-3
learning disabled *see* people with
  learning disabilities
Levy, Andrea 9
Lister, R. 28
Local Area Agreements 161
Local Area Coordination 53
local authorities
  as care managers 22
  funding for residential and nursing
    home care 21-2
  in Japan 262, 275
  in Scotland 41, 45, 48
  Swedish municipal services for older
    people 235-40, 241, 242-3
  and welfare associations in Germany
    248, 251
local government: role in community
  13-14
Local Government in Scotland Act
  (2003) 45
Local Health Care Cooperatives 50
'local' occupational groups 8
Local Strategic Partnerships 23
locality 7
long-term care *see* nursing homes;
  residential care
long-term care insurance
  Germany 12, 251-2, 253, 254, 255
  Japan 12, 261-78
low pay in care work in Australia
  213-14, 221, 223, 285
low status of care work 61, 71
  in Australia 211, 213-14, 221, 223
Lownsbrough, H. 52-3

M

McLeay, L. 211
marketisation of public services 76, 77, 87, 284
  in Australia 212-13, 216
  'double marketisation' in Germany 247, 250
  see also independent sector; private sector
Marshall, T.H. 230
maturity of paid care workers 214, 218
Mayo, Marjorie 6, 9
Means, R. 5-6, 29
means-tested social care 22, 35, 283, 284
mediation in antisocial behaviour work 116-17
medicalisation of care in Germany 251-2, 283
mental health
  befriending services 193-207
  depression in older people 187-8
  environmental factors 25
Mentoring and Befriending Foundation 207
Millie, A. 110, 111
Milton House, Bradford 150-1
minority ethnic communities *see* black and minority ethnic communities
Mirza, K. 144
'mixed communities' 10
mixed economy of care 27, 285
  in Japan 262-3, 275
Modernising Social Services (White Paper) 24, 125
Mooney, G. 45-6
moral reasoning and care 67-70, 72
motivations
  for community engagement 67-70
  domestic violence survivors 129-31
  of paid care workers in Australia 216-17, 221-3
  profession motivations 79-80
  for volunteering 181-4, 202
multicultural context
  and ethnocentric value base 149-50, 281
  regeneration workers and ethical dilemmas 82, 83
Mussenden, B. 151
'mutual recognition' 113
mutuality of volunteering 185-6

N

Naipaul, V.S. 9
'naming and shaming' 111, 116
nation state concept 11-12, 15
National Centre for Volunteering 202
National Institute for Social Work 41
National Lottery Community Fund 179
National Service Framework for Mental Health 198
National Service Framework for Older People 98, 148
National Service Frameworks 24
National Standards for Community Engagement through Communities Scotland 45
National Strategy Action Plan: *A New Commitment to Neighbourhood Renewal* 23-4, 125
National Strategy for Ageing Australia 213
need assessment
  and community care development approach 163, 164, 174
  levels of care for older people in Japan 265-8, 275, 276
  needs identified by participants 113, 115, 163, 164
  older people in black and minority ethnic communities 148-50, 152
  Single Assessment Process 148, 150
  in Sweden 232
  and allocation of resources 235-6
needs tests and supplementary cash benefits 16
Neighbourhood Care Scheme in Brighton & Hove 31, 177-90
  background to scheme 178-9
  evaluation and findings 179-90
  funding 178, 179, 189-90
neighbourhood renewal *see* community development
Neighbourhood Renewal Unit 27, 126
Neighbourhood Support Fund 170
Netherlands 14
networks
  of care 17
  community networks 166-7, 177-8
New Labour
  anti-social behaviour and respect agenda 105-17
  civil renewal and ethic of care 63-7, 71, 131
  community care policy 23-5
  and voluntary sector 177
New Managerialism 76, 83, 153
New Public Management 76, 77, 79, 212, 251, 285
'New Welfare' 76
'new youth justice' 111
NHS and Community Care Act 21-2
NHS Large-scale Workforce Change programme 33
Nichols, G. 183

normalisation and care discourse in
    Sweden 234-5, 241
Northmore, S.M. 180-1
nursing homes 21
    and informal care in Japan 271-2, 276
    shortage of places 262, 272-3
    and people with dementia 90, 92
    in Sweden 234, 235, 236

O

occupational groups 8
Office of the Third Sector 160
older people
    and active citizenship 66, 67
    black and minority ethnic
        communities 144-5
        assessment practice 148-50
        residential care 150-1
        voluntary supportive services 151-2,
            153
    civic engagement and social care in
        Germany 247-57, 281-2
    and community care development
        approach
        community lunches 171
        intergenerational issues 170, 173
    free personal care in Scotland 47-50
    Long-term Care Insurance in Japan
        261-78
    Neighbourhood Care Scheme in
        Brighton & Hove 177-90
    paid community care workers in
        Australia 211-24, 285
    Single Assessment Process 148, 150
    Swedish care system 229-43
    'young pensioner' volunteers in
        Germany 253-4
    see also home care services; nursing
        homes; people with dementia;
        residential care
Older People's Programme 186
Options for Excellence 51
Our Health, Our Care, Our Say (White
    Paper) 32-3, 177, 188, 189

P

'packages of care' 22
    Japan 265-6
paid care
    community care workers in Australia
        211-24, 285
    see also home care services; residential
        care; social care workforce; social
        workers
Pantling, K. 129
Parish, A. 198, 202

participation *see* community
    engagement; social inclusion
participatory care ethic 12, 72, 163
    and people with dementia 94-5, 96,
        99
participatory research 180
Partnership for Older People Projects
    (POPs) 33
partnership working 24, 33-4
    civil renewal and ethic of care 64
    Community Care Development
        Project 159, 162, 164-5, 171, 173-4
    and professional dilemmas 85, 285
    in Scotland 44-5, 53
    Community Health Partnerships 50-1
    unpaid carers 46-7
'patch' teams 14, 21, 178
payments
    for carers in Germany 257*n*, 284
    see also direct payments; user funding
people with dementia 89-100, 282
    care outcomes 92-5, 99
    and citizenship 100
    and ethic of care 91-7, 283
    in Germany 253, 254, 255-6
    in Japan 277
    statistics on 89-90
people with learning disabilities 90
    summer activities for children 171-2
personal care
    funding 22
    free personal care in Scotland 47-50
    see also home care services
personal qualities for care work 218-21
personalisation of social work in
    Scotland 51-2, 54
Petch, A. 49
Pollack, S. 113-14
Poole, L. 45-6
Power of Community Initiative, A (Green
    Paper) 45
private sector
    double marketisation in Germany 250
    mixed economy of care 27, 284
    in Sweden 229-30, 231, 240, 242
    see also independent sector
private sphere
    and caring 66
    gendered nature of care 61, 233-4
    paid care workers in Australia 211,
        214
    and civil renewal agenda 66, 67, 72
professional ethics 76-8
professionalisation of workforce 84
    professional distance 84-5, 87, 96-7,
        285
    welfare associations in Germany 252

public order and community cohesion 64
public participation 67-70
Public Partnership Forums in Scotland 51
public service ethos 76, 80, 87
public sphere
  and citizenship 66, 72
  restriction of domestic violence 128
Putnam, R.D. 161, 177, 189

Q

Quilgars, D. 24-5
Qureshi, T. 144

R

race equality 141, 142-3
  legislation and policy 147-8
Race Relations Amendment Act (2000) 141, 147-8
racism 144, 145, 152
rational choice theory 126
'rationality of caring' 233-4
rationing of care services 34, 36, 48
reflection as coping strategy 86
reflexivity and individualisation 75
refuge movement 123-4
regeneration professionals and ethical dilemmas 78-87
Reidpath, D.D. 111
relationship with client
  paid care workers in Australia 215-16, 218-21, 223-4
  in Scandinavian care discourse 233, 234
religion and German welfare associations 248
religious commitment and social action 68
religious support systems 149
remittances 15-16
representation and ethical dilemmas 82
resident involvement in Scotland 42
residential care 21
  in Australia 212, 213
  black and minority ethnic residents 150-1
  and informal care in Japan 268-72, 275, 276
  shortage of institutional places 262, 271-2
  and people with dementia 90, 92, 94-5
  and people with learning disabilities 90
  in Scotland
  free personal care 47-8

number of care homes 48
  in Sweden 234-5
residual social care in Japan 261, 262
respect: New Labour agenda 105, 106
Respect Action Plan 106, 112
Respect and Responsibility (White Paper) 105
'responsibilisation' and antisocial behaviour 105, 107, 111
responsibility
  and ethic of care 63, 70, 72
  people with dementia 96-7
  New Labour civil renewal agenda 65, 67
responsiveness and ethic of care 63, 71, 97
restorative justice 116
rights-based approach
  disability movement 60, 61
  unpaid carers 47
risk management and antisocial behaviour 111
Rothstein, Bo 17
Royal Commission on Long Term Care 22, 34-5
Rummery, K. 33-4
Russell, J. 197

S

Scotland 41-54
  community care development approach 161-2
  Community Health Partnerships 50-1
  devolution and policy divergence 45-50
  21st Century Social Work Review 51-4
Scottish Befriending Development Forum 197
Scottish Community Care Forum 44
Scottish Executive 43, 47-8
Scottish Health Council 51
Scottish Office community initiatives 42
Scottish Social Attitudes surveys 48
Seebohm Report 14, 21, 26, 29
segregation 8
self-government 12-13
self-interest as motive for volunteering 181, 183, 202
Senate Community Affairs References Committee 213-14
Sennett, R. 81, 84-5, 113, 117
service development process 113, 114-15
Settlement Movement 26
Sevenhuijsen, Selma 62, 63, 65, 70

shared interests *see* 'communities of interest'
short-term interventions and ethical dilemmas 82-3
Sim, D. 44
Sinclair, S. 53-4
Single Assessment Process 148, 150
single equalities commission proposal 147, 148
Single Regeneration Budget initiatives 161-2, 170
Skills for Care agency 24, 31
    New Types of Worker pilots 33
Smith, D. 77
social capital 161, 173, 177, 189, 282
    black and minority ethnic communities 152, 153
social care 6
    citizenship discourse 29, 285
    comparative views 229-79
    Green Papers 29
    and healthcare 32-4, 283
    personalisation in Scotland 51-2, 54
    see also social care workforce
Social Care Institute for Excellence (SCIE) 24
social care workforce 31-2, 284-5
    black and minority ethnic workers 146, 150
    development policies 24
    front-line professionals and ethical dilemmas 78-87, 285
    professional distance 84-5, 87, 96-7, 285
    paid community care workers in Australia 211-24, 285
    see also carers; education and training; social workers
social citizenship in Sweden 230-1, 234
social cohesion 63-7, 72, 177
social enterprise in Scotland 42
social exclusion
    befriending services 193, 199, 204-6
    and community development
    Community Care Development Project 160
    in Scotland 44
    and domestic violence 134
    and volunteering 186-8
    see also social inclusion
Social Exclusion Unit 23-4, 125, 186, 205
social groups 9
social housing: and diversity 10
social inclusion
    and anti-social behaviour enforcement 111-17
    and befriending services 205-6

and Community Care Development Project 163
    see also social exclusion
social insurance *see* long-term care insurance
social isolation
    and befriending services 197
    and depression 187-8
social justice
    and antisocial behaviour management 113, 115
    and community engagement 66, 70
social mobility 9-10
social rights 16
Social Services Inspectorate 142, 144
social services/social work
    and community development 24
    negative view of domestic violence survivors 128-9
    21st Century Social Work Review 51-4
    see also community social work; social workers
Social Work (Scotland) Act (1968) 41
social workers
    anti-oppressive practice 110, 112-17
    coping mechanisms 78, 85-6
    education and training 28, 32, 87
    ethical dilemmas 77-87
    people with dementia and ethic of care 91-5, 98, 99
    'socialisation' of care in Japan 261, 274, 277
Socialstyrelsen (Sweden) 236-41
special housing in Sweden 236, 237-8, 240-1, 241-2
Squires, Peter 25, 106, 108, 109
stakeholder participation in Scotland 42
Stephen, Dawn E. 25, 106, 108, 109
Stewart, J. 41, 43
stigmatisation
    and antisocial behaviour enforcement 111, 112-13, 116
    and befriending services 194, 203, 204
Stone, Deborah 185
Strategy for Carers in Scotland (1999) 33, 46
strengthened/stronger communities 64, 107
strengths and abilities of individuals 113, 114
subsidiarity principle 14, 31, 248
suicide incidence in Hastings 195
summer activities for disabled children 171-2
supervision and front-line professionals 85-6, 87
supplementary cash benefits 16

support services and systems
  befriending 196-207
  and black and minority ethnic
    communities 146-7, 149
  for carers 33, 46, 47, 90, 94-5, 96, 99,
    240
  community care development projects
    162-74
  for domestic violence survivors 132-3,
    134-5
  families and anti-social behaviour
    management 108-9, 111-17
  families and disabled people 145-6
  for front-line professionals 85-6, 87,
    285
  voluntary and community groups as
    151-2
  Neighbourhood Care Scheme 177-
    90
  for volunteers 184-5, 203
Supporting People Programme 124,
  160, 174
sustainability
  community care development
    approach 163, 165
  social care in Japan 276-7
Sweden 17
  care of older people 229-43, 283
  ageing demographic 236
  government bill in 2006 242-3

T

Taylor, M. 34
Taylor, Marilyn 75
territorial justice 15, 16
testimony of user groups 71
Third Way 75
time available for volunteering 183-4
Toennies, F. 6
Together: Tackling Anti-Social Behaviour
  campaign 105
Together We Can campaign 161
Trace analysis 62
training *see* education and training
Training Organisation for the Personal
  Social Services (TOPSS) 24
Tronto, Joan C. 61, 62, 63, 65, 92
trust: lack of trust and ethical dilemmas
  82
Turner, M. 28
21st Century Social Work Review 51-4

U

Ungerson, Clare 16
United Kingdom overview 21-36
universalism and communitarianism
  15-17

unpaid care *see* carers; informal care;
  voluntary and community sector
Urban Partnerships in Scotland 42
urban renewal *see* community
  development
user empowerment 24, 29
  and devaluing of care ethic 60, 61
  and partnership working 34
  in Scotland 44-5
user funding
  Australia 213
  Japan 262-3, 265-6, 273-4, 275-6,
    277-8
  Sweden 229
user groups
  lack of formation for domestic
    violence survivors 122, 127, 128
  motivations and commitments 12-13,
    67-70
  domestic violence survivors 129-31
  testimony of 71
user movements 60, 128
utilitarianism 76

V

values
  ethnocentric value base 149-50, 281
  and professional motivation 79-80
very sheltered housing 36
voluntary and community sector 14,
    30-1, 282
  in Australia 214
  befriending services 199-206
  community development and social
    care 26-7
  black and minority ethnic voluntary
    organisations 141, 146, 151-2, 153
  Community Care Development
    Project 162-74, 282
  and gender 180
  Germany
    new approach to social care 255, 256
    volunteer bureaux 254
    welfare associations 247, 248, 249,
      250, 252, 253, 254, 281-2
    'young pensioner' volunteers 253-4
  motivations for volunteering 181-4,
    202
  Neighbourhood Care Scheme in
    Brighton and Hove 31, 177-90
  Sweden 231
Volunteering into Participation (VIP)
    186
vulnerable people and community care
  development 159-60, 161

W

Waerness, Kari 233-4
Walklate, S. 122
Walsall's New Deal for Communities:
    Domestic Violence Project 126-7
Wanless review 35
Warner, S. 129
Weisbrod, Burton A. 249
Weitzman, M.S. 182
welfare associations in Germany 247,
    248, 281-2
  demise of 250-2, 253
  new approach to volunteers 254
welfare rights and citizenship in Sweden
    230-1, 234
Wilcox, P. 122, 132-3
Williams, F. 72, 133
Williams, Raymond 6, 128
Wilmot, P. 11
Wittgenstein, Ludwig 76-7
Wollmann, Helmut 13
women's refuge movement 123-4
Wood, G. 15-16
workforce *see* social care workforce

Y

Yee, L. 151
Young, M. 11
young people
  antisocial behaviour and families in
    the community 105-17
  and community development
    approach 167, 168, 170, 173, 281
    activities for disabled children 171-2
  regeneration workers and ethical
    dilemmas 83
Youth Justice Board 111-12
Youth Network in Hull 167, 170